A Historical Study of

the Grange, the Farm Bureau

and the Associated Farmers

1929-1941

by CLARKE A. CHAMBERS

1952

Berkeley and Los Angeles

UNIVERSITY OF CALIFORNIA PRESS

California Farm Organizations

UNIVERSITY OF CALIFORNIA PRESS, BERKELEY AND LOS ANGELES
CAMBRIDGE UNIVERSITY PRESS, LONDON, ENGLAND
COPYRIGHT, 1952, BY
THE REGENTS OF THE UNIVERSITY OF CALIFORNIA

to Florence

PREFACE

California's farm organizations have played a significant role in the history of the state for many years. Not only have they provided educational, social, and business services for their members, but they have also made many important contributions to the community as a whole and played an influential part in the political and economic life of California. During the depression years farm groups were particularly active in state politics.

Because of the peculiar structure of the farm economy of the Golden State, California farm groups have often deviated from the national pattern. The California Grange, for example, was markedly to the left of the national group in the period 1929-1941. This study has not, however, been concerned with the relationships of the California groups to their national organizations. Rather it has emphasized the different and often contradictory attitudes and actions of the various farm groups within the state on matters of labor relations, government unemployment relief, taxation, marketing proration, water and power, and partisan politics.

Many friends at the University of California have helped to make this study possible. I especially wish to acknowledge the guidance and encouragement given to me by Professor John D. Hicks. The suggestions and criticisms of Professor M. R. Benedict were of great value. Mrs. Helen Gray gave generously of her time and experience in the wearisome task of preparing the manuscript for publication.

CLARKE A. CHAMBERS

University of Minnesota

ACKNOWLEDGMENTS

The following organizations, newspapers, and periodicals have kindly permitted me to quote from their publications: *Business Week,* for the article "Push California Land-Labor Fight," in the August 12, 1939, issue; the *California Farmer,* for articles and editorials appearing in the *California Cultivator* and the *Pacific Rural Press;* the California State Department of Public Works, for an article in the February, 1940, issue of *California Highways and Public Works;* the California State Grange, for material appearing in the *California Grange News* and in the *Journals of Proceedings;* the *Sacramento Bee;* the *San Francisco Chronicle; Survey Graphic,* for the article "From the Ground Up" by Paul S. Taylor in the September, 1936, issue; the Office of Agricultural Publications of the University of California, for Bulletin 565, *Economic and Legal Aspects of Compulsory Proration in Agricultural Marketing,* by E. A. Stokdyk, and for Bulletin 630, *The Composition and Characteristics of the Agricultural Population in California,* by George M. Peterson; and the Commonwealth Club of California, for remarks of Philip Bancroft in the *Transactions* of December 22, 1936, and for remarks of Frank T. Swett in the *Transactions* of January 26, 1932. The remarks of Bancroft and Swett did not necessarily reflect the attitudes and views of the Commonwealth Club.

CONTENTS

1. *Economic Structure
   of Agriculture in California* 1
   Importance of agriculture — Crop specialization — Seasonal operations — Migratory labor — Intensive farming — Factors of concentration — Interdependence of agriculture, industry, and finance — Diversity and conflict

2. *The California
   State Grange, 1873–1941* 9
   Founding of the California Grange, 1873 — Economic activities — Political action — Decline, 1880–1921 — Grange in the 1920's — Sehlmeyer and Grange leadership in the 1930's — Structural organization — Membership

3. *The California Farm Bureau
   Federation, 1919–1941* 21
   Founding of the California Farm Bureau, 1919 — Leadership and membership, 1920 — Business activities — Stuctural organization, 1920's — Political activities — Structural organization, 1930's — Leadership, 1930's

4. *Economic Crisis and
   Labor Strife—The Action* 31
   Depression and California agriculture — Migratory labor — Unionization of transient workers — Agricultural strikes, 1933–1934

5. *The Associated Farmers—
   The Reaction*   39
   Founding of the Associated Farmers, 1933–1934 — Early activities — Financing

6. *Reorganization of
   The Associated Farmers*   46
   Broadening of the Associated Farmers, 1936–1937 — Leadership — Membership — Failure to expand outside the state

7. *Relationships among
   California Farm Organizations*   53
   Agricultural Department of Chamber of Commerce — Agricultural Council of California — The Farmers' Union — Isolation of Grange, 1930's — Coöperation of Farm Bureau and Associated Farmers

8. *Farm Organizations
   and Labor Policy*   60
   Importance of labor relations — Attitudes of Associated Farmers — Farm Bureau policies — Farm Labor Policy Code, 1937 — Neutrality of Grange

9. *The Associated Farmers in Action*   70
   Contra Costa pickers' strike, 1934 — Los Angeles orange strike, 1936 — Stockton cannery strike, 1937 — Madera cotton strike, 1939

10. *Farm Organizations
    and Unemployment Relief*   82
    Relief and farm wages — Government relief policies, 1933–1939 — Farm Bureau policies — Position of the Grange — New state policy, 1939 — Crisis in relief, 1939–1941

11. *The Struggle: "Hot Cargo"
    and Secondary Boycott*   98
    Labor troubles in southern California — Farmers' Transportation Association — Crises in labor relations in northern California — Initiative proposition, 1938 — "Hot Cargo" Act, 1941

12. *Criminal Syndicalism Trial
    and Labor Legislation*   108
    Sacramento trial, 1935 — Anti-Communism of Associated Farmers and Farm Bureau — Local labor ordinances — State labor legislation

13. *Tax Reform and the
    Riley-Stewart Amendment*   115
    Crisis in taxation, 1929–1933 — Tax reform legislation, 1931 — Tax initiative, 1932 — Riley-Stewart amendment, 1933

14. *Farm Organization
    Tax Policies, 1933–1941*   125
    Sales tax, 1933 — Income tax, 1935 — "Single tax" proposals — Division of Farm Bureau and Grange

15. *The Agricultural Prorate Act*   133
    Breakdown of voluntary coöperative marketing, 1929–1933 — Stokdyk report — Terms of Agricultural Prorate Act, 1933 — Farm attitudes toward proration — Legislative battles over proration policy, 1935–1939 — Alleviation of marketing problem, 1939–1941

16. *The Issue of Water
    and Power, 1919–1933*   147
    Water and power problem in California — Regulation of power rates, 1919–1935 — Role of the Farm Bureau — Taxation of public utilities — Early statewide plans, 1919–1933 — Central Valley Project Act, 1933 — Referendum campaign, 1933

17. *Struggle for Control
   of the Central Valley Project*   160
   Complexity of problem — Grange support for public ownership — Farm Bureau emphasis on irrigation — Revenue bond legislation, 1935–1937 — Garrison Act referendum, 1938 — C.V.P. legislation, 1939–1941

18. *State Politics and Reform*   174
   Weakness of political parties in California — Strength of lobbies — Dominant rural representation in state senate — Grange and unicameralism — Movements for political reform, 1935–1939 — Farm organization lobbies

19. *Farm Groups
   in Politics, 1929–1941*   185
   Farmer discontent with Rolph administration — Grange recall movement — Farmer political action, 1934 — Farm groups in campaign of 1938 — Grange coöperation with Olson administration — Opposition of Associated Farmers and Farm Bureau to Olson

20. *Summary and Conclusion*   196
   Bases of agricultural problems — Conflicting interests of farmers — The Grange — The Farm Bureau — The Associated Farmers — Labor relations — Taxation — Agricultural marketing proration — Water and power — Farm groups in politics

Appendices   203

   A. Membership of the California State Grange, 1873–1941
   B. Membership of the California State Grange, by Counties, 1929 and 1932
   C. Membership of the California Farm Bureau Federation, 1920–1941

D. Membership of the California Farm Bureau Federation, by Counties, 1929 and 1941
E. Leadership of the California State Grange, 1929–1941
F. Leadership of the California Farm Bureau Federation, 1929–1941
G. Leadership of the Associated Farmers of California, 1934–1939

Notes   217

Bibliographic Notes   243

Source material for the California Farm Bureau Federation — Source material for the California State Grange — Source material for the Associated Farmers of California — Miscellaneous source material — Personal interviews — Newspapers and periodicals — General studies — Theses and dissertations — General books

Index   263

1. THE ECONOMIC STRUCTURE OF AGRICULTURE IN CALIFORNIA

The economic, social, and political structure of agriculture in California is unique. Native Californians familiar with other parts of the country know this to be true, and visitors and new citizens of the Golden State immediately sense peculiarities in the farm economy. Although the similarities with other parts of the country are basic and of great importance, there are significant differences that explain the peculiar development and history of California agriculture in the twentieth century.[1]

California's farms produce many diverse crops, but on any single-farm unit specialization in one crop, or at the most in a few crops, is the rule. Although the state boasts of the cultivation of over two hundred different crops, the traditional diversified family farm is rarely to be found. Many specialty crops require the application of scientific and technical knowledge for cultivation, harvesting, and marketing. The farmer in California, to be successful, must be a skilled agronomist, a careful manager of labor, an astute businessman, a speculator, and certainly an optimist. California ranchers are dependent upon an often undependable water supply; many of them rely upon a large mass of transient labor; they operate under constant conditions of high cash costs and realize profits by the sale of perishable products on markets thousands of miles away. To such ranchers farming is rarely a "way of life."

In recent decades California agriculture has been characterized by a high degree of specialization, seasonality, and reliance

Economic Structure of Agriculture

upon hired migratory labor. Intensive agriculture with large capital investment in land, buildings and equipment, and water systems has been the rule. The concentration of land and other factors of production (especially in the cultivation of such crops as rice and cotton) has had particular significance, even though small farms have far outnumbered the large industrial units. The relationship of agriculture to industry has been intimate. And, finally, Californian agriculture has suffered from economic and social divisions of group interest; the migrant laborer has been pitted against his employer, the small and part-time farmers against the large industrialized farmer.

Agriculture in California is a large and important industry. In the 1930's California farms vied with those of Iowa for first place in total value of farm commodities produced. Four California counties—Los Angeles, Tulare, Fresno, and San Joaquin—as a rule led the nation. Fourteen California counties were usually counted in the leading twenty-five, and twenty-three California counties were in the first one hundred. In the production of almonds, apricots, artichokes, lemons, and olives California had almost a national monopoly. California grew over half of the country's figs, grapes, prunes, walnuts, carrots, lettuce, oranges, cantaloupes, and cauliflower; it led in the production of alfalfa, celery, cherries, grain hay, peas, peaches, pears, and tomatoes.

Conditions of climate, soil, elevation, and water supply made specialization of crop production necessary. Capital invested in vineyards and orchards was difficult to liquidate or shift to other crops. By the period 1929–1941 regional and individual specialization had settled into a well-established pattern. Even within a crop, specialization was likely; a farmer might produce peaches for canning, drying, or fresh sale, or he might grow table, raisin, or wine grapes. Farmers who knew how to grow one specialty crop were not likely to shift to the production of a crop whose peculiarities they did not understand. Constant vigilance against insects, disease, pests, frost, and drought was essential. Application of scientific knowledge, coöperation with technical experts, and expenditure of large sums of working capital upon control measures was necessary.

In many crops, processing and marketing operations were carried on for the growers through large and financially strong coöperative marketing associations.

Since the production of California's specialty crops was extremely seasonal in nature, careful planning, exact timing of crop operations, and quick and efficient marketing were essential, especially in the fresh fruit and vegetable industries. These operations depended upon the existence of a large supply of migratory labor, the demand for which was highly seasonal. During the rainy winter months, December through March, there was little demand for farm labor, but beginning in April the demand rose constantly until a peak was reached in September. In the slack winter months fewer than fifty thousand migrants were employed on California farms, but during the summer more than two hundred thousand farm workers were engaged in harvesting the state's crops.

Farm employers needed a large supply of labor for a relatively short season. For perishable commodities such as fresh vegetables and deciduous fruits, harvesting operations had to be started at exactly the right moment and completed as quickly as possible. Harvesting operations in perishable crop industries were particularly vulnerable to local labor shortages and to strikes conducted by farm labor unions. California farmers depended upon a constant supply of unorganized migratory workers, willing and able to move quickly from crop to crop and from region to region. Mobility, docility, and some skill and experience were the characteristics desired of these workers by their farm employers. California's peculiar labor needs arose from its specialized type of farming more than from the size of farm operation, because specialty crops demanded seasonal labor regardless of farm size.

The development of this type of farming was made possible by a long-continued supply of cheap migrant labor. In early days, when California was turning from extensive to intensive farming, this mobile labor was supplied by Chinese coolies, released from their labors in railroad construction. Gradually the Japanese took over the tasks of "stoop" labor; in the years preceding the First World War they constituted the primary supply of farm labor. By the 1920's, however, many of the

Economic Structure of Agriculture

Japanese had migrated to the cities or had set themselves up as farmers on small rented plots throughout the state, especially in Los Angeles County and in the delta lands of the Sacramento and San Joaquin rivers. In the 1920's this backbreaking work was performed by Mexican nationals, with the addition of some Filipino and Hindustani laborers. Throughout these years a few white men also, known as "bindlestiffs," wandered up and down the great Central Valley performing casual labor.

To the migrant worker the system brought unemployment during the winter months and underemployment during the remainder of the year, low annual income, dependence upon supplementary relief to maintain pitifully low standards of existence, difficulty in organizing for protection of wage standards, and complete lack of social status and community life. To the farm employer the system meant reliance upon laborers whom he could not possibly know or understand, upon workers who were frequently ignorant of and indifferent to the needs and problems of the farmer. Furthermore, high government relief payments to migrants in the off-seasons resulted in heavy tax burdens upon the resident landholding citizens. Because competitive bidding for labor at peak seasons tended to force wages upward, employers sought to keep labor fluid and unorganized and working at uniform wage levels.

Heavy reliance on hired farm labor was but one indication of the intensive nature of California agriculture. Specialty crops required not only large expenditures of cash for labor but also large capital investment in land with a very high value per acre in orchards and vineyards, and in specialized equipment. Large sums were spent annually for commercial fertilizers, irrigation water (whether pumped by electricity or secured by gravity flow), and for pest control. Once harvested, the crops underwent expensive processing—cutting, sorting, grading, packaging, and canning. After preparation for market, farm commodities bore high transportation, advertising, and marketing costs. Taxation, interest payments on borrowed capital, bond redemption payments in irrigation districts, and insurance premiums, all constituted further fixed cash costs. High capital investment per farm and per acre and high cash

Economic Structure of Agriculture

costs, fixed and operating, were essential features of farming in California.

California agriculture was also characterized by a high degree of concentration. Most farms were small or of moderate size, but significant acreage and production were controlled by the relatively few large farms. One study of economic concentration in California agriculture indicates that in the 1930's 10 per cent of all farms in the state received 53 per cent of gross farm income; 9 per cent spent 65 per cent of the total wage bill; 7 per cent employed 66 per cent of all farm workers and held 42 per cent of all crop lands harvested; and 4 per cent of all farms controlled 62 per cent of all farm land.[2]

Another feature of the state's farm economy was the intimate relationship between agriculture and industry. Food processing and canning industries, whose margins of profit depended in part upon prices paid for the raw agricultural commodities, naturally were vitally interested in agricultural matters. Concerned that wage levels be kept low during their seasonal operations, these industries often coöperated with farm employers in resisting the unionization of field, packing, and processing labor. The trucking industry depended upon the transportation of agricultural commodities for much of its income. The railroads and shipping firms also received a large part of their revenue from carrying farm products. California farmers, especially those who pumped underground water for irrigation purposes, were heavy consumers of electric power, and the electric power industry was therefore keenly interested in agricultural developments. Other industries interested in agriculture included those selling sugar, refrigeration, wine, agricultural supplies, paper, cardboard cases, tin cans, lumber, and milk.

In summary, California agriculture in the period from 1929 to 1941 was characterized by specialization of crop production, seasonality of farm operations, reliance upon hired migratory labor, emphasis upon intensive farming with high capital investment and high cash costs, concentration of all factors of agricultural production, and intimate relationship and close interdependence of agriculture, industry, and finance in the state's economy. These factors had an influence upon events in California, and an understanding of these factors is basic to an understanding of the attitudes, opinions, and activities of the various farm organizations.

One consequence of the peculiar structure of California agriculture was a wide diversity of interests among the various groups of farmers. Leaders of farm organizations often found it difficult to convince a cotton farmer of Kern County that he had interests in common with a poultryman of Sonoma County. A small dairyman in Humboldt County, who may have worked part time also in town or in the lumber mills, often felt that he had little in common with a large dairyman in Los Angeles County. Even growers of dry-wine grapes and producers of sweet-wine grapes often found little basis for coöperation. Diversity of interests was based on commodity, regional, and economic differences.

Part-time farmers constituted a special group in California agriculture. It is estimated that in 1929 about one-third of all farm operators in the state spent some time in nonfarm work and that, of this group, approximately one-half spent at least 150 days a year working away from the farm.[3] Some worked as managers or clerks in the coöperatives, some held public office, others had jobs in small rural communities but lived on tiny ranches at the edge of town. Others, especially in northern California, worked part time in the lumber mills. Some small farmers who lived in coastal areas supplemented their income by fishing. Part-time farmers rarely felt a common bond with either the migrant laborer or the larger farmer.

The small family farmers also constituted a group by themselves. Thousands of them, often growing specialty crops, were underemployed during a large part of the year, a condition that contributed to their low annual income. Occasionally such farmers had to employ small numbers of casual workers to help at the harvest rush, but more often they drew their hired labor from workers resident in the area rather than from the migrants. Small farmers had little in common with larger employers of labor.

These small farmers, who did most of their own work but hired labor for short periods at harvest time, probably constituted the largest single group of farmers in the state. Although they competed with the larger growers, they were nevertheless, like them, property holders, and this fact constituted a bond of common interest between the two groups. The small farmer was often at a competitive disadvantage. His fixed costs were relatively high as compared with the gross income he might expect to receive; he had few capital reserves to draw upon in hard years; he lacked capital for investment in adequate machinery; and he did not always enjoy the marketing facilities that many of the larger farmers employed. On the other hand, the small farmer often had "staying power" during times of economic depression because he operated with relatively low cash costs and could absorb the shock of hard times by utilizing family labor more fully and by accepting a lower standard of living. The introduction of small tractors and other new types of farm machinery also helped to alleviate the economic disadvantages of this group.

More fortunate were the larger farmers, those with sufficient acreage, equipment, and capital to permit efficient operations. Most of them farmed according to the best technical, scientific, and managerial practices. Locally they were often prominent in community affairs and in politics. Firm advocates of coöperative marketing, they produced efficiently and marketed with astute business acumen. But these ranchers, too, had their problems—migratory labor, taxation, high cash costs—and often in the depression years they saw their margins of profit wiped away by drought or frost, by wildcat labor strikes, or by sudden drops in market price.

Finally, there was a group of large industrial and corporation farmers, many of whom lived in the cities and delegated supervision of their agricultural interests to resident managers. For them, farming was secondary to their interests in real estate, finance, and industry.

Social stratification and conflict of group interests thus marked California's agriculture in the period 1929–1941. Each of the groups engaged in farming—the migrant laborer, the small family farmer, the substantial commerical farmer, and the corporate industrial farmer—had its own peculiar problems, advantages and disadvantages, and its own economic, social, and political outlooks. It is against this background of specialization, concentration, diversity, and conflict that the farm organizations of California in the depression decade must be viewed to be understood.

2.

THE CALIFORNIA STATE GRANGE 1873–1941

The history of the California State Grange from its beginning in July, 1873, until it came under the leadership of George Sehlmeyer in 1929 paralleled very closely the development of the National Grange. During the decade after the Civil War California farmers labored under many of the same disabilities that plagued farmers throughout the country as a whole—low prices, heavy mortgage indebtedness, high rates of interest on borrowed capital, a rigid, inelastic system of currency and credit, and high transportation rates. But the farmers of the Golden State had additional burdens to bear—manipulation of grain prices by a local monopoly of commission merchants, uncertain land titles, confused water rights, periodic droughts, extreme conditions of monopoly in the ownership of land and water rights, and a completely corrupt state government operating under an inadequate and faulty constitution.

To alleviate these ills California ranchers, like farmers in others parts of the country, began to organize. At first, from 1871 to 1873, the aggrieved ranchers formed independent Farmers' Clubs, but the members of these clubs soon saw the advantages of affiliation with a national organization and turned to the Patrons of Husbandry for assistance in creating a strong statewide organization. A national deputy was sent out from Iowa to help establish "Subordinate Granges," the basic organizational units, and upon these local groups a state organization was formed. On July 15, 1873, delegates from twenty-eight Subordinate Granges met in Napa to write a constitution for the California State Grange. By the time of the first annual convention, which met in October, 1873, the organization had grown to include one hundred and four Subordinate Granges with a total membership of 3,168 farmers. By the fall of 1874 the organization had mushroomed into two hundred and thirty-one Subordinate Granges with 14,910 members. Membership was centered primarily in the counties of Napa, Sonoma, Santa Clara, Sacramento, San Joaquin, Santa Cruz, Sutter, El Dorado, and Los Angeles. The members were, for the most part, growers of grain.[1]

The State Grange at once inaugurated a program of coöperatives to secure higher prices for wheat and lower costs of production and marketing. Late in 1873 the Executive Committee designated the San Francisco company of Morgan's Sons as shipping agents for Grange members. Morgan's Sons was to purchase the wheat grown by Grange members and to arrange for its shipment to Liverpool, England. The introduction of this competition into the local wheat market bid up the price to a level hardly warranted by the price on the world market. As a result of this situation, combined with the fact that the crop in 1874 was nearly double that of 1873, Morgan's Sons, working with insufficient capital, went bankrupt trying to purchase great quantities of wheat at artificially high prices. The failure of the company brought ruin to many Grange members and nearly destroyed the State Grange itself.[2]

To take the place of the defunct company, the Grange set up the Grangers' Business Association to purchase supplies for members and to arrange for the sale of their grain. But this Association, along with the Grangers' Bank of California and the Grange-sponsored California Mutual Fire Insurance Company, suffered from insufficient funds, poor management, and lack of patronage and consequently was but indifferently successsful. Farmers by the thousands withdrew from the Grange in disgust and disappointment over the failure of these business ventures. By 1876 membership had dropped to 7,660, and by 1879 only 3,262 farmers still remained in the organization.[3]

After these initial setbacks in the economic field the Grange turned to political action. The Farmers' Clubs had participated in the election of the reform candidate for governor, Newton Booth, in 1871, and two years later the Grange had joined with the People's Independent Party, which sought legislation to regulate railroad monopoly, but by 1875 this movement for political reform had collapsed. By this time the financial panic that had struck the rest of the country in 1873 had finally reached the West Coast, and as depression spread throughout California the plight of the farmers became more severe. When the Workingmen's Party of San Francisco, led by the young Irish agitator Dennis Kearney, began to draft demands for political reform and for the writing of a new state constitution, the Grange saw in this movement a means by which the farmers of the state might be able to secure constitutional and legislative relief.

Delegates to the annual convention of the State Grange meeting in October, 1878, drew up a list of reforms and demanded their incorporation into the proposed new constitution. Among the reforms demanded were state regulation of railroads, guarantees that taxes would not be levied upon growing crops or upon improvements on the land, heavy taxation upon uncultivated lands held for speculation, limitations on the debt-creating and taxing powers of state and local government, provision for a graduated income tax, regulation of interest rates on borrowed capital, and elimination of political corruption. The Grange endorsed and supported for election as delegates to the constitutional convention those candidates who promised to incorporate these reforms into the new instrument of government.[4]

In the convention the Grange-inclined farmer delegates held a balance of power between the Workingmen's Party and the conservative bloc. Although the farmer and worker delegates were somewhat suspicious and distrustful of each other, the two groups were able to work together, since they shared many of the same grievances and sought many of the same reforms. Parts of the new constitution were based upon the suggestions of the Grange: a Railroad Commission was created, with authority to fix rates and to prevent pooling and discrimination; a State Board of Equalization was established, with power to assess railroad properties and to equalize assessments from county to county; land, cultivated or uncultivated, of the same quality and of similar situation, was to be assessed at the same evaluation and rates; the state legislature was authorized to levy a graduated income tax; lobbying was made a felony; farmers were protected against the forced sale of their homesteads; and provision was made for state regulation of irrigation water. In the close balloting for ratification of the new constitution, rural citizens voted affirmatively in sufficient numbers to overcome the negative vote cast by the cities.

The Grange in 1879 had sufficient influence to take a leading role in determining some of the provisions of the new constitution, but the organization was soon so weakened that it was unable to force the enactment of reform legislation that the new document had authorized. In 1880 the Grange lost more than 2,000 members; when the state convention assembled in October of that year only 1,276 members were enrolled in the various Subordinate Granges throughout the state. From that time until 1921 the Grange grew slowly, failing by far to keep pace with the great increase in the number of farms and in the size of farm population. In 1905 the Grange claimed 2,600 members; by 1915 there were about 3,000 active Grangers in the state; and in 1921, when George Harrison became Master, the organization could boast a membership of slightly less than 4,800. This membership was almost entirely in northern California, especially in Sonoma, Santa Clara, Siskiyou, and Modoc counties.

The failure of the Grange to expand its membership to keep pace with the spectacular development of agriculture in these years may be traced to the fiasco of Grange business activities in the 1870's and to the competition for membership with other farm groups. Most of the grievances of the earlier period disappeared as California agriculture turned from extensive wheat farming to the intensive farming of diverse specialty crops, as large landholdings were subdivided, as water rights were stabilized, as coöperative marketing associations were formed, and as the market for California's farm commodities continued to increase.

From 1880 to 1921 the California State Grange played a relatively insignificant role in the history of the state. In the first decade of the twentieth century the California Grange endorsed programs for the extension of political democracy—the direct primary, the direct election of senators, woman suffrage, and the initiative, referendum, and recall. But the small total membership and the isolation of the local groups from each other rendered the organization relatively ineffective in the field of politics. Until the 1920's the Grange remained, for the most part, a fraternal and social organization with few political or economic interests. In its concern with education and self-improvement, in its interest in youth, and in its crusade against intoxicating liquors, the saloon, and even tobacco, the Grange reflected predominant Protestant, rural, nineteenth-century ethics.[5]

In 1921 George Harrison was elected Master of the State Grange, a position which he held for the next eight years. During the 1920's the Grange again became interested in political action, probably in response to the economic grievances that began to bear down upon the farmer in the postwar years. Stimulated by the competition for membership on the part of the Farm Bureau, the Grange increased from approximately 4,800 members in 1921 to slightly more than 8,300 in 1929. Interested in government economy, lower taxes, a high protective tariff, and regulatory agricultural legislation, the Grange coöperated with other California farm organizations on these issues. The unique contribution of the Grange in this decade was its continuing interest in moral affairs. It spent much time and energy in opposing organized gambling, immoral movies, and cigarette smoking among teachers and in urging the strict enforcement of prohibition. Under Harrison the State Grange was conservative in outlook, Republican in politics, and deeply concerned with problems of morality. The formulation of political programs was largely in the hands of S. S. Knight of Petaluma, a farm leader whose conservatism was strict and narrow. But in the fall of 1929 two events coincided to revolutionize the program and policy of the State Grange: the stock market crash, which marked the beginning of a long descent into economic depression and despair; and the election of George Sehlmeyer as Master of the State Grange.[6]

George Sehlmeyer was born into the Grange movement since both his father and mother had been active in that organization. He had planned to study for the legal profession, but upon his father's death when George was still a youth, he had to give up his desire to become a lawyer to support himself and his widowed mother. He took over operation of the family homestead, a 116-acre ranch near Elk Grove in Sacramento County.'

George Sehlmeyer entered actively into Grange work. In 1907 he was elected Master of Elk Grove Subordinate Grange, and two years later he was elevated to the office of Master of the Sacramento County "Pomona" Grange. In the same year he was elected to the post of Assistant Steward of the California State Grange, a position concerned primarily with ritualistic ceremonies at the annual conventions. In 1911 he was reëlected to this office and also was appointed to serve on the Standing Committee on Taxation for the state organization. At the annual convention in 1913 he was elevated to the office of Steward of the State Grange and also was selected to become a Deputy of the State Master for Sacramento County. The duties of county deputy were primarily those of organizing new local units and promoting Grange membership. Because of the progress he made in promoting purchasing coöperatives in Sacramento County, he was appointed in 1916 to serve on the Standing Committee on Coöperation for the state organization. Because of an interest in legislative matters, he was appointed to the Grange Legislative Committee in the following year.

He was elected Lecturer for the State Grange in 1921 and again in 1923, a position in which he was able to influence the formulation of political and economic policy since it was the duty of the Lecturer to plan and guide the educational programs of the Subordinate and the Pomona, or county, Granges. As State Lecturer, Sehlmeyer stressed the importance of public ownership of water and power and also interested himself in the taxation problem. He was chosen by Harrison to represent the state organization as Deputy for San Joaquin County in 1927.

By 1929 there was hardly an office in the Subordinate and Pomona Granges or the State Grange that he had not held, and he had also served on nearly all the key policy-making committees of the state organization. This experience taught him the workings of the Grange at every level, and as a State Grange officer he established many contacts with influential Grange leaders throughout the state. This background, combined with his own wit, parliamentary skill, and political instinct made him a logical candidate for the highest office in the State Grange.

In the early days of the California Grange, when emphasis had been placed on the purely fraternal aspects of the organization, the honor of being State Master had rotated among Grange leaders every two or four years. In the 1920's, when the Grange reëntered the political field in earnest, state office was sought for the political influence it would have. Harrison was able to stay on as Master for eight years, and Sehlmeyer, after his election in 1929, won reëlection year after year.[8]

The sources of Sehlmeyer's continuing power were many. Throughout the depression years he initiated policies that were designed to relieve the economic disabilities of the small farmers of California. He worked tirelessly to maintain friendly contacts with Grange members, traveling up and down the state visiting the Subordinate and Pomona Granges. Grangers who came to visit him at his state offices were always assured of a sympathetic hearing, friendly advice, and quick and often effective action to solve their many personal troubles. Through his power to appoint deputies, he was able to keep leaders friendly to his own program in influence in every Grange county. As secretary of the Board of Governors of the Farmers' Automobile Inter-Insurance Exchange, a company closely affiliated with the Grange though not part of it, he controlled a source of patronage in the form of appointments of local agents for this insurance company.

There was occasional opposition to Sehlmeyer's leadership, to be sure, but he probably kept majority opinion on his side on most issues. Many Grangers were interested in the Grange primarily for its social and fraternal activities, and this group was usually content to swing along with the State Master on policy matters. An organized conservative minority attempted in 1933 and again in 1941 to overthrow Sehlmeyer, but each time he was able to win reëlection comfortably. In 1931, 1935, 1937, and 1939, Sehlmeyer was reëlected without opposition.

The formulation and execution of Grange policy was controlled primarily by the Master and an Executive Committee of three members. Membership on the committee was kept within a small group of leaders, all of whom were personally loyal to Sehlmeyer and in sympathy with his program. Leadership from 1929 to 1941 was drawn entirely from Grange counties in northern California.

The California Grange organization was never as well financed as other farm groups in the state. Initiation fees and annual membership dues were low, and the Grange received no outside financial support, direct or indirect. When Sehlmeyer became Master, the Grange operated on an annual budget of around $6,000. By 1941 membership had increased to such an extent that the state office expended approximately $26,000 a year. The *California Grange News*, which began publication in January, 1932, was financed independently by subscription and advertising receipts.⁹

Men and women became eligible for membership in the basic unit, the Subordinate Grange, at the age of fourteen. Membership was held on an individual basis. The Pomona, or county, Granges were formed from the membership of the Subordinate Granges and were a ritualistic step above them. The Masters of the Subordinate and Pomona Granges and their wives were the official delegates to the annual state convention. Nonvoting delegates were urged to attend the annual meetings to participate in the ceremonies, of a higher ritualistic degree than those of the Pomona Granges. Statements of official policy were drawn up at these meetings by the passage of resolutions based upon suggestions submitted for the consideration of the convention by Subordinate and Pomona Granges. These proposed resolutions were submitted to the various standing and special committees of the State Grange, the members of which were appointed by the Master, and, after revision, they were presented to the voting delegates for debate and approval, amendment, or rejection. Actions of the state officers during the year were based on convention resolutions, but actually the Master enjoyed and exercised wide latitude in speaking and acting for the Grange. It is interesting to note that the programs publicized by the *Grange News* were not always in exact agreement with the policies laid down by the delegates to the annual conventions. In general, the editorial policies of the official journal were further to the left than those formulated at the annual conventions and dealt with many issues that the Grange delegates avoided.

The Grange, despite its renewed interest in political matters in the 1930's, remained primarily a fraternal order. As the editor of the *California Grange News* held:

Lying beneath these principles and having a deep, reverent meaning is *fraternalism*. This is the very key to success, the tie that binds; it is the brotherhood of man, without which success is not possible. Fraternalism bears a spiritual significance, an obligation to help one another, and this is the foundation stone of the Grange.[10]

For many farmers, especially in isolated rural areas, the Grange was the center of social and educational community life.

Under Sehlmeyer's leadership, the California Grange increased in size from 8,335 members in eighty-two Subordinate Granges in 1929 to 23,492 members in three hundred and four Subordinate Granges in 1941. In 1929 there were Subordinate Granges in twenty counties, all in northern California, and in 1941 there were active Grange units in forty-eight counties, including all the counties south of the Tehachapi except Imperial.[11] The Grange had a large membership in Sonoma and Santa Clara counties (resting primarily on a historical base), but otherwise it was strongest in those counties of northern California that were relatively unimportant from the viewpoint of total annual value of agricultural production.

In the period from 1929 to 1941 the California Grange nearly tripled in size, whereas the national organization increased only from a reported 576,563 members in 1929 to 638,804 members in 1941.[12] The California Grange extended into many new counties in these years. Lacking a large executive staff and operating on a relatively small budget, it extended outward from well-established centers of Grange strength. In 1935 the Executive Committee decided to send State Deputies south of the Tehachapi to found Subordinate Granges in that part of the state. There were requests from farmers in that area for the creation of Granges, and, at the same time, the Executive Committee believed that the political influence of the Grange would be greatly enhanced if it could validly claim to speak for farmers in all regions of the state. During 1935 Granges were organized in Riverside, San Bernardino, Orange, and San Diego counties, and during 1937 the counties of Santa Barbara, Ventura, and Los Angeles were added to the Grange fold. Grange units in southern California possessed little influence, however, until after 1941.[13]

The causes of the spectacular growth of the Grange in this period were many. Undoubtedly the depression induced many small farmers to join the Grange to seek alleviation of their economic grievances; the dynamic leadership of Sehlmeyer can hardly be overestimated; and the liberal program of political action probably had some influence. The Grange itself stated the causes it considered important in this upward swing in an editorial in the *Grange News*.

What has the Grange accomplished to warrant this great increase in membership? Certainly there must be a reason. Glancing at the record we can see that Grange leaders have stood valiantly for certain fundamental principles which have been in the minds of farmers for years, but which they were unable to advance for lack of leadership. Equality in taxation; the right of public ownership of utilities; reform in our banking system; protection of the small farmer against the injustices of so-called Big Business; representation before canners and packers of both fruits and livestock; demand for reduction in power rates and for water conservation; insistence on economy in government; and proper administration of our public offices....

But legislation and important positions are not the only evidences of progress. Better homes, improved community life, happy evenings of entertainment, all go to make up a successful year. Many a fear has been banished, many a load lightened by a Granger's extending a helping hand. This is the true measure of fraternity.[14]

In California the Grange membership consisted primarily of small and part-time farmers and included some persons who were not farmers at all. Time and again leaders of the State Grange stated publicly that the great part of its membership was composed of farmers who owned and operated small family farms.[15] That nonfarm members were sought by the Grange was indicated in an article in the *Grange News* that urged each

Subordinate Grange to work toward the goal of enrolling every teacher in the community as a member.[16] An independent study made in 1938 pointed out:

... the Grange, instead of growing more conservative as its parent organization in the East has tended to become since the original crusading zeal of the powerful "Grange movement" died out, has all along the Pacific tended to become the refuge of the more discontented farmers, who feel that all is not well with the official agrarian philosophies and activities. The Grange in California has accelerated this tendency of late years by taking in large numbers of part-time farmers who live on the edge of cities and who are semi-agrarian, and semi-industrial in their economic philosophy.[17]

There is evidence, too, of the type of farmer who joined the Grange in the kind of policies that the State Grange supported. A resolution passed in 1934 urged that corporation and large-scale farming be discouraged. The Grange in 1936 passed a resolution that suggested a graduated tax on chain ranches starting at a charge of $1 for the first ranch owned by any single person or corporation and increasing to a charge of $500 on each ranch in excess of ten. In 1938 the Grange stated its opposition to a proposed bill that would have forced all farmers to pasteurize their milk, objecting on the grounds that such a statute would throw the small dairy farmer out of business and thus benefit the large dairy ranchers. The Grange in 1939 vigorously supported a bill relating to the licensing of fishermen that would have operated to the benefit of the small fishing interests, because, as the Grange pointed out, many Grange members living in coastal areas supplemented their farm income by engaging in part-time fishing. In 1940 the organization opposed the imposition by the state of strict regulations for dairy barn construction and equipment, on the grounds that such restrictions would eliminate the small dairyman who could not afford to invest in the expensive equipment required under the proposed regulations. Delegates to the Grange convention in 1940 objected to the size of the checks that small farmers were getting from the Agricultural Adjustment Administration as compared with those paid to large operators and recommended that $1,000 be set as the maximum size of a government check to any single farmer. In 1941 the Grange supported a bill to permit home slaughtering of calves, on the grounds that small dairymen could realize significant additional revenue from the sale of meat if they were not forced to take their calves to a slaughterhouse for butchering. On each of these issues the Grange took its stand on the side of the small farmer.[16]

There were, of course, many kinds of farmers in the Grange, but the dominant group in the organization was composed of small, home-owning, family farmers. This fact, together with the fraternal aspects of the order, the traditional moral outlook of Grange members, an early history of social protest against economic monopoly and political corruption, the dynamic leadership of George Sehlmeyer, and the omnipresent fact of economic depression, accounts for the policy, program, and actions of the California State Grange from 1929 to 1941.

THE CALIFORNIA FARM BUREAU FEDERATION

3.

1919–1941

The Farm Bureau movement in California, from its earliest days to the present time, has paralleled the development of the same organization in other states; names and places have been different, but the general pattern has been identical. In the years just preceding the First World War, local Farm Bureaus were organized in various rural areas of California to coöperate with the Extension Service of the College of Agriculture of the University in its program for disseminating the technical information that was being developed in the Experiment Stations and in the University. The Smith-Lever Act of 1914 provided for the granting of federal funds to the states, on a dollar-matching basis, to pay the salaries of county agents (or farm advisers, as they came to be known in California), who were to teach farmers the principles of farm management and the practice of scientific methods of crop production. The farm advisers were hired and their salaries paid jointly by the United States Department of Agriculture and the Extension Service of the College of Agriculture, and their expenses (mileage, office rent, and supplies) were paid by appropriations made by county boards of supervisors. They conducted their educational activities through local Farm Bureaus and county Farm Bureaus, organized for that specific purpose.

The original aims of the Farm Bureaus were, therefore, educational in nature. The bureaus were independent, local organizations, which coöperated with the Extension Service and with the Department of Agriculture but were in no way connected with them; they were merely agencies through which the farm advisers could carry their work to the farmer. But, as farmers came together to hear lectures and to observe demonstrations, they soon began to realize that they had other things in common and that their organization could, if it wished, exert great influence over more than purely technical and managerial matters.

The organization of county Farm Bureaus was accelerated by the war, and by the end of the war various county units were contemplating the formation of a statewide group. Late in 1918 a special delegation from the San Joaquin County Farm Bureau visited Thomas Hunt, Dean of the College of Agriculture, and Professor B. H. Crocheron, director of the Agricultural Extension Service, to request that the latter take the initiative in calling a convention of Farm Bureaus at which a state organization might be formed. These two educators apparently thought that such a movement might involve the entire Farm Bureau setup in politics and thus imperil the educational program, which to them was the most important matter. Throughout the following year, however, other county Farm Bureaus added their requests to that of the San Joaquin group, and Professor Crocheron sent out an invitation for a meeting to be held in Berkeley October 22–23, 1919. Delegates from thirty-one county Farm Bureaus, along with the farm advisers of those counties, answered the invitation and assembled at Berkeley to organize the California Farm Bureau Federation. A short time thereafter, on November 12–13, 1919, the newly formed California Farm Bureau Federation (C.F. B.F.) joined with several other state organizations to form the American Farm Bureau Federation.[1]

Membership in the Farm Bureau was based on the family, rather than on the individual as in the Grange. During the first decade of its history the California Farm Bureau Federation increased its membership from 10,794 families in 1920 to 18,939 families in 1929. Membership was concentrated chiefly in the upper San Joaquin Valley and in southern California, with the counties of Los Angeles, Tulare, San Joaquin, Fresno, Orange, Riverside, Imperial, and Kern usually topping the list.[2]

Like the Grange in its formative years, the Farm Bureau attempted to help its members by going into the business of buying and selling grain and purchasing machinery and other

The California Farm Bureau Federation

supplies. A California Farm Bureau Exchange was set up as an independent business association by the Marketing Department of the C.F.B.F. in 1921, but by 1924 it had collapsed. The familiar causes for failure were present—inadequate financing, lack of customers, and inexperienced management. Unlike the Grange, however, the Farm Bureau was not seriously damaged by the failure of its business venture, and local Farm Bureaus continued, though on a smaller scale, to buy supplies and to sell commodities for their members.

From the beginning the Farm Bureau had a large and complex organizational structure. In 1921, in addition to an executive department composed of seven regional directors, there were special departments for Coöperation with State and Federal Institutions, Publication and Publicity, Public Utilities, Legislation, Education, Community Improvement, and University Farm Support, plus seven commodity departments and four technical departments. It is entirely possible that the State Farm Bureau suffered from overorganization during this formative period, but by 1929 a more rational structure had been worked out.

The California Farm Bureau, on both the local and state levels, was active in many areas throughout the 1920's. The local Farm Bureau centers and the county Farm Bureaus engaged in the purchase of fuel, fertilizer, and feed for their members. They held auctions for the sale of livestock. They coöperated with the Extension Service in promoting disease, pest, and weed control and in encouraging better methods and techniques of farm management and practice. They set up cow-testing associations. They coöperated with the home demonstration agents of the Extension Service for the improvement of family diets and housing. They fostered youth clubs, which soon developed into the 4-H movement. They assisted in the organization of labor bureaus for the rational recruitment of seasonal workers. They entered actively into local politics, influencing the budgeting activities of the county supervisors and organizing special fire and irrigation districts. They sponsored community projects for securing better mail service, for planting trees, and for staging bigger and better fairs. They organized coördinated drives against coyotes, squirrels, rats, and predatory animals. In short, the local Farm Bureau centers and the county Farm Bureaus responded to the every need of the farmers.

On the state level the Farm Bureau concerned itself with legislative matters, of both major and petty significance. A multitude of bills were written and sponsored by the group: bills for the establishment of a state bee inspection service, for the eradication of bovine tuberculosis, for the regulation of trespassing, for licensing seed dealers and commission merchants, for the improvement of market news service, for the regulation of warehouses, for soil conservation measures, for clarification of the water code, for establishment of uniform standards for California agricultural commodities, for the forcing of a strict labeling law upon California canners. All these were matters to which the state organization turned its attention.

The California Farm Bureau, in the 1920's, was careful and conservative in almost all it did. It rarely took an official position on any issue without first thoroughly investigating all aspects and phases of the issue. On controversial matters on which there was likely to be a serious divergence of opinion within the group, the Farm Bureau took no stand. Although it was operating in a dominantly Republican decade, and its policies and actions were usually in sympathy with the program and outlook of that party, the Farm Bureau kept aloof from partisan politics and refused to endorse candidates for office. Its major achievement in the realm of politics was the sponsoring and securing of an amendment to the state constitution that based election of state senators on county units instead of the former "equal population" districts. This amendment, which was also supported by the Grange and other farm organizations, gave the rural areas predominant representation in the upper house of the legislature and greatly enhanced the political power of organized farmers in state politics. In the field of state fiscal policy, the Farm Bureau launched an investigation of the tax structure with the purpose of evolving plans for legislation to reduce reliance of government upon the general property tax. In the formulation of labor policy the Farm Bureau represented the interests of the farm employers.

The California Farm Bureau Federation

When R. W. Blackburn assumed the presidency in 1929, the Farm Bureau had a large membership concentrated in the most important agricultural counties of the state; the organization was well organized and adequately financed, and it was prepared to act upon diverse political and economic matters. The general character of the California Farm Bureau was established in the first ten years of its existence, and it rarely deviated from this pattern in the period 1929-1941.

The basic organizational unit of the Farm Bureau was the county group, but it was in meetings of the local Farm Bureau centers that the farm advisers and the home demonstration agents of the Extension Service did their educational work. In most parts of the state the farm centers were organized strictly on a locality basis, but, because of the production of hundreds of diverse specialty crops in many areas, a number of farm centers came to be organized on a commodity basis as well. Thus, in Ventura and Los Angeles counties the local farm centers were not community affairs, but instead were organized on the basis of the commodity produced by the farmer—apricots, citrus fruits, walnuts, truck crops, milk, field crops, livestock, and poultry.[3] The county units, resting upon the mass membership of the local Farm Bureaus, had their own boards of directors, executive officers, commodity departments, and policy committees.

Before 1931 the state organization was governed by a Board of Directors on which each county unit had one representative, and by an Executive Committee composed of representatives chosen by the eight regional districts into which the state was divided; the executive officers were elected annually by delegates to the state convention. On October 31, 1931, however, the California Farm Bureau Federation was legally constituted a nonprofit corporation with a constitution that provided for major changes in the state organizational structure. Under the new constitution, each county was authorized to send to the annual convention one voting delegate for each three hundred members. County delegates within each of the eight regions now selected one of their number to serve on the Board of Directors. These regional directors served two-year terms, with half of the directorships falling vacant each year. The delegates to the annual convention were empowered to elect a president and a vice-president, whose terms of office ran for two years. The state leader of the farm advisers and the state chairman of the Farm Home Department were made ex officio members of the Board of Directors. The secretary treasurer, an officer previously elected annually by the delegates to the convention, was now selected by the Board of Directors and was made responsible to that group. This constitution remained in effect throughout the remainder of the period under discussion.[4]

The House of Delegates, which met in November of each year, had the responsibility of formulating policy for the state organization on the basis of resolutions submitted for its consideration by the local Farm Bureau centers and by the county Farm Bureaus. From one convention to the next, however, the Board of Directors and the executive officers had to exercise great latitude of judgment in interpreting policy statements and in working out specific proposals based upon general programs.

The state organization had the following service departments in 1929: Farm Home Department, Publicity Department, Law and Utilities Department, Tax Research Department, and Insurance Department. By 1941 there had been added a Director of Marketing, a General Counsel, and an Organization Department. The Farm Home Department coöperated with the Extension Service in planning and executing the programs of the farm home demonstrators. The Publicity Department supervised the publication of the *Farm Bureau Monthly* and also handled general press releases.[5] The Law and Utilities Department, created in November, 1920, handled work concerned with electric rates, water and power legislation, and miscellaneous legal matters; its chairman often appeared before the State Railroad Commission in cases involving the regulation of utilities. The Tax Research Department, organized in 1927, soon dropped the "tax" from its title and assumed the task of conducting research on all legislative matters. From its inception in 1927 this department has been under the direction of Von T. Ellsworth, who has also served as chief lobby representative of the Farm Bureau before the state legislature. The Insurance Department was dropped in 1931, when it was decided that the sale of various types of insurance should not be an integral part of Farm Bureau activities. The Organization Department, which had functioned briefly during 1923, was reëstablished in December, 1929; its main function was that of supervising membership drives. The Director of Marketing and the General Counsel did miscellaneous work in the fields indicated by their titles.[6]

The commodity departments of the Farm Bureau were also of great importance. By 1941 commodity departments had been established for citrus fruits, deciduous fruit, livestock, cotton, edible nuts, poultry, dairy products, field crops, and vegetables. The departments were directed by delegates from the commodity departments or committees of the various county Farm Bureaus. These delegates annually elected state chairmen to direct the activities of the various departments. The commodity departments worked in close coöperation with the Extension Service in executing programs for controlling disease and pests, increasing farm efficiency, improving crop quality, and rationalizing marketing operations; they were also active in securing protective and regulatory legislation for the various crops concerned.[7]

After the failure of the California Farm Bureau Exchange in 1924, the state organization was reluctant to enter into other business enterprises either for the purchase of supplies for its members or for the sale of their commodities. Many county Farm Bureaus, however, continued to operate their own purchasing and marketing associations. During the 1930's some of these continued to be managed by local Farm Bureau units; some developed into independent coöperatives; others were sold to private interests; still others were discontinued. In most cases the county Farm Bureaus chose to work in close coöperation with existing coöperative associations rather than set up their own independent and competing companies. Farm Bureau leaders were often active in setting up new coöperatives and in strengthening those already in existence, whereas the associations, in return, encouraged their membership to join the Farm Bureau. At the state level the Farm Bureau and the coöperatives worked together on legislative matters. The Farm

Bureau did not enter into direct business activities on a large scale again until after 1941.[8]

Farm Bureau membership varied little from 1929 to 1941 either in total enrollment or in distribution by counties. In 1929 the C.F.B.F. claimed a membership of 18,939 families throughout the state; the figure fell to 15,259 in 1933, but by 1941 it had risen to 22,154. The counties with the largest number of members continued to be Los Angeles, Tulare, San Joaquin, Orange, Riverside, Ventura, and Fresno, although their positions relative to each other shifted slightly from year to year. The counties with the largest percentage of all farmers enrolled as Farm Bureau members were Colusa, Santa Barbara, Ventura, Yolo, and Lassen. The center of Farm Bureau membership and influence lay in southern California and in the upper San Joaquin Valley.[9]

The educational activities of the Farm Bureau were financed jointly by federal, state, and county governments, but all other activities of the Farm Bureau were financed entirely out of annual membership dues. The state organization expended $70,679.23 in 1929; the figure fell to $55,873.00 in 1933, but rose again to $67,934.06 in 1941. The largest expenditures for any one year were made in 1937, when $76,857.45 was spent by the state organization. To these sums should be added the substantial expenditures of the various county units.[10]

Leadership in the California Farm Bureau was more widely distributed than it was in the State Grange, which George Sehlmeyer and a small Executive Committee dominated. The provision for eight regional directorships meant that each of the major geographic areas of California was always represented in the state organization. The numerous service and commodity departments drew many farmers into active participation in Farm Bureau affairs, and some assumed positions of leadership. There was, however, a natural tendency to keep in office those men who proved themselves able and who had the money and leisure to take an active part in the affairs of the organization. In this way men with experience and with well-established contacts could maintain a continuity of policy and execute that policy with a maximum of efficiency and effectiveness.

Most of the Farm Bureau leaders were substantial farmers, owning or operating large farms, and many of them had business interests other than those in agriculture. R. W. Blackburn, president from 1929 to January, 1938, operated a 320-acre farm in Riverside on which he cultivated sixty acres of grapes, ten acres of grapefruit and tangerines, one acre of figs, and one acre of date palms. He served as president of the Mecca Growers' Association (a coöperative marketing association for grapes and figs) and as a director of the First National Bank of Indio. He was also active in several other marketing coöperatives. He resigned as president of the C.F.B.F. in January, 1938, to become secretary treasurer of the American Farm Bureau Federation.[11] Ray B. Wiser, who served as vice-president from 1931 to January, 1938, and who succeeded to the presidency at the latter date, owned and operated a 120-acre farm in Butte County. On about half of this acreage Wiser produced alfalfa, grains, and beans, and on the other half he raised peaches and a few prunes and almonds.[12]

U. Butte Tyler, vice-president from 1929 to 1931, farmed 2,000 acres of grain and also operated a 12-acre apricot orchard and a 24-acre almond orchard. On this farm he ran eight hundred head of cattle and four hundred hogs. In addition to these agricultural interests he was employed by the Tehama County Bank.[13] E. C. Kimball, director for Region 2 from 1934 to January, 1938, and vice-president of the state organization from the latter date to 1941, was a walnut and citrus grower from Ventura County. He was active in two marketing associations and was a director of the Union National Bank of Ventura. The economic interests of the regional directors of the Farm Bureau were similarly substantial.[14] The leadership of the California Farm Bureau Federation was, then, furnished by large farmers with substantial economic interests. Many of them were also active in the economically powerful marketing associations of California.

It is more difficult, however, to determine what kind of farm operator made up the basic membership of the Farm Bureau. A large proportion of the larger, more prosperous, more progressive farmers of the state undoubtedly were active in the organization, but owners of small and medium-sized farms probably made up the bulk of the membership.[15] John Pickett, editor of the *Pacific Rural Press*, made this observation of the character of the Farm Bureau convention that met in 1938:

> The annual convention and banquet of the California Farm Bureau Federation at Sacramento... at least 1,500 farmers who farm their farms present... representing all parts of the State... some who specialize in criticism call it an organization of Big Farmers... young, progressive President Ray Wiser, Butte County farmer, directed attention to those present in the banquet room at Merriam Hall, State Fair Grounds... many little farmers, a lot of middle size farmers, very few big farmers... perhaps one might correctly say that the audience was a cross-section of middle class farmers, men and women who are richer in service and in civic conscience than in land...[16]

During the 1930's the policies of the Farm Bureau and the Grange were often contradictory. Their contrasting forms of organization, the differences in the type and location of their membership, and their disparate kinds of leadership—all serve to explain their variances in outlook and action.

4. ECONOMIC CRISIS AND LABOR STRIFE THE ACTION

Underlying every social and political problem in California during the period 1929–1941 was the inescapable fact of economic depression. Every problem of California agriculture—labor relations, taxation, controlled marketing, ownership of electric power—was related to and aggravated by economic prostration. Fixed cash costs continued at a relatively high rate but the market price for California's specialty crops, always sensitive to effective demand, dropped to levels that frequently failed to yield sufficient gross returns to cover total operating costs. And, even with prices at these low levels, national purchasing power was so weak that great surpluses of California crops could not be taken off the market. California farmers sought to cut operating costs. But tax, interest, and insurance payments could be lowered but little, and operating expenses for electricity, water, fertilizer, sprays, and transportation decreased only slightly.

The farmer did have some control over at least one cost item, however—wage payments to hired migratory labor. Hourly or piece-rate wage levels, and total wage payments to agricultural labor in California, fell faster and farther and stayed depressed longer than gross farm income, net farm income, and total expenses.[1] Many farm employers found they could stay in production only by cutting wages. Wage costs had to be low enough to justify the employment of labor in the final production steps of harvesting and marketing. If prices were not high enough to allow the payment of wages to labor, the crops were left to rot in the fields or the fruit to drop unpicked from the trees. Wages sufficient to give laborers even a minimum standard of existence were often too high for the farm employers to pay. When the price situation improved employers were often reluctant to increase wages, for wage rates were virtually the only cash cost item they could manipulate so as to return to themselves the highest net profit.

Here, then, was the basis for class conflict and strife in California agriculture. Here want in the midst of plenty was a stark reality. Urban unemployed were occasionally just as hungry as agricultural migrants, but the latter could actually see the crops destroyed, the milk dumped, and the fruit rotting on the ground. The paradox of gnawing want in the midst of plenty was nowhere more apparent than in the warm fertile valleys of California.

Aggravating the situation still further was the influx of thousands of white migrants in this decade, emigrating largely from the states of the southern Great Plains. "Blown-out and tractored-off," the "Okies" and "Arkies" fled from drought and debt to the promise of the Golden State. Two hundred thousand of them entered in the years 1936 and 1937 alone. The total number of such migrants entering the state during the period 1930–1940 has been estimated at about 1,200,000.[2] Urban unemployment, and the fact that most of the migrants had been farmers, drove these thousands into an agricultural labor market already glutted with an oversupply of workers.

These migrants added a new complex to the historical pattern of farm labor. They were white; they were experienced farmers and good workers, although hardly trained for the type of labor required by California crops; they carried with them traditions of democracy that earlier, alien groups had lacked; they came with their families, and traveled with all their earthly possessions. Welcomed at first, they soon came to be ridiculed, disliked, and feared. Dr. Clements, of the Los Angeles Chamber of Commerce, candidly described the nature of the migrant problem as follows:

This year [1936] 90 per cent of the labor consisted of migratory labor from the south, mid-south, and south-east. This labor, mostly white, is supposed to supplant the former Mexican laborers who were what might be termed versatile labor, since when the 150 days of agricultural labor were over they could turn their hands to manual labor of rough industry and ... tighten their belts and exist on the minimum of subsistence.... They were impossible of unionizing; they were tractable labor. Can we expect these new white transient citizens to fill their place? The white transients are not tractable labor. Being American citizens, they are going to demand the so-called American standards of living. In our own estimation they are going to be the finest pabulum for unionization for either group—the A.F. of L. or the subversive elements. They are not going to be satisfied with 160 working days.[3]

The plight of the migrant in this decade was investigated, documented, and publicized as few other social problems have ever been. Pamphlets, novels, government reports, doctoral dissertations, and newspaper accounts all discussed the problem at length, and with partisanship and passion. From this plethora of material one can gather certain obvious and unchallengeable conclusions concerning the living conditions of the migrants: rural housing was poor at the best, and degrading at the worst; sanitation facilities were inadequate; health, especially that of the children, was substandard; education was generally poor; hourly wage rates may have been higher in California than in other states, but unemployment and underemployment made annual earnings dangerously low.

These conditions led to movements for unionization of agricultural workers. The drives often resulted in spontaneous, short, and violent strikes when demands for better conditions, higher wages, and union recognition were met with active resistance by farm employer groups. The organization of these unions among agricultural workers was one of the principal factors that led to the formation of the Associated Farmers of California.

The first union to take advantage of the desperate conditions in the early years of the depression was the Cannery and Agricultural Workers' Industrial Union (C. and A.W.I.U.). This organization was avowedly a part of the Communist Party. It had no mass membership, existing in leadership only. It was subordinate to the Trade Union Unity League, which in turn took orders from the Red International of Labor Unions, which in its turn was part of the Communist International.[4] The central strategy of this union was to assume leadership of the many spontaneous strikes breaking out all through the rich valleys of California. In the one year 1933 the C. and A.W.I.U. furnished leadership for three-quarters of all the strikes and for four-fifths of the 48,000 workers on strike.[5] This union, it was charged, was interested only in the disruption of the economy for the purpose of causing its collapse and disintegration. The union itself admitted that this was an ultimate goal but insisted upon the sincerity of its actions in helping the downtrodden farm workers to secure better wages and conditions.

The effectiveness of this union in stirring up trouble is attested by the way in which farm employers reacted to the threat. Pat Chambers, his colleague Carolyn Decker, and many of their assistants were often escorted unceremoniously from the scene of strikes by vigilante groups. The trial of the top leaders of the union at Sacramento for violation of the Criminal Syndicalism Act in 1934–1935 put an end to the union, for its leaders were found guilty and sentenced to prison. Some of them were later released upon appeal in 1937, but by then the crisis had passed.[6] The C. and A.W.I.U. became defunct in the summer of 1934, and, following the new policy of the Communist International to bore from within and to unite with liberal and reform organizations, the parent body, the Trade Union Unity League, was formally dissolved in 1935. Because of the new Communist line of promoting the "Popular Front," it became ever more difficult to trace the influence of Communists in subsequent agricultural unions.[7]

Following the collapse of the C. and A.W.I.U. there was relative quiet on the labor front for a time. The lack of leadership among agricultural workers and the upswing in income and wages from the desperate depths of 1930–1933 promoted peace in rural areas. The strikes that did occur in 1935 and early 1936 were precipitated largely by Mexican and Filipino unions or by unorganized workers acting in desperation.

The American Federation of Labor, however, soon took notice of the vacuum created by the lack of unionization in the agricultural counties. Believing that its urban position would be better consolidated if the hinterland were organized, it began to lay plans for a "march inland." Coöperating in this movement were the International Longshoremen's Union and the Teamsters' Union, both of the A.F. of L.[8] A conference composed of delegates from various A.F. of L. unions in addition to several unaffiliated unions of Mexican, Filipino, and Japanese workers was held in Stockton, June 6–7, 1936. This conference was led by Edward Vandeleur of the State Federation of Labor; the honorary chairman was Norman Thomas. Plans were laid to set up statewide agricultural locals and to fight for better conditions and wages among rural workers.[9] In putting the program into effect, Edward Vandeleur was quoted as saying:

There never has been a stable or responsible organization of farm workers in California and, as a result, we have had twenty-five years of intermittent turmoil and bloodshed as symptoms of bad conditions. The California State Federation of Labor's participation in organizing the agricultural workers means the conservative and responsible labor movement is at last moving into a field that heretofore has been left to left wing agitation.[10]

The A.F. of L. Executive Council consistently refused to charter a statewide agricultural union, however, insisting that field and processing unions should be kept separate. On the other hand, the local unions themselves (as yet without charters) insisted that their strength lay in unity of the two groups. A conference of agricultural workers was held in San Francisco in February, 1937, attended by delegates from fourteen A.F. of L. locals, fifteen locals of a Mexican farm labor union, four Filipino labor unions, and the Japanese Agricultural Workers' Association. This conference called for one big union of cannery and field workers.[11]

In the meantime a National Committee for Agricultural Workers had been established in Washington, D.C., for the purpose of establishing industrial unions in the fields and in the canneries. In its organ, the *Rural Worker,* it called for progress and unity. In the June, 1937, issue of this paper a call was sent forth by forty-four A.F. of L. unions and eight independent unions for a meeting to be held in Denver: "The policy of the CIO in successfully organizing in industry-wide unions and their policy of aggressively assisting the organization of the unorganized with advice, funds, and organizers makes it necessary for us to seriously consider affiliation to the CIO."[12] In reaction to this pronouncement the California

A.F. of L. ousted all local officers suspected of being Communists or pro-C.I.O. and revoked the charters of such locals as were mistrusted.[13] The conference was held in July, 1937, with ninety-seven delegates, representing some 100,000 workers, in attendance. The delegates voted almost unanimously to affiliate with the C.I.O. and laid plans first to unionize cannery and packing-house employees and then to extend into the field. The name adopted by the new organization was the United Cannery, Agricultural, Packing and Allied Workers of America (U.C.A.P.A.W.A.).[14]

To meet the challenge of this rival organization the A.F. of L. established a National Council of Cannery and Agricultural Workers in December, 1937, to represent all field, shed, cannery, and winery workers. The president of this group was Charles W. Real, a teamster official from Alameda County. By 1939 this group had organized some 70,000 workers in canneries, citrus packing houses, vegetable packing houses, dairies and creameries, and wineries and distilleries, but it had not attempted to unionize field workers.[15]

The U.C.A.P.A.W.A. likewise was slow to organize field labor, finding it difficult to do so without a firm base in the canning and processing plants. The best it could do was to send organizers into localities where strikes were threatened or had already been called by independent groups. This union never had a large mass membership in California. It did assume leadership of a number of strikes from 1937 to 1939, but many of them were poorly planned and ended in failure. By 1940 it could claim a national membership of 26,000 in agricultural industries and 75,000 in one hundred and fifty nine field locals scattered throughout the country, but its main strength lay outside of California.[16]

Most of the numerous short-lived agricultural unions organized in California during the 1930's were formed spontaneously for the single purpose of conducting strikes to secure better wages, better working conditions, and union recognition. This tendency was especially pronounced in the unions of field workers; these unions rarely held together after their strikes were broken or, even if their strikes were successful, after the short season had ended and the workers had moved on to harvest crops in different parts of the state. There was little opportunity for effective collective bargaining by these short-lived unions of field workers. Often situations developed that made it easy for radical leaders to assume control of a strike. This brand of leadership brought to the field experience gained in other strikes, skill and training in the techniques of disruption, a unity of purpose that tended to give temporary cohesiveness to otherwise diverse and unorganized groups, and a philosophy that made them willing, and even eager, to accept threats to their persons.

There were two peaks of strike activity during this period: one in 1933, when more than 50,000 workers were involved in more than thirty major strikes in the field, and another in 1936, when approximately 13,000 workers participated in twenty-four strikes.[17] It is interesting to note that the chief impetus for the original formation of the Associated Farmers came during the fall of 1933, when strikes in agriculture reached an intensity not approached before or since. After the upsurge in strike activity in 1936 the Associated Farmers was reorganized on a wider basis.

A series of radically led strikes staged during the period from 1930 to 1934 furnished the immediate cause for the organization of the Associated Farmers of California. The fact that so many of these strikes were led by the radical C. and A.W.I.U. tended to intensify the farm employers' fear and hatred of all agricultural unions. Three strikes especially—the Lodi grape strike in October of 1933, the cotton strike in the upper San Joaquin Valley in the fall of 1933, and the vegetable pickers' strike in the Imperial Valley in 1934—were of such size and intensity as to inspire farm employers to organize for the purpose of preventing similar disturbances in the future. Each of these strikes was characterized by violence on both sides. In each strike farm employers organized themselves into vigilante groups to take the law into their own hands, although the members of these groups were often deputized by local sheriffs to give to them a semblance of legality.

At Lodi, Colonel Walter E. Garrison, later to become president of the Associated Farmers, led the farmers in their resistance to the workers. Here the strike was broken, but not before much of the grape crop had rotted unpicked and sunscorched on the vine.[18]

The cotton strike of 1933 in Kern, Kings, Tulare, and Fresno counties was the largest of the three. The growers offered wage rates of 60 cents per 100 pounds of cotton picked and maintained that they could not afford to pay more. The workers, under radical leadership of the C. and A.W.I.U., demanded $1 per hundred, union hiring, and the abolition of the labor contract system. A Farmers' Protective Association was organized to resist these union demands. Violence soon broke out, reaching a peak October 10 when three strikers were killed and a score injured. Attempts by government agencies to mediate the strike met with slight success. On October 24, the growers finally announced that they would accept a 75-cent rate, a figure suggested earlier by Governor Rolph's fact-finding committee. It was planned to deny federal relief to all workers who refused to accept employment at this rate. When the union refused this compromise offer and continued to hold out for 80 cents, federal relief was cut off and protection was given to nonstriking workers by the state highway patrol and county deputies. Strike leaders were forcibly evacuated from union headquarters at Corcoran and some were jailed. The strike was broken, and by the end of October cotton picking had returned to normal. The farm employers had learned that by banding together and by taking direct and drastic action the demands of agricultural workers could be successfully resisted.[19]

The vegetable pickers' strike in the Imperial Valley the following spring repeated the familiar pattern—low wages and unemployment, widespread discontent, subversion and violence, coöperation of employer groups and local government officials to keep the peace, mass arrests, and eventually the breaking of the strike.[20] Such events, repeated in nearly every agricultural area of California, led to the formation of the Associated Farmers.

5.

THE ASSOCIATED FARMERS
THE REACTION

The first group to feel a need for forming some sort of farmers' organization to meet the threat of unionization and strikes was the Agricultural Labor Subcommittee of the State Chamber of Commerce. Meeting in Los Angeles, November 6, 1933, just after the long, violent, and costly cotton strike in the San Joaquin Valley, the Subcommittee submitted for the consideration of the Agricultural Committee of the State Chamber a resolution calling for action to put an end to Communist agitation through enforcement of the State Criminal Syndicalism Act and to cut off all relief to persons voluntarily idle during a strike. The Subcommittee also suggested that the Chamber's Farm Labor Committee be enlarged into a broader Citizens' Committee.[1]

The Board of Directors of the State Chamber of Commerce, meeting November 10, 1933, approved these recommendations and called for the formation of a Citizens' Committee to include civic and business groups.[2] S. Parker Frisselle was given the task of organizing this Citizens' Committee. He had been manager of a 5,000-acre ranch near Fresno, an active leader in the Agricultural Labor Bureau of the San Joaquin Valley, a director of the Kern Sunset Oil Company, and a prominent member of the State Chamber of Commerce.[3]

Frisselle, in a letter to Frank J. Palomares of the San Joaquin Agricultural Labor Bureau, dated November 15, 1933, gave an indication of what directions this new committee might take. He wrote:

It is my thought that this group can become the nucleus of a State-wide organization and can develop policies for immediately handling whatever situation may develop.... Possibly it will be necessary to further organize on a county basis in each county in which strike difficulties are imminent, in order that the citizens may come to understand in advance many of the experiences of other countries including the type of Communist leaders dealt with, the vicious methods which they have used ... and probably the most important political methods which have been successful in other countries in dealing with acute problems.⁴

An organizing committee met in the Palace Hotel in San Francisco, November 28, 1933, with Frisselle presiding and R. N. Wilson of the State Chamber of Commerce acting as secretary. Twenty-four persons were present, including representatives from the Pacific Gas and Electric Company, the Southern Pacific Railroad, the California Packing Corporation (Calpak), and the Bank of America. Here it was moved and carried: "That the President of the State Chamber and the President of the California Farm Bureau Federation name a few men to constitute an executive committee to carry out the ideas developed during this meeting."⁵ It was agreed that the influence of the Citizens' Committee should be extended into local regions where agricultural disturbances were anticipated.

After another such meeting at Modesto on December 13, 1933, an Executive Committe was chosen by the method indicated above.⁶ This committee was to act as a policy-making body only, however; Edson Abel of the Farm Bureau and R. N. Wilson were to carry on the actual organization work.⁷ The Chamber of Commerce and the Farm Bureau sent letters to their representatives in the various communities of California, suggesting that meetings of local leaders be held to discuss the situation. Representatives of the utilities and banks, processors and distributors of farm commodities came to these secret gatherings. Of these meetings, R. N. Wilson noted:

... The Farm Bureau usually has 5 [representatives] including the county Farm Bureau president and the heads of the 4 different departments. This will leave room for about 10 others, and these should include the sheriff, district attorney, the chief of police and the chairman of the Board of Supervisors.⁸

Meetings of this nature were held in various parts of the state during the winter months of 1933–1934. Wilson and Abel met with groups in eight counties and had them organized into Citizens' Committees by the end of January, 1934. By the

The Associated Farmers—the Reaction

middle of March twenty-one counties had been visited with satisfactory results.⁹

On March 28, 1934, a meeting of delegates from the various local Citizens' Committees was held in Fresno with Frisselle presiding and Wilson acting as secretary. To this gathering came thirty-five representatives, fourteen of them registering as county representatives of the Citizens' Committees that had been established. The chief decision made at this meeting is reported in a letter from Mr. Wilson to F. A. Stewart, dated April 4, 1934, stating that more than twenty-seven counties had been visited and that:

... more than twenty counties have passed picketing ordinances and a few have passed camp ordinances. In addition, the respective counties have in most cases perfected some type of organization to meet whatever communistic troubles may develop.... Each county has been asked to appoint a county representative to meet and form a statewide organization....

On March 28, an Executive Committee, representing the southern counties and the county representatives of some seventeen northern counties, met in Fresno and decided to form a definite statewide group to be called the Associated Farmers of California, or the California Farmers' Committee, the final determination of the name to be left to the Executive Committee.[10]

At this meeting in Fresno a constitution for the new organization was drawn up, and a new Executive Committee, composed of nine members, was selected to carry on the work begun by the Citizens' Committees. S. Parker Frisselle was named chairman of this new committee.[11]

On May 21 the Executive Committee adopted the constitution and bylaws drawn up in March, and the Associated Farmers (A.F.) was soon thereafter incorporated as a nonprofit organization. The members of the Executive Committee formally named themselves the Board of Directors of the Associated Farmers, and these nine men constituted the sole membership of the organization for the next two years. Throughout 1934 and 1935 the Executive Committee of the state group made no effort to secure mass membership for their organization. The original local Citizens' Committees remained small or became inactive. Only three county units of the Associated Farmers were formally incorporated during these two years, and these units remained autonomous and without representation in the state group until the latter was reorganized on a mass membership basis in 1936.

This small group then faced the problem of how best it could achieve the goals that it had set for itself. The local Citizens' Committees had already tackled one phase of the problem by promoting the adoption of local antipicketing ordinances. It was decided that this program should be continued and expanded. The group also planned a publicity program designed to educate the public to the danger of Communism and to secure popular support for a concerted attack on radically led agricultural unions. The Committee felt that if the radical leaders of the C. and A.W.I.U. could be successfully prosecuted under the Criminal Syndicalism Act (a legal procedure that had already been followed with some success in Imperial County) the consequent loss of leadership might bring the collapse of the unions.

But all this would take money. Where was the money to come from? It was only natural that the Executive Committee should turn for funds to the same groups that had sponsored the organization in the beginning—the agricultural interests that had previously worked through the State Chamber of Commerce or the Farm Bureau and the industries that were closely allied with the farming business of the state and had immediate and personal interest in the volume and costs of agricultural production and in the general stability of social and economic conditions.

The problem of how the needed funds were to be raised had already been discussed at a meeting of the Board of Directors of the Chamber of Commerce on April 20. At this meeting the Chamber appointed four of its members to assist the Associated Farmers in the collection of funds: Colbert Coldwell, a real estate agent; Leonard E. Wood, president of Calpak; R. E. Fisher, vice-president of the Pacific Gas and Electric Company; and R. N. Wilson, who was to serve as secretary of the committee. Colbert Coldwell set to work immediately to organize a subcommittee to serve under him. His appointees consisted of leaders of various industries: Preston McKinney, vice-president of the Canners' League of California, was to collect money from the canners' group; Arthur Oppenheim, president of Rosenberg Brothers, was to collect from the utility interests; F. L. Burckhalter, vice-president of the Southern Pacific Railroad, was to get contributions from transportation groups; Philip H. Patchin, president of Standard Oil of California, was selected to approach the oil interests of the state; Roger Lapham, chairman of the Board of Directors of the American-Hawaiian Steamship Company, was to collect from intercoast shipping groups; Charles McIntosh, an official of the Bank of America, was to get contributions from his friends in the financial world; and Atholl McBean of Gladding-McBean and Company, was to collect from miscellaneous interests.[12] Coldwell testified concerning the work of this subcommittee:

When the request was made that San Francisco make a contribution toward the budget of the Associated Farmers, the point was very strongly made that San Francisco business had a very selfish interest in this, outside of any general public interest; that selfish interest being that if the crops for that year were not moved that industry and business in general in San Francisco would suffer.[13]

This subcommittee enjoyed little success. Lapham and McBean were too busy with their own troubles on the waterfront to bother much with the problems of the farmers. Of the $36,000 that was supposed to be raised by this subcommittee, however, a little less than $7,000 was actually collected. Consequently, on June 26, 1934, Leonard Wood took over Coldwell's task.[14] Wood secured the coöperation of his colleagues in Calpak for the collection of sums from various industrial groups, although he later maintained that he had collected funds for the Associated Farmers as an individual and not as an executive of Calpak. Wood insisted that he called upon his friends for their services as "patriotic citizens." The fact remains, however, that solicitation letters were sent out under the letterhead of Calpak and donors usually referred to their gifts as solicited by Calpak and not by Wood personally. By July 30, 1934, Wood had collected $17,574.25—enough money to give the Associated Farmers a good start in life.[15]

The funds collected by Wood in 1934 were sufficient to finance the organization until October of that year. From

The Associated Farmers—the Reaction

October to January of 1935 the Industrial Association of San Francisco furnished the chief subsidy. Then, from January to March, 1935, the Calpak group again assumed the task of keeping the Associated Farmers solvent. Alfred W. Eames of Calpak managed the collection of funds this time. From March to May, 1935, the Industrial Association of San Francisco once more assumed the task of subsidization. Throughout this entire period there were many times when the funds of the Associated Farmers were dangerously low, and it was only by last-minute contributions from either the Calpak group or the Industrial Association that the organization was able to keep going. But by the fall of 1935 the Associated Farmers was almost completely without funds, and its activities were at a standstill.[16]

The upsurge of unionism and strikes in 1936, however, caused a revival of interest in the Associated Farmers. In this year the Association was reorganized on a mass membership basis, with emphasis upon local county units. The expansion of the activities of the Associated Farmers necessitated the raising of ever more money. From May, 1934, to November, 1939, the Associated Farmers collected $184,231.00; of this sum, $175,002.58 was disbursed.[17] As part of the reorganization in 1936, the county units assumed more and more responsibility in the collection of funds. Part of the money was kept by the local units for use in functions that had previously been carried on by the state organization; the rest was used by the state organization for those activities that could be handled best on a statewide basis. In the earlier years of the organization the northern California interests had carried almost the entire burden by themselves. Another change in the financial structure came as industries and agricultural interests in southern California began to contribute large sums. The heaviest contributors from the southern part of the state were Southern Californians, Inc., the Crown-Willamette Paper Company, and the Southern California Edison Company.[18]

Contributions from industrial interests continued to be of major importance. The ten largest contributors to the Associated Farmers, though constituting but the smallest fraction of 1 per cent of all contributors, provided 44.3 per cent of all funds. These ten were, in order of the size of their total donations: the Industrial Association of San Francisco; the Dried Fruit Association of California; the Canners' League; the Southern Pacific Railroad; Southern Californians, Inc.; the Atcheson, Topeka, and Santa Fe Railroad; the Pacific Gas and Electric Company; the San Joaquin Cotton Oil Company; the Holly Sugar Corporation; and the Spreckels Investment Company.[19]

Since it was impossible for the Associated Farmers to keep its sources of income secret, the group was constantly attacked as a "front" organization for big business. To meet these charges, which tended to discredit the organization and to lessen its effectiveness, the Associated Farmers made available for public consumption a leaflet that explained the organization and financing of the group in the following terms:

BY WHOM ORGANIZED

By farmers, run by farmers, with a farmer directorate, and financed (except for emergency expenditures) by farmers—in spite of all propaganda to the contrary put out by those whose subversive efforts are handicapped by the existence of such organizations as the Associated Farmers of California, Incorporated.

HOW FINANCED

By a nominal assessment upon agricultural commodities in this State. This apportionment is set and approved by the commodity groups themselves. It is so small that it may be considered negligible, but in the aggregate will furnish ample finance to properly take care of the agricultural situation.[20]

6.

REORGANIZATION OF THE ASSOCIATED FARMERS

The reorganization of the Associated Farmers on a broader base in 1936 was, as mentioned in a preceding chapter, a response to the increase in unionization and strike activity of farm labor. Although the strikes in 1936 reached neither the size nor intensity of those staged in 1933, they nevertheless constituted a real threat to the stability of California agriculture. Some of the leaders in the Associated Farmers soon began to urge renewed activity. As early as November 23, 1935, Frisselle wrote to Clements of the Los Angeles Chamber of Commerce: "... the situation is quite as serious today, and perhaps more serious than it was in 1933."[1] The letter mentioned knowledge of secret plans of the Communist Party to disrupt agriculture. In response to these alleged plots, the Executive Committee hired John Phillips, conservative Republican Assemblyman from Riverside County, as field representative to organize local units.

However, not all of the members of the groups that had previously furnished the primary support of the Association were convinced of the need for reorganization. The California Farm Bureau Federation, for example, which had coöperated in the creation of the Associated Farmers in 1934, did not participate actively in the reorganization of the group in 1936. And when E. Clements Horst, president of the E. C. Horst Company which was engaged in the raising and processing of canned and dried fruits, and himself a large grower of hops, was asked to contribute to the organization, he replied, on December 27, 1935:

We have employed every year for many years last past, many thousands of harvest hands, without having the slightest labor troubles. This makes us feel that the best way for farmers to overcome so-called red activities is to improve the working conditions for harvest help.

Until such time as we feel that harvest help is unreasonable in its demands, we do not feel like taking any part in any antilabor campaign.

It has been our experience that our own help makes life so unpleasant for reds on our various ranches, that they move to other farms whose pay or working conditions should be corrected.[2]

It was this attitude that the Associated Farmers had to overcome if it were to succeed in its reorganization. Magazine articles, written by leaders or friends of the Associated Farmers, began to appear in such magazines as the *California Journal of Development*, official organ of the State Chamber of Commerce. Roy M. Pike, general manager of El Solyo Ranch, was responsible for one such article published in January, 1936. In this article he warned of the dangers to California agriculture inherent in unionism and radicalism. As remedial action he advised that businessmen, large and small, urban and rural, should learn more about their government and about what the "reds" were doing, elect reliable men to local offices, and educate school children and the adults of the community to realize their responsibility toward the government and toward the maintenance of law and order.[3]

In 1933–1934 the emphasis had been on breaking the one union in the field at that time (the C. and A.W.I.U.) through legal action brought under the terms of the State Criminal Syndicalism Act. Now the emphasis was on breaking all strikes through the mass deputization of farmers; this action was to be accompanied by proper publicity and press notices and to be bolstered by political pressure upon local and state government.[4] Colonel Walter E. Garrison later summed up this shift in policy and strategy in a speech before a local unit, April 21, 1937, reported as follows:

State President Walter E. Garrison of Lodi, told a meeting of 150 Associated Farmers here last night that when first they were organized some years ago a large membership was not sought lest this give them the appearance of "vigilantes," and because members could not sit as jurors in trials of labor agitators. "Things have changed now," he said, "We've made up our minds it is more important to enforce the law than to sit on juries."[5]

Reorganization of Associated Farmers

Each one of the new county units was a separate entity; each was independently incorporated and had no legal connection with the state group except as it chose to affiliate. Actually, of course, the units worked in close coöperation with each other and with the state group. Henry L. Strobel, in testifying before the La Follette Committee, emphasized the point that each county unit was autonomous, that each one controlled its own activities with no supervision "... except upon the request of the different counties that the State will step in and aid them in any problems that they might have."[6]

A survey of the officers, and members of the Executive Committees of the state group clarifies the matter of leadership and control. The original officers, appointed in May, 1934, continued to serve until February, 1936, with but a few changes. S. Parker Frisselle continued as president and C. E. Hawley as vice-president; Guernsey Frazer, R. N. Wilson, and Gilbert H. Parker served as administrative officers. The Executive Committee chosen in March, 1934, continued in power with the subsequent addition to this body of Philip Bancroft, Holmes Bishop, Charles A. Worden, and David S. Bell. Ernst Behr and F. A. Stewart, ceased to be active in the organization during these years.[7]

In February, 1936, before reorganization on a county level had been achieved, a new set of officers and a new Executive Committee were chosen to serve for the remainder of that year. Walter E. Garrison became president and Philip Bancroft and C. E. Hawley were chosen as vice-presidents representing northern and southern California respectively. John Phillips and H. C. Morgan were selected as organizers.[8]

By the time officers were elected in December, 1936, a number of county units had been organized and representatives from these county units were admitted to the Board of Directors. That body was thus greatly expanded from the 9 members it had had in 1934 and 1935, and the 21 members it had had in 1936, to 63 members representing thirty different county units. Leadership, however, was kept within the same group; Walter E. Garrison was reëlected president, and Holmes Bishop and Henry L. Strobel became vice-presidents. Fred Goodcell was kept on as executive secretary, and Stuart Strathman was made field secretary.[9]

Reorganization of Associated Farmers

In December, 1937, the following year, the constitution of the state group was amended to divide the state of California into seven districts, each composed of several adjoining counties with similar interests and each with authorized representation on the Executive Committee. In addition provision was made for two representatives at large from southern California and two from northern California. Holmes Bishop was promoted to the presidency, and Philip Bancroft and Hugh Osborne were selected as vice-presidents. Henry Strobel, Fred Goodcell, Harper Knowles, and Stuart Strathman were chosen to serve as administrative officers. The Executive Committee was stabilized at 14 members, and the Board of Directors was expanded to include 86 members from thirty-five different counties.[10]

At the annual meeting of the Associated Farmers in December, 1938, further changes in the structure of the organization were made. The Board of Directors, which had become much too large and unwieldy, was reduced to 42 members, one representative from each county unit. Holmes Bishop continued as president during 1939, and John Watson and Ray E. Badger served as vice-presidents. W. B. Camp, H. E. Pomeroy, Stuart Strathman, and Robert Franklin served as administrative officers.[11]

The changes made by the Board of Directors in December, 1938, were more than formal and constitutional in nature. There was a division of opinion within the group as to what program and strategy should be adopted for 1939. One group favored a continuation of direct action; another group preferred to make more effective use of publicity and propaganda. The leaders worked out a compromise by which Bishop, generally considered a "middle-of-the-road moderate," was allowed to continue as president, and the all-important position of executive secretary was given to Harold Pomeroy, formerly administrator of the State Relief Administration. *Business Week* reported on the shift in leadership and policy as follows:

In December, 1938 [sic], a transformation began. Blunt, impulsive, military-minded Col. Walter E. Garrison, wine grower, and believer in direct action, stepped out and Holmes Bishop, orange grower and ex-choir singer, became president. Actual direction was assigned to young, smooth, hard-boiled Harold Pomeroy, an experienced political organizer, and former liaison man between California municipalities and various New Deal agencies. A silk glove has been drawn over the A.F. iron fist. Smooth strategy, political pressure and "campaigns of education" have replaced direct action. The A.F. has become smart.[12]

In December of 1939 John Watson, who had been active in the state organization for only one year, serving as vice-president for northern California during 1939, was selected to head the organization for 1940.[13] The La Follette investigation into the Associated Farmers had just begun, and it may be that the delegates therefore decided to select a man who had not been too intimately associated with the organization in its earlier years. At the Fresno convention in December, 1940, the delegates elected Don Stevning to serve as president during the following year. Phil Bancroft again became vice-president for northern California, and Edward Backs was selected as the southern vice-president. Harold Angier became secretary, and Henry Strobel treasurer.[14]

From this survey of the leadership of the Associated Farmers, two facts are clear: first, the county units became more influential after 1936 and contributed more direction to state policy with each succeeding year; and, secondly, the real power and authority remained in the hands of the same small group that had originally created the organization. The Associated Farmers maintained many of the older, more experienced men in positions of leadership to ensure continuity of policy and the most efficient execution of that policy.[15]

Membership in county units is shown in the following chart, compiled by the La Follette Committee:[16]

Year	Dues-paying members	Other members including mailing list	Total
1934	.....	.....	.....
1935	45	.....	45
1936	187	.....	187
1937	3,874	334	4,208
1938	6,296	1,075	7,371
1939	5,578	5,682	11,260

The Associated Farmers in 1939 claimed a membership of nearly 50,000. In light of the revelations of the La Follette Committee, this claim and all other official A.F. membership statistics must be regarded as gross exaggerations.

The local units of the association were similar in nature to the parent organization. The Associated Farmers of Sutter and Yuba counties were controlled by boards in which only one-third of the directors were actual growers; the remainder were directly associated with banks, canneries, chambers of commerce, lumber companies, petroleum interests, real estate firms, and law enforcement agencies. The Monterey County group was closely allied with the Grower-Shipper Vegetable Association; the Imperial County unit was controlled by the Western Growers' Protective Association; whereas the Kern County association was financed and controlled by cotton-ginning and fruit interests.[17]

The widespread attention given to these facts, and many others, at the time of the La Follette Committee hearings in San Francisco and Los Angeles in December, 1939, and January, 1940, prompted the Associated Farmers to defend their organization in a special editorial entitled "Who Are the Associated Farmers?"

> You, the individual members, not only are the Associated Farmers, but you know that in your county, and the state as a whole, the AF are you, your neighbors, and thousands of other farmers banded together in order to grow your crops, harvest your crops and transport them to market, under the rights guaranteed by the American form of government....
> ... Our strength has lain in the strong membership of our county units. Our effectiveness has been that tillers of the soil have stood shoulder to shoulder in protection of their civil rights, so that the only way that these radical and subversive groups can even attempt to curtail our activities is by trying to create the false impression that the Associated Farmers are not farmers.[18]

In spite of such assertions, however, the effectiveness of the organization was undermined, for the time at least, by the revelations of the La Follette hearings.

Attempts to spread the influence of the Associated Farmers to other parts of the country met with slight success. In December, 1937, the Associated Farmers of the Pacific Coast was formed, with state units in California, Arizona, Oregon, and Washington. The purpose of this new group was to coördinate migratory labor policies of farm employers in these states. None of the other state groups, however, ever approached the California organization in strength or influence. An attempt the following summer to sponsor a nationwide organization failed utterly. The Associated Farmers remained a California phenomenon.[19]

7. RELATIONSHIPS AMONG CALIFORNIA FARM ORGANIZATIONS

The California State Grange, the California Farm Bureau Federation, and the Associated Farmers of California all exercised great influence upon events in the 1930's. They were not, however, the only farm groups in California. Nor were they always, on all issues, the most important. Three other organizations—the Agricultural Department of the State Chamber of Commerce, the Agricultural Council of California, and the Farmers' Union—were often of equal significance. No detailed analysis of these latter groups will be attempted in this study, but a word or two must be said about each so that their role in the events discussed in subsequent chapters may be understood.

The Agricultural Department of the State Chamber of Commerce often sought to coördinate the activities of the other farm organizations. When a unified policy on labor relations seemed desirable, for example, this group took the initiative in organizing a conference to discuss the problem. To this conference came representatives from the Farm Bureau, the Associated Farmers, the Farmers' Union, and the Agricultural Council.[1] It will also be recalled that it was the State Chamber of Commerce, with the coöperation of the Farm Bureau, that originally helped to found and finance the Associated Farmers. The Agricultural Committee set up under the Agricultural Department of the Chamber of Commerce met frequently to discuss problems affecting agriculture and allied industries. Serving on this committee at one time or another during this period were such farm leaders as Alex Johnson, secretary of the California Farm Bureau Federation; Ray Wiser, president of the C.F.B.F. from 1938 on; A. C. Hardison, president of the same group from 1923 to 1925; S. Parker Frisselle, president of the Associated Farmers during 1934 and 1935; Roy Pike, another active leader of the Associated Farmers; R. V. Garrod, president of the Farmers' Union of California; and Ralph Taylor, executive secretary of the Agricultural Council of California. Through service on this committee, farm leaders from the various organizations got together, heard discussions by agricultural experts, and discussed their common problems. No prominent Grange leader served on this committee during the period 1929–1941.[2]

The Agricultural Council of California was formed in 1919, the same year that the California Farm Bureau Federation and the State Department of Agriculture were created. (The latter was legislated into existence in 1919 to unite thirteen separate boards and commissions dealing with agricultural problems.) In November, 1919, delegates to the annual convention of Fruit Growers and Farmers, meeting under the auspices of the new State Department of Agriculture, passed a resolution recommending the creation of an Agricultural Legislative Committee to serve as a clearinghouse for information and to help draft and secure the passage of agricultural legislation. In December, 1919, this committee was formally organized, with eighteen coöperative marketing associations forming its nucleus of membership. By 1929 the committee represented twenty-nine such groups with a stated membership of around 70,000 persons. Since the 1930 census showed only 36,120 farmers reporting any coöperative marketing, however, it may be assumed that there was much overlapping of membership among these groups.[3] Membership was held by the marketing association, not by the individual producer.

In the 1930's the Agricultural Legislative Committee changed its name and became the Agricultural Council of California. Ralph H. Taylor, executive secretary of the organization since the early 1920's, was almost solely responsible for making and executing policy for the group. Because of the financial strength of the coöperatives that he represented, Taylor was able to exert great influence over all phases of agricultural legislation.[4]

During the 1920's all farm organizations coöperated actively with this group, but in the following decade the Grange, under

Sehlmeyer, refused to go along with its policies. Senator J. C. Garrison, Grange senator from Stanislaus County, in debating a proposed piece of dairy legislation, asserted that the Agricultural Council represented not the farm producers but rather the large packers and the "manufacturing end of the farming business."[5] It was because of its belief that the Agricultural Council did represent primarily such groups that the Grange, which always claimed to speak for the "dirt farmer," refused to support the legislative program of the council except on routine matters.

The California unit of the Farmers' Union was founded in 1909. In 1920, R. V. (Vince) Garrod was elected president, a position he held throughout the period. The California unit was always more conservative than the national group and, as a result, finally lost its charter. It was reorganized in 1947 under another name, the California Farmers, Incorporated. Its membership was relatively small, and it enjoyed influence only in Santa Clara and Stanislaus counties. Garrod was an active lobbyist before the state legislature, where he usually aligned his group with the Farm Bureau, the Agricultural Council, and the Associated Farmers.[6]

Farmer membership in these California organizations naturally overlapped in many cases. A farmer might join the Farm Bureau to take advantage of the advice offered by the commodity departments or to participate in the educational programs of Extension Service and the Farm Home Department, and at the same time he might join the Grange for the social fellowship it provided as a fraternal lodge. If a strike threatened to disrupt the harvesting operations of a farmer, he might possibly join a local unit of the Associated Farmers. If he were a member of a marketing association, he would automatically be associated with the Agricultural Council. Politicians, lawyers, town merchants, and doctors often accepted nominal membership in these organizations for the political and economic contacts they provided. Still, despite this overlapping of membership, each organization had its own peculiar characteristics and policies.

Until 1929 there was usually close coöperation among all the various farm organizations in California, and, although there may have been some divisions of opinion within each group and between the different groups, a compromise program could usually be agreed upon. In the 1930's, however, the State Grange began to dissociate itself from the programs and activities of the other organizations. During the period 1929–1941 the California State Grange generally played a lone hand. To some, at a later date, Sehlmeyer was known facetiously as "the lone Granger." This inclination to withdraw from close coöperation with other farm groups may be attributed partly to the personality of the State Master, but it also rested upon the differing interests of the dominant members of the Grange.

Occasionally, coöperation on a local level was possible. The Grange, the Farmers' Union, and the Farm Bureau occasionally formed joint committees to carry out some community project. But, in general, examples of such coöperation are of interest only because of their rarity. Such coöperation as did occur took place largely in the years 1929–1933, when all farm organizations were working together to secure tax reform legislation. Although individual Grange and Farm Bureau members might have been able to agree, and probably did in many instances, coöperation between the two groups at a local level was extremely limited and coöperation on a state level proved to be impossible.[7]

Opposition of the Grange to the Farm Bureau was based not only upon idiosyncrasies of leadership and upon conflicts of interest but also upon Grange jealousy of the connections of the Farm Bureau with the Extension Service of the College of Agriculture. Time and again the Grange displayed irritation over the fact that the Farm Bureau enjoyed the support and facilities of the College of Agriculture and the aid of county farm advisers whose expenses were paid by county government. This resentment was based upon the feeling of the Grange that in the race for increased membership it was at an unfair disadvantage because of the quasi-public character of its rival, the Farm Bureau.

An article in the *California Grange News* of June, 1932, complained that government funds were being wasted by College of Agriculture professors, farm advisers, home demonstration agents, and extension personnel in general. The article observed:

We shall halt this silly and ceaseless running up and down the state in automobiles at our expense, doing things which might well be left undone....

As for the home demonstrators who teach our wives to retrim hats and upholster furniture, they must walk the plank as well. The hats have been turned up so many times they are falling apart, and we can't afford to pay for any more gimcracks to decorate them. Besides, the milliners are all on strike because we do not patronize them and help them pay their expenses. There are plenty of more important items in farm home economics than hats and foot stools.[8]

In a less captious mood, the delegates to the State Grange convention in October, 1936, commended the Agricultural Extension Service for the excellent work it had done but insisted that, because it was supported in part by funds of the federal and county governments, it should be dissociated from any general farm organization.[9]

There was not absolute unanimity within the Grange on every policy matter, however. When the Canning Peach Committee of the California State Grange met in Sacramento, March 29, 1937, to formulate a program for marketing the peach crop, it endorsed the program of the Associated Farmers to protect the farmers against labor troubles. This event suggests that some Grange members, the representatives of the canning-peach growers at any rate, were not entirely in accord with the more prolabor attitudes of the state organization.[10]

It has already been noted how the Farm Bureau helped to found the Associated Farmers in 1933 and 1934. The interests of these two organizations continued to be similar throughout this period. Many Farm Bureau members were also active in the Associated Farmers and allowed the latter group to take the lead in direct action against labor unions. This arrangement undoubtedly worked to maintain unity within the Farm Bureau. Many of the smaller farm members of the C.F.B.F. were not entirely in accord with the interests and policies of the larger farm employers, who dominated the Farm Bureau, and they probably would not have gone along with the organization had it been forced to do the work that the Associated Farmers did in its place.

There is considerable evidence of coöperation between the two groups at a local level. It was tacitly understood that the Associated Farmers would handle all labor trouble, with the moral and sometimes the financial assistance of Farm Bureau members. It was recognized, at the same time, that the Associated Farmers was not to engage in other activities that might compete with those of the local farm centers or of the county Farm Bureaus. The action to be taken by the Associated Farmers in relation to local labor disturbances was often discussed and even determined at meetings of the boards of directors of the county Farm Bureaus.[11]

Coöperation at the state level was also important. In November, 1934, the annual convention of the California Farm Bureau Federation strongly endorsed all activities of the Associated Farmers. Philip Bancroft, at the same time that he was an officer of the Associated Farmers, was also chairman of the Deciduous Fruit Department of the State Farm Bureau, and he appeared before legislative committees in both capacities. R. W. Blackburn, president of the C.F.B.F., appeared before the fourth annual meeting of the Associated Farmers at San Jose to assure that group that the Farm Bureau would do its part to help lift the Teamsters' Union blockade in Los Angeles. At the annual convention of the Farm Bureau in November, 1937, the Cotton Department reported that it had worked closely with the Associated Farmers to forestall labor strife and to improve housing conditions for migratory laborers. In November, 1938, Holmes Bishop, president of the Associated Farmers, addressed the annual convention of the Farm Bureau on the subject of "Labor and Agriculture."[12] These are but a few of the many indications of top-level coördination of activities between the two farm groups.

In 1937 and 1938, at a time when the Associated Farmers was reorganizing on a local basis, there was some discussion within the C.F.B.F. as to what new relationships between the two groups should be developed. Alex Johnson, secretary of the C.F.B.F., apparently thought that some of the local units of the Associated Farmers had been too militant.[13] S. Parker Frisselle, in a letter to Johnson, complained that the drive of the Associated Farmers for members in Kings County had bogged down because local Farm Bureau leaders believed that Secretary Johnson and S. G. Rubinow, publicity director of the C.F.B.F., were not in full sympathy with the Associated Farmers. Frisselle promised to try to hold local groups in check, and observed in closing:

... There is not a man on our Board of Directors or Executive Committee, as far as I know, who is not a member of your Bureau. ...
As you know, the organization is now entirely divorced from the Chamber of Commerce and is in reality a program led by and carried out by leaders in your organization.[14]

Several months later E. C. Kimball, soon to be made vice-president of the State Farm Bureau, wrote to Secretary Johnson to assure him that the Associated Farmers were under control.

Labor relations is undoubtedly the livest issue before our farmers here in the south. Associated Farmers is receiving a lot of attention, some members and liberal financial support from the coops. Undoubtedly it is in instances a counter attraction but Farm Bureau people are for the most part running it and so far I have not noted any tendency to stray from the one problem. I believe we should encourage our Farm Bureau leaders and members to be active in it and thus guide its policies. It is our baby and must be guided.[15]

Other letters written at about the same time indicate that it was by common consent that labor relations were left for the Associated Farmers to handle and that on all matters there was close coöperation between the two groups. A community of interests drove these two organizations to coöperate on labor policy and on other matters.[16]

The relationship between the county Farm Bureaus and the local Chambers of Commerce was also close during this period. In some areas, the two organizations shared the same offices and worked on community projects together. This cordiality is hardly surprising, based as it was upon the intimate interdependence of agricultural and urban economic interests and upon the community of interests shared by all property holders.[17]

8. FARM ORGANIZATIONS AND LABOR POLICY

Of all the problems that California farmers faced in the depression decade, the crisis in agricultural labor relations probably attracted the most widespread attention. The 1930's were a decade of labor unionization and labor strife in both city and country, and every citizen of the state was, in one way or another, vitally concerned with the outcome of these struggles. Over the nation as a whole, the average citizen heard or read little about California's tax reform program or about its program of agricultural proration, but John Steinbeck's *Grapes of Wrath* was a national best seller and nearly everyone was familiar with the dramatic, tragic plight of the Dust Bowl migrants in California.

To the Associated Farmers the labor problem was paramount. The Farm Bureau, though it let the Associated Farmers take the lead in these matters, was itself often active in this field. The Grange was less concerned with problems of agricultural labor, for small and part-time farmers could, to a large degree, hold themselves aloof from problems that plagued large farm employers; the relatively few Grange members who were farm employers probably held membership in either or both of the other two groups as well and let those organizations act for them in matters of labor policy.

The Associated Farmers constantly maintained that farm employers should pay their hired labor as much as they were able to. Its argument ran as follows. The producer of agricultural commodities operated under conditions of high fixed costs and high cash operating costs. The farmer had little control over the prices he paid for electricity, fertilizer, and transportation and no influence over the prices he received for his commodities on the market. In many years a net profit at the end of the season could be achieved only by adopting the most efficient methods of farm management, by making economies wherever possible, and by controlling wage costs strictly. To permit the unionization of agricultural labor was to surrender control over this cost item and, in addition, to allow an unsympathetic group arbitrarily to disrupt harvesting operations. To be forced to pay higher wages cut into the farm employer's profits; to suffer a strike at harvesttime often meant total loss. The Associated Farmers further observed that unionization and strikes often had far more serious consequences for farm employers than for industrial employers: many industries could pass the increased cost of higher wages along to the consumer, and in most industries strikes did not result in absolute loss of the entire year's production operations.

Philip Bancroft argued these points in an extemporaneous speech before the Commonwealth Club of San Francisco in December, 1936.

We customarily employ in our harvests all the male workers in our respective localities, as well as numerous transient workers. The wages are, as a rule, fully as high as the farmers can afford to pay, and average twice as much as those of our principal competing states.... If the wages are acceptable to our men and if, after we have started harvesting, outside agitators come in to stir up trouble, and by threats, coercion and intimidation prevent our men from picking for a week, or in some cases for only as much as two or three days, we may lose practically our entire crop—*and this we will not tolerate;* nor will we willingly permit our farms or our packing sheds to become unionized, for we will not give any group of irresponsible union officials (often alien radicals) the power to ruin us at will.[1]

It should be noted, however, that the concept of "ability to pay" was subject to many definitions and interpretations. What any individual farmer was capable of paying depended on many factors—the going market price, the level of other cash costs, the natural advantages of his own land and equipment, his own ability as a farm manager, and his concept of what constituted an "adequate return" for himself. Agricultural employers had one idea of what they could afford to pay; agricultural workers another. Wage levels were usually determined, moreover, not by "ability to pay," or by the "economic needs" of the workers, but by the relative strength of those two groups when engaged in collective bargaining. To strengthen their own bargaining position laborers formed unions; to improve their strategic position farm employers often turned to the Associated Farmers.[2]

To the Associated Farmers the only "good" union was the distant union, the union that in no way threatened them, directly or indirectly. In 1936, before the American Federation of Labor had begun to organize in rural areas, S. Parker Frisselle could say to A.F. of L. leaders:

> We are in no way in opposition to the American Federation of Labor: We are tremendously interested in the welfare of agriculture, particularly, and we want you to understand that our cards are on the table; that there is no opposition here to the American Federation of Labor in any way, shape, or form; and we want your coöperation.[3]

But after the Stockton conference in 1936, at which the A.F. of L. had laid plans to "march inland," those A.F. of L. leaders who were active in this move were at once labeled "Communist" or "Communist-controlled."[4] When both the C.I.O. and the A.F. of L. advanced into rural areas, Holmes Bishop, the president of the Associated Farmers, announced: "The one group was dominated by Communists and the other was led by racketeers, so take your choice."[5]

If unions were not to be permitted, neither could any of the traditional weapons of organized labor be countenanced; especially to be resisted was the forcing of techniques of urban, industrial unionization upon the agricultural economy without modification. Thus the Associated Farmers opposed the closed shop, the hiring hall, and picketing—union practices that it was willing to concede might be necessary in industry but regarded as impractical and even disastrous when applied to agriculture. Colonel Walter E. Garrison argued, when interviewed by Frank J. Taylor for a nation-wide farm journal, that the Associated Farmers opposed the closed shop on the grounds that it prevented farmers from coöperating with one another in the harvesting of crops, kept college students from summer work, and forced seasonal workers to pay annual dues for the privilege of working a couple of months. Similarly, Garrison continued, the Associated Farmers opposed the hiring hall because it ran counter to the tradition that farm workers were to be treated like members of the family, whereas picketing was wrong because it led to the destruction of crops and, moreover, subjected farm homes and families to the hazards of labor strife.⁶

The Associated Farmers repeatedly insisted that it believed in the right of labor to organize and bargain collectively. But, it added, the employer should bargain only with those men in his own employ. Henry Strobel, one of the most militant of A.F. leaders, in testifying before the La Follette Committee, declared that, whereas he was always willing to bargain with his own employees, he would never talk with a man who was not going to work for him.⁷ This refusal to deal with an "outside agitator" made meaningless any assertion regarding the right of labor to organize, for the right of a union to delegate to its leaders the authority to bargain for its members was absolutely essential to labor.

That the Associated Farmers realized this fact is indicated in the text of a confidential memorandum sent by the Labor Relations Committee of the state organization to all county units in December, 1937. This memorandum advised farm employers to refuse to deal with any labor organizer.

The organizer, after all, is the individual who should be dealt with summarily at the very outset.... It may be well to remember that no organizer—no matter how suave or smooth—has anything to offer except trouble.... He wants only one thing, and that thing is *control* through the worker.... At the very outset, then, it will be wise for every farmer to refuse flatly to meet with any organizer.⁸

The memorandum offered advice as to what A.F. members should do when threatened with unionization or with a strike. First, it stated, a special strategy committee should be created, whose job it would be to compile lists of farmers who would be available for law enforcement work. The local sheriff should then be given these lists and be assured that sufficient deputies could be secured by calling upon the strategy committee. The committee, the memorandum continued, should establish good public relations with local newspapers and with civic groups of citizens' associations so that their support would be assured in case of trouble. If a strike should occur, production and marketing operations were to be maintained at all costs. This would entail the protection of all nonunion men willing to work and the importation of workers if local nonstriking labor was insufficient. Mass action was to be used only as a last resort.

In this fashion did the Associated Farmers oppose all unionization and all activities of unions, and thus did it move from theory to action. The psychological outlook of members and leaders of the association was a determining factor in all it did. Philip Bancroft, in a formal address before the Commonwealth Club, suggested some of this aggressiveness underlaid by fear when he said:

... we would regard the unionization of farm labor as absolutely ruinous to us, as well as injurious to the laborers themselves.... In the case of the average farmer, he has spent eleven months and all the money he can borrow, as well as his life's savings, in producing his crop; and if he is prevented from harvesting this by a strike, he loses not only his whole year's profit, but the much larger amount representing his whole year's production costs.... We are not willing to give any group of labor agitators the power to destroy us at will—*and we are not going to do it.... Gentlemen, the farm workers of California are going to be protected and the farmers of California are going to harvest their crops!* [9]

The California Farm Bureau Federation has long been interested in the problems of agricultural labor. In the 1920's this organization had often taken the lead in determining wage levels for various commodities and areas in an attempt to keep wages uniform and to ensure that employers would not force labor costs upward by competitive bidding.[10] Constantly concerned with the supply of "stoop" labor, the Farm Bureau had taken steps to prevent the passage of proposed federal legislation to restrict Mexican immigration. Interest in the supply and condition of agricultural labor naturally continued throughout the 1930's.[11]

A discussion at a meeting of the Board of Directors of the San Joaquin County Farm Bureau in September, 1936, indicates that the outlook of that group was similar to that of the Associated Farmers. The directors discussed the matter of housing for agricultural labor and concluded that some sort of migrant camping facilities would have to be provided if labor were to be secured. The board expressed the belief that labor had the right to organize and that all the trouble came from Communist agitators who worked through the unions to disrupt production. Some members complained that many farmers had contracted for sale of their crops to canners early in the season at such a low price that to allow labor costs to rise would cut deeply into the farmer's net profit.[12] A resolution passed by the same group a few months later complained that labor, during a strike, often usurped powers rightfully exercised only by a political unit and declared that the government must protect the farmers in the harvesting of their crops.[13]

The Extension Service of the College of Agriculture, through its connection with the Farm Bureau, helped in the formulation of the Bureau's labor policy. In the spring of 1938 a series of meetings, sponsored by the Extension Service, was held in various rural counties throughout California. At many of these conferences resolutions concerning labor were passed. These resolutions endorsed the following principles: that wages be as high as possible, consistent with the ability of the farmer to pay; that adequate and sanitary housing be provided for the migrants; that the relief scale of government agencies be adjusted to prevent competition with going wages in the field; that labor unions be made to incorporate so that they would be legally responsible for their acts; and, finally, that the program and activities of the Associated Farmers be endorsed.[14]

At the annual convention of the Farm Bureau in November, 1936, the delegates passed a resolution outlining their policy on labor relations. Such a statement probably seemed necessary in the light of renewed activity among agricultural workers in that year. The resolution stated that great harm had been done to California agriculture by strikes, many of which had been instigated or controlled by Communists against the will of the majority of the workers. Then followed a four-point program: 1) that every effort be made by farm employers to improve conditions of labor so that justifiable causes for conflict would be removed; 2) that uniform county and municipal ordinances be passed regulating picketing and trespassing; 3) that agriculture never accept the hiring hall or the closed shop; and 4) that the Farm Bureau reaffirm its support of the Criminal Syndicalism Act.[15]

By the spring of 1937 labor troubles were so widespread that it seemed advisable for the various farm organizations to meet together to formulate a common policy. The Agricultural Department of the State Chamber of Commerce took the initiative, and at its invitation representatives from the California Farm Bureau Federation, the Associated Farmers of California, the Agricultural Council, and the California Farmers' Union met in June, 1937, and worked out a Farm Labor Code.

This eleven-point code recommended that farm employers take measures to improve conditions of labor upon the farm; that housing be improved; that attempts be made to make farm work more continuous throughout the year; that an agency be created to determine and coördinate labor requirements; that education facilities for children of migrants be extended; and that employers pay a "maximum wage consistent with the farmer's ability to pay." With regard to labor relations and collective bargaining, the delegates maintained that all workers must be protected from union coercion when they continued to work even though the union declared that a strike existed. The conference recommended that unions be made responsible before the law to the same degree as employers. It opposed the closed shop and hiring hall, citing the perishable nature of agricultural commodities as its reason for this stand. Further, the delegates held that the worker should be free to bargain with his employer individually or collectively, just as he desired. They also declared it essential that there should be no interference with the free flow of goods from farm to market. Finally, the code urged that "agricultural employers in the exercise of their responsibility of leadership freely avail themselves of every opportunity to educate the people as to the value of the American form of government and economic system and general welfare."[16]

The California State Grange did not participate in the formulation of this Farm Labor Code. Nor did it ever endorse the principles enunciated at that meeting. The Grange, unlike the other farm groups, usually assumed a middle or neutral position during agricultural labor disturbances; in this respect it more closely followed the role played by farm groups in other parts of the country, that of mediating between industry and labor.

The Grange and the Farm Bureau often disagreed over matters of labor policy. At a time when the Farm Bureau was lobbying in Washington to prevent the passage of legislation restricting Mexican immigration into the United States, State Master George Sehlmeyer was declaring that 90 per cent of the Mexicans who entered California did not go into the fields but went instead to the cities where, by working for low wages, they broke the buying power of labor and thus hurt both agriculture and industry. In the same year, 1930, the delegates to the annual convention of the State Grange went on record as opposed to the importation of large numbers of foreign laborers and stressed the need for legislation to curb the illegal entry of such people. Again, in October, 1933, the Grange delegates declared that, "as members of the Grange . . . a portion of whom are laborers," they were opposed to the employment of cheap Filipino labor by farm employers.[17]

Occasionally the Grange allied itself openly with labor. In the spring of 1934 the Stanislaus County Pomona Grange expressed its feeling of unity with labor in the following resolution:

> The great majority of farmers in Stanislaus County earn their bread by the labor of their hands and the sweat of their brows. Their interests are largely the same as those of the industrial wage earner. Stanislaus County Grange is a non-partisan, non-sectarian farm organization striving for better conditions for all farmers. We invite men and women who derive their livelihood from agricultural pursuits to join our membership. Farm employees are eligible for membership and stand on an equal footing with all other members. We are not allied with, nor under obligation to, any organization whose policies are derogatory to the farmers' and the laborers' interests.[18]

Occasionally, too, the Grange expressed labor policies similar to those of the Farm Bureau. Resolutions passed at the annual convention of the State Grange in October, 1937, stated that many radically controlled unions were irresponsible and that they conducted strikes and engaged in violence without regard to law or property. The delegates then went on record as favoring recognition of only such labor unions as were organized along sound and constructive lines and urged the Executive Committee to investigate legislation to make unions responsible before the law.[19]

More often, however, the Grange took a middle position between employers and labor and insisted that the answer to labor strife lay in enactment of legislation that would provide machinery for the mediation or arbitration of strikes. There is an expression of this viewpoint in the Chaplain's report to the annual convention in October, 1933.

> Keen sympathy is felt for the farmers who are confronted with strikes at this critical time, but it is lamentable that violence and lawlessness are used as weapons to settle their difference. We deplore the shots fired by farmers who were provoked to a degree of revenge thus making a very dangerous relationship between the grower and labor. In our extreme situations let us submit our differences to mediation and arbitration in the beginning instead of at the end of the fight.[20]

In October, 1937, the delegates to the state meeting noted the losses that labor disturbances brought to producers of perishable products and passed a resolution favoring mediation or arbitration of labor disputes and directing the State Master to appoint a special Grange Labor Mediation Committee to act as a disinterested third party when invited to do so.[21]

All the other farm organizations had agreed upon a common labor policy in June, 1937, when they endorsed the eleven-point Farm Labor Code. The Grange, in October, 1938, worked out its own statement of policy in a resolution that was considered the greatest achievement of that year's convention. This resolution expressed the general sympathy of farmers for labor in the following terms: "The California State Grange has had the cooperation of organized labor in much progressive legislation for the benefit of agriculture. We should avoid any hasty action which would break down the spirit of friendship on those issues of mutual interest."[22] The delegates admitted the right of labor to organize and bargain collectively and to strike but denied that it had a right to engage in violence, coercion, or intimidation. They stated that they held sacred the constitutional right of private ownership and control of property. They insisted upon the security of the farmer to produce, harvest, process, and market without governmental regulations of hours and wages and without the hazard of having his products labeled "unfair." They denounced jurisdictional disputes, violence, and vigilantism by either labor or capital. They demanded the preservation of free speech and assembly. Finally, they suggested the creation of mediation boards as one remedy for labor strife.[23]

Such were the general principles and policies of these three farm groups on labor problems. Only against this background can their activities during rural and urban strikes, their stands on local and statewide labor legislation, and their opinions on social legislation be completely understood.

9.

THE ASSOCIATED FARMERS IN ACTION

There seems to have been a tacit understanding among farm employer groups in the state in dealing with labor problems; the Farm Bureau was to take the lead in legislative matters and in the formulation of general policy, but when trouble struck the Associated Farmers was to take command in the field. When union leaders moved into an area, when workers began to organize, when strikes occurred, it was the Associated Farmers that moved quickly and directly to meet these threats.

The tactics used by the Associated Farmers varied with the time, the place, and the situation, and the group was active at many times, in many places, and in many different situations. There was, for example, the strike in the spring of 1934 in Contra Costa County. Workers demanded an increase in wages above the prevailing $17\frac{1}{2}$ cents an hour, and, when growers refused to negotiate, union members began to picket the roads and orchards of the county. Seventy-five growers, soon to organize themselves into a unit of the Associated Farmers, were deputized. Picket leaders were arrested for technical violations of the law; other strikers were escorted to the county line and persuaded not to return. Peace was soon restored, and picking resumed at established rates.[1]

To forestall a recurrence of trouble the Associated Farmers of Contra Costa County worked out a project for labor registration and control, a scheme that came to be known as the "Brentwood Plan." This plan provided for the setting of a uniform wage level by a growers' committee in advance of the harvest season. All migrants seeking employment were registered with a central labor bureau, which was operated by the Associated Farmers through the sheriff's office. By use of informers and by exchange of information, these files could be used to exclude from employment all applicants with known records of troublemaking. Finally, munitions, principally gas bombs, were purchased for use in case of extreme emergency by those members of the Associated Farmers who had been selected for deputy service.[2]

The Associated Farmers was also active during the orange pickers' strike in Los Angeles County in the spring of 1936. There a union composed largely of Mexicans threatened to disrupt the wage structure of the citrus industry. The Associated Farmers organized protection for nonunion men who were willing to work. Regular police and county officers were augmented by deputized farmers and by private guards. Four hundred and fifty guards were hired by the growers and sworn in as deputies. Scab orange pickers were daily convoyed to and from work. The strike was soon settled with but a slight increase in wages.[3]

In Stockton during April, 1937, the Associated Farmers helped to break a strike that had tied up operations in the canneries. Growers, many of whom were in debt to the canneries for financial advances in the form of crop loans, had to be able to deliver their produce for canning or face still deeper indebtedness. Furthermore, the canning companies had helped to finance the Associated Farmers and to keep it going; perhaps the time had come for the A.F. to repay a long outstanding debt. Over twelve hundred farmers were sworn in as deputies, organized on a military basis, and armed by the Associated Farmers with clubs, rifles, and shotguns. The sheriff turned over complete command of these deputized vigilantes to Colonel Walter E. Garrison of the A.F.

As a result of a mediation meeting the union notified the sheriff and the canning plants that its members would return to work pending further negotiations. But the Associated Farmers, with the consent of the canners, had decided upon a show of force. As the first workers began returning to the factories, they were surprised and mobbed by an armed force of one hundred and fifty deputies stationed inside the Stockton Food Products Plant. An open battle occurred, despite attempts by union leaders to get the workers to retreat. The strike was broken for the time, but public opinion turned against the canners and against the Associated Farmers because of the violent actions they had taken, and the union therefore won a satisfactory compromise on most of the issues.[4]

One strike more is worthy of narration, the violent cotton strike in the Madera area in October, 1939. Here, written large, were features common to much of California's agricultural strife: low wages and substandard living conditions, agitation by militant union leaders, complex national minorities problems, coöperation of Associated Farmers with peace officers, open warfare between deputized vigilantes and unionized workers, attempts by state government officials to mediate the dispute, and manipulation of government relief payments to influence the level of wage payments. Although, because of its size and intensity, this strike may hardly be considered typical, it provides a good case study.

The cotton industry had not been without its disturbances; the cotton strike in the fall of 1933 had been long, costly, and bloody, and minor disturbances had broken out in subsequent years. In Kern County in September, 1938, a strike had been called by the United Cannery, Agricultural, Packing and Allied Workers of America, C.I.O., after growers had offered 75 cents per hundred pounds of cotton picked in response to the union demand of $1 a hundred. The Associated Farmers had taken up the challenge, refused to deal with the union, run key organizers out of the community, kept certain growers from raising wages to the level of the union demands, and furnished protection for nonunion men who continued to work. There had been a mass arrest of pickets. Harold Pomeroy, then head of the State Relief Administration, had set a policy of refusing relief aid to any able-bodied man who refused to accept work at the prevailing wage rate of 75 cents per hundred. Neighboring counties had set up shotgun patrols to keep cotton pickets and union leaders from spreading the strike to other counties. The Associated Farmers had organized resistance and announced publicly: "We do not regard the wage dispute as a strike since cotton-picking is progressing despite the constant effort of a group of reds and pinks to create dissatisfaction among the workers."[5] On October 25, one hundred strikers had been arrested and charged with "conspiracy to break and enter with intent to incite a riot."[6] Growers who had raised the wage rate to 85 or 90 cents per hundred pounds had been urged by the Associated Farmers to reduce those offers to 75 cents, and most of them had complied. By a combination of these actions the strike had finally been broken, but it had left a feeling of discontent among the cotton workers and added to ill-feeling on both sides, and thus it contributed, in part, to the outbreak that occurred the following year.[7]

Trouble occurred early in the 1939 season in Madera when a walkout, originally sponsored by the Workers' Alliance, was called as a protest against wage rates of 20 cents per hour or 75 cents per acre for cotton chopping. The workers, later under U.C.A.P.A.W.A. leadership, asked for $27\frac{1}{2}$ cents per hour or $1.25 per acre. Carey McWilliams, chief of the State Division of Immigration and Housing, investigated conditions and reported that $27\frac{1}{2}$ cents an hour constituted a "fair" wage rate. This rate was then accepted by the State Relief Administration as a base below which relief clients would not be forced off the rolls. The farmers of Madera County maintained that this order, in effect, established a higher wage rate than the growers could afford to pay. These disputes, which occurred in May, 1939, added to the tension that was slowly developing.[8]

The real trouble came in September, however, when the cotton-picking season began. The Agricultural Labor Bureau of the San Joaquin Valley had set wage rates for the coming season at 80 cents per hundred pounds. Many workers were dissatisfied with this rate, especially since the amount of work available had been severely cut by the federal Agricultural Adjustment Administration (A.A.A.) crop control restrictions, which had reduced cotton acreage in California from 670,000 acres in 1937 to 340,000 acres in 1939, and, as a result, there were surplus workers available for cotton picking, and weekly and monthly income seemed certain to be decreased because of underemployment.[9]

On September 21, 1939, Governor Olson appointed a seven-man board that was given the task of determining what the "prevailing" wage was for cotton picking that year and what would constitute a "fair" wage. The results of this investigation were to be used by the State Relief Administration in determining relief policies for the area. This committee was composed of the following members:

    Professor R. L. Adams, University of California
    Ray B. Wiser, President of the California Farm Bureau
    George Sehlmeyer, Master of the State Grange
    William B. Parker, State Director of Agriculture
    Carey McWilliams, State Director of the Division of Immigration and Housing
    H. C. Carrasco, State Labor Commissioner
    Mrs. H. E. Erdman, State Democratic Party leader from Berkeley

This committee held open hearings in Fresno September 27–29. The investigations of the committee were hampered, however, by the fact that most of the growers refused to testify, on the grounds that the state had no power to set wage rates in agriculture. The committee, of course, had no intention of directly setting wages; its purpose was to establish an equitable state relief policy.[10] Ben Hayes, president of the local Associated Farmers unit, announced that the growers would not participate in the hearings because: "The hearings will be a rally for radicals and a Roman holiday for people loafing on relief at the expense of the taxpayer."[11]

After hearing testimony for three days the committee retired to write its report. The report, which was released October 5, was divided into three parts: remarks endorsed by the whole committee, a majority report, and a minority report. The whole committee reported that the workers had testified that they could not gain sufficient income for themselves and their families at any wage less than $1.25 per hundred but that the growers, on the other hand, had complained that they could not afford to pay more than 80 cents per hundred. The committee pointed out that the conflict was thus one between the needs of the workers and the ability of the growers to pay. The committee also recognized that poor conditions of housing, sanitation, and education prevailed in the area. In its summary, the whole committee commented on the difficulties to be faced.

If the State Relief Administration suspends relief and thereby forces relief clients off the rolls to accept employment at tasks they are not fitted to perform, and thus fail to earn an adequate income, the Relief Administration is remiss in its duty. Should the Relief Administration fail to recognize this fact and release for employment those not fitted for the type of work available they will reduce the prevailing wage rate by contributing to the relative oversupply of labor.[12]

The committee further observed that if the State Relief Administration set the rate for suspension of relief higher than the base wage rate being paid in the area, the growers would contend that this relief rate tended to establish a base rate not in accord with their ability to pay. In short, the group concluded that no solution would be entirely satisfactory to all parties.

The majority report, signed by Adams, Sehlmeyer, Wiser, and Parker, noted that the amount of income an individual could earn by picking cotton was determined not only by the wage rate but also by the picker's particular skill, experience, sex, age, stamina, and crop conditions over which he had no control—conditions such as the crop yield, the height of the bush, and the thickness of the growth—and that his net income was further influenced by the cost of his transportation to and from work and the cost of his housing and food. In its conclusions, the majority report did not attempt to lay down what it considered a satisfactory or "fair" wage; instead, it summarized its findings in general terms: "Relief clients should not be removed from relief rolls unless, in each instance, they are able to earn at least the equivalent of the budget which they are receiving under the State Relief Administration rules and regulations."[13]

The minority report, signed by McWilliams, Carrasco, and Mrs. Erdman, went further in its recommendations. First, it maintained that the 80-cent base rate could not be considered a "prevailing" rate, since it was set by the growers alone before seasonal conditions could possibly have been determined. It stated that at 80 cents per hundred the average worker could earn but $9.60 per week or $38.40 per month, whereas the State Relief Administration budget requirements were $43.45

a month. Moreover, it was observed that neither of these amounts was sufficient to maintain a man doing hard physical labor in the field. The minority report further noted that the growers had hoped to harvest the crop without the use of men on relief, a group that constituted less than 10 per cent of all workers available for cotton picking in the area, and that, therefore, the setting of a higher relief rate, below which workers would not be released for field labor, would not necessarily mean that cotton pickers would actually be paid a higher rate. In conclusion, the three members submitting the minority report noted the difficulty of conducting an investigation when many of the agricultural interests refused to submit evidence and "confined their contentions to generalized claims of inability to pay, entirely unsupported by tangible evidence of that fact" and stated that, in their opinion, $1.25 per hundred was the best figure for the State Relief Administration to use in its administration of relief.[14]

The Associated Farmers commented on the proceedings as follows:

... Grower organizations refused to participate in the hearing. ... Practically the entire hearing was given over to the presentation of propaganda by radical leaders of groups attempting to organize the agricultural workers. ... The farmers charged that Carey McWilliams, who advocates collective agriculture despite his oath of office to uphold the American form of government, was the leader and coordinator of the groups attempting to use the state administration to promote strike agitation.[15]

On October 2, some one thousand union men—Dust-Bowlers, Mexicans, Negroes, and native Californians—assembled in the Madera County Park to demand a wage rate of $1.25 per hundred pounds.[16] A week later a strike was officially called by the U.C.A.P.A.W.A., provoked, according to Donald Henderson, president of the national union, by the "insistence of growers in paying starvation wages."[17] Picketing in large auto caravans began on October 12. On this first day 143 pickets were arrested by the sheriff for parading without a permit in violation of Madera County Ordinance 168. Auto caravans continued to picket the next couple of days, however, and, as the jails became crowded to overflowing, pickets were released on the advice of the district attorney, who observed that parading without a permit was a "trivial offense."[18] By October 15, it was reported that the strike was approximately 75 per cent effective.[19]

Stuart Strathman, field organizer for the Associated Farmers, arrived in Madera on October 14 and found local growers puzzled and confused. He was instrumental in setting up a Grower's Emergency Committee of sixteen members, fourteen of whom were members of the Associated Farmers. This group began to organize public relations and finances and to draw up plans to give protection to those workers not on strike. Feeling was running high, as evidenced by the following editorial in the *Madera Daily Tribune and Mercury* for October 16:

There is one little item that has been overlooked by the radicals—the history of the rise and cause for the sudden crackup of the I.W.W. [Industrial Workers of the World]. History always repeats itself.

Enthusiasm for the I.W.W. ceased when a few were found suspended from a bridge near a Colorado village early one morning. So far as anyone has ever been able to prove, they were letting themselves down with ropes, the ropes slipped and became entangled about their heads.[20]

On the same day the Associated Farmers sponsored a mass meeting at which Stuart Strathman advised the growers that men who wished to work must be given protection, but that violence should be avoided. A committee headed by Ben Hayes, president of the Madera County Associated Farmers, announced that all willing workers should appeal to their employers for protection. Two days later, October 18, the Associated Farmers organized "flying squadrons" and provided members with armbands so that they could easily be identified in case of conflict.

In the meantime the C.I.O. continued its organization drive. Pickets patrolled cotton fields and the Madera County Park, marching and singing such songs as this:

> JOIN THE PICKET LINE
> (I've Been Working on the Railroad)
>> Fight for Union recognition,
>> Fight for better pay,

> Fight to better your condition,
> In the democratic way—
> Eighty cents won't even feed us,
> A dollar and a quarter would be fine,
> Show the farmers that they need us,
> JOIN THE PICKET LINE.[21]

In a pamphlet the union stated the reason for the strike.

... Guess all of us know what the strike is for by now. It is for better wages, wages we can feed ourselves on. The Associated Farmer wants us to pick his cotton for 80¢ which is a starvation wage. We ask only for enough to live half ways which is $1.25 per hundred and which the farmer is more than able to pay. So the only way we are able to get more for our labor is by organizing and sticking together so that is the purpose of the strike and the picket line. We don't go out there breaking the law or acting out of order but only try to be peacefully law abiding. ... It is better to die on your feet than to live on your knees.[22]

The first open violence occurred on October 19, when a group of Associated Farmers attacked a union picket line with clubs. Following this incident, Governor Olson sent Lieutenant Colonel Charles Henderson of the National Guard to Madera to observe conditions. The Associated Farmers declared that, unless Henderson saw to it that the strike leaders were immediately imprisoned, the growers would be forced to take the law into their own hands. Henderson replied that he was powerless until martial law had been proclaimed. On the same day fifteen hundred ranchers mobilized and threatened to march on the C.I.O. encampment; only Strathman's appeals for moderation kept the farmers from precipitating a battle at that time. Strathman convinced the growers that the wisest course of action for them would be to return to their own ranches and protect their own property. In the meantime, more pickets and union leaders were being arrested for violation of numerous ordinances and statutes.[23] On October 20 the growers asked Governor Olson for the arrest of five strike leaders, for the prohibition of all strike rallies in Madera County Park, and for the prevention of all picketing by auto caravans. At this point Colonel Henderson suggested that the dispute be mediated, but this offer was turned down by the growers. On Saturday, October 21, occurred the incident that set off several days of violence, violence that soon led to the breaking of the strike. On that hot afternoon over two hundred carloads of growers, organized by the Associated Farmers, assembled and moved to the vicinity of Madera County Park, where the union was holding one of its daily mass meetings. The farmers came armed with pick handles, rubber hoses, auto cranks, and fan belts. Some three hundred of this group moved on the park and proceeded to break up the meeting. The strikers—men, women, and children—were routed from the scene of the battle. This scene was witnessed by Colonel Henderson, the sheriff, Captain Tores of the state highway patrol, and fourteen other members of the highway patrol, eleven of whom were armed with gas guns, but none of these law-enforcement officers made any move to stop the vigilante action. The riot was finally ended by several shots of gas, but only after the main attack had succeeded.[24] The Associated Farmers reported this incident as follows:

Literally seizing the county park in Madera, the group [the U.C.A.P.A.W.A. union] broadcast over a loud-speaking system a vile language and name-calling contest, calling respectable farmers of the county every dirty name at their command.

Crews were driven out of the fields by caravans flaunting their violation of the county's anti-parade and anti-picketing ordinances. Workers' families were threatened. Farmers were threatened with fire. . . .

Finally, the farmers and merchants and their employees, fed up by intimidation and threats, dictatorial and fascistic methods by the strike agitators, many of whom they knew were communists—blew up.

One Saturday afternoon, these people came to town and cleaned out the park of the reds and radicals, the strike agitators, the misled workers who were beginning to believe that the reds were in control of the community. . . .

The next day the cotton pickers, freed of the fear and intimidation of the agitators, went back into the cotton fields.[25]

The union gave its side of the conflict in a leaflet headed by a cartoon entitled "Portrait of an Associated Farmer," depicting a boll of cotton wearing a silk top hat. This leaflet said:

Gathered in the Madera County Park, the weaponless CIO workers were rushed from two sides by the Associated Farmer "goons.". . . The screams of clubbed women, the clouds of gas covering the prone, bloody bodies of beaten men were a fitting climax to the wave of terror which the Associated Farmers tried to down the strike in Madera.

So far not one striker has committed any violence; not one farmer has been arrested for the brutal attacks made on defenseless strikers.... If our economy in this state is to survive the Fascist tactics of the Associated Farmers, already in alarming control, it will take the combined efforts of all fair-minded citizens working hand in hand with thousands of agricultural workers to accomplish.[26]

The difficult position in which the farmers found themselves was suggested by Governor Olson in a statement to the press.

I believe the growers find themselves in a difficult spot on the wage scales. They are under contract to the gin owners and are unable to pay picking wages. They are willing to pay higher scale, but are unable to do so. A strike under these conditions is really a strike through the growers at the financial interests controlling cotton.[27]

It was further reported at the same time that C. L. Baker, president of the Madera County Farm Bureau, had broken down in tears at a growers' meeting and said that he had been ruined financially by the strike. "We can't stand this any longer," he said.[28] Bitterness, fear, and economic frustration underlay the farmers' violence.

The incident of October 21 did not immediately end the strike. New union committees were formed as labor leaders were packed off to jail. A. L. Wirin, attorney for the American Civil Liberties Union, was escorted from the county and warned against returning. Governor Olson finally sent a large complement of highway patrolmen to the scene to assist local peace officers in preventing further interference with civil liberties. By October 25, the union had lowered its demands to $1 per hundred pounds, and union men began to go back to work at this rate. On October 27, R. F. Schmeiser of the Associated Farmers reported that picking was proceeding at 90 per cent of capacity and at the original 80 cents per hundred, although other reports indicated that many workers were getting up to $1 per hundred for their labor.[29]

Of the union leaders who had been jailed, twenty-one were still behind bars on October 29. Several days later the American Civil Liberties Union asked Attorney General Earl Warren to prosecute all known violators of civil liberties, especially those farmers who had participated in the incident of October 21 in Madera County Park. Delegates later reported of this meeting with Earl Warren that he had "given a courteous hearing, but did not commit himself."[80] In January, 1940, the last thirteen of the union leaders were indicted, but they were freed when the indictments were ruled insufficient.

10. FARM ORGANIZATIONS AND UNEMPLOYMENT RELIEF

The emphasis placed on government relief policy in determining wage rates for the Madera cotton pickers during the 1939 strike indicates the degree to which unemployment relief was a matter for dispute throughout this period. The constant surplus of agricultural workers, even at seasons of maximum demand, meant that there was always a large group of migrants dependent upon one form of relief or another. California agriculture depended upon a supply of migratory labor. If sufficient harvest hands were to be available at harvest time, a large mass of labor had somehow to be financed through seasons of low labor demand. Government relief payments to migratory labor, then, constituted an indirect subsidization for farm employers.

When employers needed labor the migrants had somehow to be taken off relief and drawn into the fields to harvest the crops. During the harvest season, extending roughly from May through October, the level of relief payments indirectly affected the wage levels that would be paid by employers. This relationship was inevitable in view of the relief policy of releasing a worker from the rolls only when the money he could earn in the fields would bring him enough income to equal or better the monthly relief payments allowed him by the government. Employers had to pay wages high enough to give the worker at least the equivalent of what he was getting from the government. If government payments were relatively high, the employer would have to pay high wages to secure sufficient labor; on the other hand, if government relief payments were relatively low, the employer could pay low wages and still secure enough harvest hands. If agricultural workers were forced, by the denial of all relief payments at harvesttime, to accept employment regardless of the wage offered, wages were depressed still further. Farm employer groups constantly sought to secure low government relief payments and the establishment of a general policy of stopping government relief payments entirely during the harvest season. The problem of granting relief to workers voluntarily idle (that is, on strike) arose in times of agricultural strikes. Farm employers argued that relief granted to strikers was in reality subsidization of the strike.

There was a further aspect to this problem of unemployment relief policy. Government aid to unemployed migrants had to be paid for somehow, and the funds for relief payments eventually had to come from the taxpayers of the state. High relief payments made high taxes necessary. Funds had to be raised not only for direct cash subsistence payments but also for public health services, education, and housing. The opposition of farm employers to higher taxation, even though funds raised by such taxes were used to subsidize the mass of cheap labor employed by these same groups, was a consistent and natural policy.

From 1933 to 1935 unemployment relief policy was formulated by the Federal Emergency Relief Administration and executed by the State Emergency Relief Administration. To qualify for federal funds, the State Emergency Relief Administration had to follow the policy laid down by Harry Hopkins that relief must be judged by need and not by the existence of any controversy in which the client might be involved. It was in conformity with this policy that relief was granted to striking cotton workers in the fall of 1933 and to the vegetable pickers in the Imperial Valley in the early spring of 1934. Without such assistance, these strikes undoubtedly would have been broken more quickly than they actually were.[1]

But by December, 1935, this form of federal assistance had been withdrawn, and responsibility for unemployment relief consequently rested directly upon the state, though federal funds continued to be used in the state in various works projects programs. The California Unemployment Relief Act of 1935 established the State Relief Administration (S.R.A.), which, working with state funds, was to provide funds for the unemployed. Unemployables (that is, the blind, disabled, and aged) were still to be cared for by the various County Welfare Departments, working with some contributions from the state government. In the summer of 1936 Governor Merriam selected Harold Pomeroy to head the State Relief Administration. He remained as director until Culbert Olson was inaugurated as governor in January, 1939. No statement of policy was outlined in the Unemployment Relief Act of 1935, and Pomeroy was therefore left entirely free to establish policy and to modify it at his own discretion. The fact that the State Relief Administration was not protected by civil service requirements made it peculiarly susceptible to political pressure.[2]

Under Pomeroy state relief policy was conservative, and its administration careful and efficient. The State Relief Administration operated on principles designed to provide sufficient labor for farm employers at a moderate wage level. The "prevailing wage" concept was the rule of thumb used to determine policy in any particular situation. That is, relief was denied to any worker who refused to accept work at the going wage rate. If the growers offered a certain wage and workers demanded a higher rate, the former was the one accepted as "prevailing" by the S.R.A., and those who refused to work for that rate were released from the relief rolls. This policy was usually modified to allow the worker to continue as a relief recipient if working involved the risk of physical harm (as in crossing a picket line). In general, however, unemployment relief was made available only as a last resort after all other resources had been exhausted.[3]

Harold Pomeroy summarized the policy of the State Relief Administration under his administration as follows:

> We can't use public relief to change conditions throughout the state. That would mean bankruptcy for the state. We haven't enough money from tax funds to do that.
>
> If business, agriculture, or industry can only pay a certain wage, then we can't give relief to those who refuse to work at that figure....
>
> Our position, therefore, is that relief will be denied wherever work is available under conditions that are prevailing. Of course, we will not have our organization used to help those who would chisel under prevailing standards, but otherwise our position stands.[4]

On the whole, the policy and administration of Pomeroy were entirely in accord with the position of employer groups. As E. F. Loescher of Fresno put it in a speech before the Agricultural Department of the State Chamber of Commerce in 1937:

> It appears that the relief situation will continue to be with us for a long time, and we are pleased that the State Relief Administration is being administered in such a practical manner. Under Mr. Pomeroy's administration most of the complaints of farmers have been eliminated, including coddling clients, unnecessary red tape, improperly feeding strikers, freezing clients within limited areas, etc. I am glad to extend to Mr. Pomeroy this hearty commendation.[5]

The policies of the State Relief Administration were obviously in accord with those of the Associated Farmers, too. One of the first publicity programs carried out by that organization, in 1934, had called for denial of relief to strikers. To the Executive Committee of the Associated Farmers this was known as the "No Work—No Eat" program. The Associated Farmers convention in December, 1937, passed a resolution condemning the practices of distributing relief to able-bodied men and of maintaining relief projects at times when agricultural crops were suffering in the fields because of the lack of labor to harvest them.[6]

The California Farm Bureau also declared its support of Pomeroy's administration. As early as November, 1933, the state convention resolved against the granting of aid to the "voluntarily idle."[7] Two years later, at a time when the liberal federal policy was still in effect, delegates to the Farm Bureau convention declared that the administration of relief in California decreased the supply of agricultural labor and established wage scales that hurt agriculture. At this time a four-point program was proposed: 1) that no relief be granted to the physically able if work were available; 2) that no wage scales or relief appropriations be at such levels as to encourage loafing; 3) that competition between agricultural areas be considered in setting relief wage payments (a reference to the Works Progress Administration wage rates in Texas and Florida as compared with those in California); and 4) that exceptional cases not be used to establish general rules.[8] In

1938 the Farm Bureau insisted that the Public Employment Service should be made available to agricultural workers and employers "without respect to labor disputes; and that the Employment Service be by law permitted to recruit workers for employment regardless of the existence or non-existence of a labor dispute."[9]

The Farm Bureau did more than pass resolutions. During the year 1935, officials of the organization established contacts with relief administrators to secure policies more in accord with the desires of farm employers. In that year the Deciduous Fruit Department of the Farm Bureau succeeded in arranging for the removal from relief rolls of "those persons who were in a position to furnish the labor necessary for harvest."[10] In the same year, after several county farm bureaus had complained of the difficulty of securing farm labor because of federal relief policy, C.F.B.F. Secretary Alex Johnson discussed the matter with State W.P.A. Administrator Frank Y. McLaughlin and won the assurance of this government official that he would coöperate in making farm workers available from relief rolls.[11]

The Farm Bureau, along with other farm groups, was successful in bringing about a stiffening of relief policy during the harvest season of 1937. On September 3, 1937, Governor Frank Merriam, in an address at a banquet given by the Farm Bureau during the annual State Fair, stated that reliefers would have to take jobs in the harvest or get off relief. Four days later, a directive issued by the California State Employment Service declared:

> His Excellency, Frank F. Merriam, Governor of the State of California, has issued an edict to the effect that persons on relief must either accept employment when it is offered by the California State Employment Service, or get off the relief rolls. His initial action follows the appeal of agriculturists throughout California for workers to harvest important crops.[12]

The statements of the California State Grange on government unemployment relief policy were not always consistent. Evidence suggests that there were three groups within the Grange, each with its own approach to this problem. One group, led by Sehlmeyer, was opposed entirely to the dole system of relief. In 1932 and 1933, before the program of the

Federal Emergency Relief Administration had been established, the *California Grange News* publicized a proposal that California's fruit surpluses be peddled from door to door by the country's ten million unemployed.[13] Several months later this suggestion was abandoned in favor of the following scheme, which was even more impractical:

... If our state government would put the unemployed to work on state projects, pay them in scrip which would be good for the payment of debts or taxes, and appoint an agricultural commission to fix fair prices for agricultural products, the production and distribution of which would be under coöperative majority rule, we could feed ourselves, and pay our own debts, without much help from outside. Shipments of agricultural products to the rest of the United States might be arranged in the same manner as this government arranges for shipments to foreign countries when the monetary rates are different.[14]

Similar schemes were suggested from time to time in the next few years. Each, in turn, was dropped and never mentioned again.

In a resolution passed by the delegates to the annual convention in 1935, the Grange recognized that relief for the unemployed was a serious problem but asserted that relief for the taxpayer should be considered as well. At this time the Grange endorsed the "production for use" plan, which had been part of the "End Poverty in California" (E.P.I.C.) scheme.[15] Sehlmeyer, in his annual address of 1937, stressed his group's opposition to the dole system of relief. He stated that to foster the feeling among relief recipients that the government owed them a living was to undermine democracy. He insisted that the unemployed had to be helped to find employment and that no relief money should be granted except in return for work or service.[16]

A second group within the Grange, a group that seems to have been more conscious of the conflict between employer and worker groups over unemployment relief policy, took its stand on the side of labor. In May, 1936, cotton choppers in the San Joaquin Valley were offered wages of 75 cents per acre or 20 cents per hour. In keeping with official policy, persons on relief were removed from the rolls to accept work at these prevailing wages. Among these were about fifty workers who were cut off from W.P.A. work. It was in protest against this situation that the Subordinate Grange of Weed Patch in Kern County passed the following resolution:

Whereas, only through raising the level of farm commodity prices and the wages of workers will we overcome the depression, and

Whereas, the present effort to force unfortunate WPA workers to accept wages even lower than the subsistence allotment set by relief,

Therefore, be it resolved, that Weed Patch Grange repudiate any self-appointed labor committee who only represent speculative interest in labor and soil. Those starvation wages set by said gentlemen who do not toil will foster class hatred and crime.

We protest the use of Kern County public funds and public officials to be used by big landowners to intimidate by threat of starvation jobless citizens to work for wages insufficient to provide a decent living.[17]

This stand must be taken as an expression of minority opinion within the Grange, for no similar resolution or statement by any other Grange unit has been found and no such opinion is expressed in the various proceedings of the State Grange.

The third group within the Grange seems to have carried the majority of Grange opinion with it on unemployment relief policy. This group led the Grange to accept the attitudes of the other farm organizations. Leadership of this group seems to have come from the newly formed Granges of southern California, and it is possible that many of these new Grange members were, unlike most Grangers in northern California, employers of migrant labor. A resolution passed in October, 1936, stated that, since "the farming industry of southern California, finds it difficult at times to secure the necessary help to facilitate the handling of crops, and other ranch work," relief should never be made more attractive than work. This resolution proposed that all deserving and able unemployed should be registered with a state employment bureau to which employers could apply for workers; that relief clients who accepted work should not thereby lose their position on the relief rolls if they again became unemployed; and that those who refused to accept work should be forced to forego all future aid.[18] Another resolution, passed the following year, restated this policy, but added that relief clients should not be dropped from the rolls if they refused to accept work unless the wage offered was at least the equivalent of relief rates.[19]

With the Olson administration in 1939 came the establishment of a new relief policy. There was evidence that the former "prevailing" wage theory would be replaced by a new "fair" wage policy, that is, that relief clients would not be released from the rolls unless the wage rate offered by employers was judged a "fair" one by relief administrators. When the cotton choppers in the Madera region threatened to go on strike in May, 1939, the State Relief Administration first decided to accept the 20 cents per hour offered by the growers as the prevailing wage and to release workers from relief unless they accepted employment at those rates. But then Carey McWilliams, Chief of the Division of Immigration and Housing, was sent by Olson to hold a wage hearing in Madera on May 9. At its conclusion McWilliams reported that 27½ cents per hour would constitute a "fair" wage. On the basis of this report, Relief Administrator Dewey Anderson ruled that workers would not be forced off relief to accept employment at less than this rate.

Alex Johnson, speaking for the Farm Bureau, objected at once, saying that the operation of this policy would keep men in idleness on state allowances that were smaller than the income laborers could earn if they worked for the 20 cents per hour offered. The Cotton Department of the Farm Bureau announced that this new policy was a "racket" directed against the growers and insisted that it be reversed at once even if this involved blocking all legislative appropriations for relief until assurance was given that the State Relief Administration would return to the former "prevailing" wage policy.[20]

Resistance of farm organizations to the new policy was so immediate and vehement that Governor Olson decided to call a conference of farm leaders and state officials for the purpose of working out a program that would be acceptable to everyone. The first meeting was held on June 12, 1939, and to it came Ray Wiser, R. V. Garrod, Harold Pomeroy (formerly administrator of the State Relief Administration and at that time executive secretary of the Associated Farmers), Ralph Taylor, R. N. Wilson, William B. Ayres (editor of the *California Grange News*, present as a personal representative of George Sehlmeyer, who was indisposed), and ten state officials including Dewey Anderson (the new director of the State Relief Administration), Carey McWilliams, William B. Parker (director of the State Department of Agriculture), Sidney G. Rubinow (publicity director of the Farm Bureau from 1936 to 1938, at the time of this meeting Assistant Director of the State Department of Agriculture, and later State Relief Administrator himself), and others.[21]

Dewey Anderson opened the meeting by expressing the opinions of the Olson administration. He stated that, though the S.R.A. could not constitute itself a wage-fixing board, neither could it release workers to accept employment at wages that the administration felt were inadequate. As he stated it: "Governor Olson is not going to have people put into the position of accepting substandard pay and existence in agricultural harvesting... we are trying to determine whether it is advisable to set a fair wage."[22] Ray Wiser of the Farm Bureau admitted that the relief problem was a complex one and that agriculture would be unable for many years to care for its agricultural workers without government assistance, but he also insisted that the farmers' costs had mounted to a very high level and that farm employers could not pay wage rates in excess of what they could afford. Ayres, for the Grange, pointed out that, unlike the manufacturer, the farmer could not stop his production, that he had no control over the price of his commodity on the open market, and that he was not able to hold his crop off the market for any length of time. He concluded that the operation of these factors made the item of wage costs an essential one. At the first conference the delegates talked around the problem a good deal, and little was accomplished. It was agreed, however, that the representatives present should report back to their organizations and then return for a second meeting two weeks later to try to reach some ground for common agreement.

On June 27 the same group met again.[23] Discussion centered around the Olson administration's proposal to create an independent agency with power to hold wage hearings for the purpose of determining at what wage levels workers should be released from relief rolls by the S.R.A. Ray Wiser came to the meeting with recommendations drawn up by a special conference of the Labor Relations Committee of the Farm Bureau. He reported that the Farm Bureau opposed intervention by government agencies in matters of agricultural wage scales, objected to any attempt to fix or influence agricultural wages through the S.R.A., and decried the "exploitation by any person or organization of unemployed and relief recipients by any means, including the collection of organization dues, and political activity." (This last objection was directed against the Workers' Alliance, an allegedly Communist-controlled union of unemployed workers, which was, at that time, putting great pressure upon local and state offices of the S.R.A.) Wiser urged instead the following policy:

1) A Relief Administration policy that will encourage a maximum of private employment and self-support while relieving actual need and discouraging the movement of unemployed and dependents from other states into California.

2) Private employers to at all times refrain from taking advantage of competition for employment and to pay the highest wages economically possible.

3) That, as a policy, the SRA remove clients from relief rolls when the income from private employment exceeds the monthly rate on relief.[24]

McWilliams pointed out that it was very difficult to estimate just what monthly income a worker would get at the going wage, for many of the workers who would be released from relief would be able to secure only part-time work. Wiser replied that the interests of the workers were not the only ones involved and that the economic concerns of the farmer had to be given equal consideration. After prolonged discussion the following three-point policy was agreed upon:

Subject to the other recommendations herein, agricultural workers and their families shall be turned off the relief rolls of the State Relief Administration when the earnings from agricultural employment for all employable members of the family will be equal to or in excess of the relief budget of the family for the period they will be off relief.

No agency in the State government should fix a wage which agricultural employers are required to pay.

That it is recognized by this group that the Relief Administration must use such appropriate reasonable means as are convenient and necessary to determine what are prevailing wages and conditions of employment...[25]

This policy was agreed to by all the delegates except Ayres of the State Grange, who was under instructions to be present as an observer only. The policy followed closely the recommendations made by the Farm Bureau and represented a concession by the Olson administration to organized farmers of the state.

Still farm employers were not entirely satisfied with the relief setup. They were afraid that progressives within the Olson administration—men such as Carey McWilliams, Leigh Athearn, and H. C. Carrasco—might reinstitute their program for the determination of a "fair" wage. Then, too, there was evidence that financial corruption, party politics, and Communist activity within the S.R.A. were reducing the efficiency of the administration of government relief funds. Furthermore, as full-time jobs became available with the beginning of the defense boom, there seemed to be less need for unemployment relief payments. And, finally, farm employers had never been fully satisfied with the State Relief Administration, even as it had been managed under Pomeroy.

Farm employers had always wanted the granting of relief to be controlled and administered by county officials (using state and federal funds, of course) under the direction of county boards of supervisors. County supervisors were often under the complete domination of farm employer groups; they always considered the interests of the taxpayer first and above all else; they were hard-headed men who had little sympathy with "reliefers" and "loafers"; and they could be relied upon to be sensitive to the need of farm employers for harvest hands. The S.R.A. had never been and never could be as dependable in these matters or as subject to the control of farm employers as county officials were.[26]

In 1939 the Associated Farmers and the Farm Bureau launched a concerted campaign to secure the return of relief

Farm Organizations and Unemployment Relief

administration to the counties. In this campaign they were joined by other agricultural and industrial groups. The campaign was unintentionally aided by maladministration in the S.R.A. under a succession of Olson appointees, none of whom was able to straighten out the political, financial, and ideological mess into which the S.R.A. had stumbled.[27]

Delegates to the annual convention of the Farm Bureau in November, 1938, called for the return of relief administration to the counties with a minimum of state or federal supervision but with funds coming primarily from the state.[28] The Grange convention, a month earlier, had not gone that far, but it had recommended that relief should be denied to anyone who quit his job voluntarily without just cause or who refused employment at reasonable wages and conditions.[29] The following spring, however, while the state legislature was debating relief appropriations, Sehlmeyer granted State Relief Administrator Dewey Anderson the use of the monthly Grange radio hour to defend continued state control of relief and to ask for farmer coöperation in a program of construction works projects for rural areas.[30]

Administration forces were still strong enough in 1939 to prevent the destruction of the State Relief Administration and to secure adequate relief appropriations from the legislature. But funds granted for relief purposes were exhausted sooner than had been anticipated, largely because S.R.A. rolls were augmented by unemployed workers released from W.P.A. projects. To meet the deficit in the relief budget, special legislative sessions had to be called in January, 1940, again in May, and again in September.

In the meantime, throughout 1939, there had been continued expressions of dissatisfaction with the S.R.A. County Farm Bureaus complained that relief clients were spending government checks on liquor and gambling and suggested that payments in food and rent would be preferable to cash subsidies. They also requested that the names of relief clients be published. Finally, they asked that the administration of relief be returned to the counties.[31] The California Grange joined in this criticism of the administration of relief. It recommended that relief grants be in kind, rather than in cash, and that lists of relief recipients should be published. But it still refused to endorse the return of relief to the counties.³²

The special session of the state legislature that met in January and February, 1940, dealt primarily with the relief problem. When the legislature convened in late January, ten Democratic assemblymen joined with the Republicans to defeat Paul Peek, the Olson administration's choice to succeed himself as Speaker, and elected in his place Gordon Garland, an anti-Olson Democrat from Tulare County. Seth Millington, Assemblyman from Butte County and a close friend of Ray Wiser of the Farm Bureau, was the brains of this "economy bloc," and Garland, the new Speaker, had always worked closely with the powerful Farm Bureau of Tulare County. The formation of an anti-Olson coalition of Republicans and conservative Democrats meant that the Farm Bureau and the Associated Farmers now had greater influence than they had enjoyed during the 1939 session. The main issues under consideration were the amount of money that should be appropriated for relief, the duration of the period over which the grants should be budgeted, and the reforms that should be made in the administration of these funds.

Before and during this session, the various county Farm Bureaus held special meetings, to which, in many cases, local assemblymen and senators were invited. For example, Assemblyman George A. Clarke was invited to attend a meeting of the Merced County Farm Bureau held on January 20, 1940. At this meeting Clarke assured the Farm Bureau that he would work for the return of relief administration to the counties. This meeting also passed a resolution calling for the publication of the names of all relief clients in the county.³³ It was with regard to this point that the editor of the *Livingston Chronicle* (Merced County), recalling that farmers had themselves depended upon federal agricultural adjustment payments throughout the 1930's, observed: "... were that done the names of many farm bureau members, especially the big farmer members, would have to be posted, for, called by any other name a rose is a rose and relief is relief."³⁴

A meeting of Associated Farmer groups from seven counties assembled at Stockton on February 16, 1940, and concluded that, because of the "extravagance" of the State Relief Administration and because of the subversion of the S.R.A. by radical groups, the administration of relief should be returned to the counties.[35] The California Grange, however, supported the Olson administration in this matter, as it had in others. A meeting of thirty deputies of the Grange held on February 10–11, 1940, in Sacramento opposed the return of relief administration to the counties, stating that such action would necessitate increased taxes upon homes and farms and would increase the cost of administration.[36]

In the first special session the legislature passed an emergency appropriation of $12,200,000 for unemployment relief. Governor Olson vetoed the appropriation bill on the grounds that the sum was inadequate to cover needs, but his veto was overridden in both houses. The governor also vetoed a bill that would have returned relief to the counties. In this case, his veto was sustained; the assembly failed to muster the necessary two-thirds majority.[37]

Relief funds again were expended at a faster rate than had been planned, and the legislature had to be called back in May, 1940, to face the deficit problem once more. In the meantime the Yorty investigation of the State Relief Administration had uncovered evidence of purported Communist activity within the S.R.A. Forces opposed to Olson seized upon this evidence to justify their refusal to grant the $50,000,000 the governor had requested to cover relief costs through June 30, 1941. The legislature instead voted $24,347,091 to last only through March 31, 1941. The results of this session as a whole, however, constituted only a partial victory for the "economy bloc," since a bill to return the administration of relief to the counties under state supervision and with joint state and county financing, proposed by Senator John Phillips, failed to pass.[38]

In July, 1940, the governor appointed Sidney G. Rubinow as State Relief Administrator. Rubinow had been associated with the Farm Bureau for a number of years and had the confidence of that group and of other farm organizations, though he did not favor the return of relief to the counties at that time. It was largely this confidence in Rubinow that persuaded the legislature to pass another emergency appropriation for the

S.R.A. in a third special session called in September.[39] But Rubinow's tenure of office was even shorter than that of his predecessors during the Olson administration. His program of economy, his wholesale dismissal of personnel, and his drastic reorganization of the administration of relief offended too many loyal party workers who had been rewarded for past services with jobs in the S.R.A. Furthermore, these policies ran counter to those of Olson and his closest advisers. By December of 1940 Rubinow was out. His dismissal permitted the legislature to attack and to destroy the S.R.A. when it met in regular session in January, 1941.

Sehlmeyer and the Grange gave the Olson administration their wholehearted support throughout the 1941 session. In October, 1940, the Grange endorsed a plan for self-help coöperatives and called for maintenance of state control over relief. In a lengthy resolution it was pointed out that a large proportion of those on relief were migrants who moved from county to county and that it was impossible for county officials to keep check on these transient workers. It was further stated that the lack of a centralized coördinating authority would lead to inconsistent relief regulations and to inequitable relief allotments.[40] In the winter of 1940–1941 Sehlmeyer made a tour of Subordinate Granges throughout the state, delivering lectures in which he sought to gain local support for the administration's program of maintaining state control of relief and instituting a program of work relief. In these speeches Sehlmeyer said:

If counties had the administration of relief, the supervisors would be obliged by law to prevent suffering, and when need occurred that had not been provided for in the state budget, the counties, whose taxes come from farmers and other small taxpayers, would have to bear this additional expense. If relief is returned to the counties, your taxes will be increased by about 25 per cent.

There are too many people today looking to relief as a mode of living, too many businesses looking to the government for subsidies. Cash subsidies to farmers is relief, and no thinking farmer looks upon a subsidy as a permanent remedy. The vital part of any relief program should be provisions enabling the recipients to rehabilitate themselves and earn their own livings.[41]

Farm Organizations and Unemployment Relief

In 1941 the legislature passed a bill, endorsed by the Farm Bureau and presented by Senator John Phillips, that provided for the return of the administration of relief to the counties. This legislation was blocked, however, when Governor Olson's veto was sustained by a slim margin in the senate. The legislature retaliated by refusing to appropriate any more funds for the S.R.A. This action automatically threw both the administration and financing of unemployment relief back upon the counties.[42]

By this time, however, the relief problem had nearly disappeared. The upswing in business activity associated with the defense boom brought nearly full employment in the state, as in the nation. In a very short time the labor market in the state manifested a shortage rather than a surplus of workers. One of the most crucial problems of California agriculture in the 1930's had been solved—or, more correctly, temporarily alleviated and postponed—not by anything that farmers, laborers, economists, or politicians of the state had done, but by the economic consequences of war.

11. THE STRUGGLE "HOT CARGO" AND SECONDARY BOYCOTT

Los Angeles had traditionally been an "open shop" city. It had entered the race for industries some years after its rival, San Francisco, and had offered low wages as an important attraction for capital. The constant migration of people into the area, attracted by other than economic factors, had kept the labor market flooded. The continued success of Los Angeles industry depended in part at least upon continued relatively low wage rates, and to keep wages low it was necessary to resist the unionization of labor. Until 1937 employers were largely successful in their program of keeping Los Angeles an "open shop" city, but protective federal legislation and the renewed agitation of labor leaders in that year seemed to indicate that labor's big drive to establish unionism in southern California could not be held off much longer.

The A.F. of L. Teamsters' Union led the way. Several weapons that it used to consolidate its position in the area hurt the farmers, who depended upon Los Angeles as an outlet for their commodities. First, the teamsters refused to handle any commodities that were not processed and packed by union labor. Fruit, nuts, and truck crops handled by nonunion labor often were declared "hot cargo" and would not be touched. Secondly, the teamsters required that every truck carrying into the area any kind of produce, including agricultural commodities, be driven and unloaded by union workers. The consequences were apparent—either farm employers would have to begin to employ union labor or they would have to break the power of the unions.

The county Farm Bureaus in southern California saw the danger implicit in the move of unions into the Los Angeles area as early as 1936. When it became apparent that the big drive was under way, the Labor Relations Committee of the Los Angeles County Farm Bureau called a general meeting of all employer groups and public agencies in the area. These groups evolved a uniform policy toward labor unions that the Farm Bureau claimed was instrumental in keeping trouble under control throughout that year.[1]

Labor unrest deepened throughout 1937, however, and the Farm Bureau finally decided that more direct action would have to be taken. Sidney G. Rubinow, publicity director of the California Farm Bureau Federation, was sent to Los Angeles in December, 1937, to work out a public relations program that would stress farmer discontent with unionization in the Los Angeles area. On January 15, 1938, representatives from the Los Angeles county and state units of the Farm Bureau and the Associated Farmers and from numerous coöperatives in southern California met together. At this meeting Rubinow worked for the adoption of a common policy that would cement these groups into a united front in opposition to the Teamsters' Union of Los Angeles. The coöperatives, however, were afraid of possible union reprisals. Jim Cook, secretary of the California Fruit Growers' Exchange (distributors of Sunkist citrus fruit), insisted that the Farm Bureau and the Associated Farmers conduct the campaign entirely by themselves. It was this viewpoint that prevailed.[2]

The Farm Bureau made two contributions to the campaign against unionization. First, Rubinow directed a publicity campaign that educated the general public to the dangers for agriculture inherent in labor unionization. Secondly, an agreement was worked out between the Los Angeles Farm Bureau and the Truck Drivers and Helpers Union No. 692 under the terms of which the union agreed to let any bona fide farmer load and unload his own products in the markets of the Los Angeles area. Possession of a Farm Bureau membership card was recognized as proof that the driver of a truck was really a farmer. By the operation of this system the Farm Bureau intended to protect the smaller farmers of the area, growers who handled their own transporting and marketing operations.[3]

It was left to the Associated Farmers to execute a program of more direct action. In February, 1938, the Associated Farmers set up an organization known as the Farmers' Transportation Association, which undertook the task of registering all truck owners and truck drivers who were willing to deliver goods under any circumstances. Drivers who pledged that they would drive agricultural commodities through picket lines were given special cards or licenses. Members of the Associated Farmers and of allied groups agreed not to transport any produce except by use of trucks and drivers properly licensed by this association. If these nonunion truck drivers encountered difficulty in delivering their goods to markets in Los Angeles, they were directed to call the Associated Farmers' office in that city, which was to dispatch guards (usually legally deputized) to protect them against possible violence at the hands of members of the Teamsters' Union.

The Farmers' Transportation Association operated from February, 1938, through September, 1939, with a budget of $9,800. Southern Californians, Inc., an employer group in that area, raised most of the funds, and the Associated Farmers of Imperial County did most of the organizational and administrative work. Licenses were granted by the association on a monthly basis; if any trucker failed, for any reason, to deliver the goods assigned to him, his certificate was not renewed. By the autumn of 1939, the attempt of the Teamsters' Union to unionize commercial trucking in southern California and to force employers to hire only union labor had been dissipated. The Farmers' Transportation Association was dissolved, but not before it had won substantial success in coöperation with other rural and urban employer groups.[4]

Farmers in northern California faced similar troubles in the San Francisco Bay Area. Not only did the Teamsters' Union frequently refuse to allow trucks with nonunion drivers to enter the Bay Area, not only did unions refuse to handle products that had not been processed by union labor, but also recurring longshore strikes frequently tied up port facilities, on which farmers depended for the export of many of their commodities. In the Bay Area, farmers faced two unions, not one. There the troubles of farmers were threefold—transportation blockades, "hot cargo" and secondary boycott, and idle warehouses and docks. Jurisdictional disputes between the teamsters and the longshoremen aggravated the troubles still further.

The idea of a counterboycott against cities that allowed organized labor to harass farmers with union boycotts appealed strongly to farm organizations. Actually, of course, such proposals were rarely taken seriously even by the farmers themselves, for most of them recognized the impossibility of establishing an effective boycott of either the Los Angeles or San Francisco market. Nevertheless, counterboycotts were occasionally threatened, largely for propaganda purposes. A resolution passed by the Associated Farmers at its annual convention in December, 1937, declared:

Resolved, That although we are opposed to Boycotts in principle, that we recommend that if any city persists in allowing any California farm products to be barred from its markets through boycotts or failure to protect the farmers in the delivery of their products, that all farmers of California consider seriously the advisability of launching united defensive boycotts against such cities—upon the principle that no city that boycotts the products of the farmer is entitled to the trade or support of the farmer.[5]

The California Farm Bureau passed a similar resolution at its annual convention in 1937.[6] And even the Pomona Grange of Stanislaus County resolved that "no city that boycotts the products of farmers is entitled to the trade or support of farmers."[7]

Occasionally farm groups attempted to resolve these problems by dealing directly with San Francisco unions. In September, 1937, officials of the Associated Farmers met with officials of the Teamsters' Union to arrange some sort of truce. This conference reached a compromise agreement whereby the teamsters agreed to allow farmers to drive their own trucks into the city. But the agreement was temporary only, and trouble recurred throughout the next several years.[8]

A more serious and more constant grievance of farmers in northern California was the series of longshore strikes that plagued the Bay Area almost every year. When port facilities were paralyzed, the prices of dried prunes, apricots, peaches, pears, raisins, grains, and rice were apt to fall. San Francisco's strong employer groups had been unable to destroy or to reach lasting agreements with Harry Bridges and his longshoremen. Where these groups had failed, there was little hope that farm organizations would be any more successful.

The Farm Bureau passed resolutions condemning these strikes and blaming the trouble upon Communist control of the longshore unions. These resolutions frequently requested federal or state intervention and mediation or arbitration of the disputes.[9] There was little else that could be done. Demands from Farm Bureaus in Kern and Tulare counties that the state organization be more aggressive evoked this explanation from E. C. Kimball:

> We [the Board of Directors of the California Farm Bureau Federation] realize that labor relations is only one of the problems CFBF is obligated to serve its members in and that the involved character of this problem tends to compel us at times to proceed slowly in order that the balance of our program be not interfered with.[10]

The Grange, with its membership located primarily in northern California, took little notice of the labor troubles in the Los Angeles area, but it did feel obliged to act when labor disputes tied up business in the Bay Area. During the first big waterfront strike in the summer of 1934, the *California Grange News* commented that, although the port tie-up hurt the farmers' market, "Farmers should be sympathetic with labor." Grange spokesmen declared that industry was as much at fault as labor and suggested that the request of employers for arbitration should be viewed with suspicion because "disinterested" arbitration committees always seemed to favor industry. Again in 1937, when another longshore strike hit San Francisco, the *Grange News* suggested that "Capital must be content with smaller profits and a fairer wage." The article suggested that arbitration of the dispute or formulation of a plan for profit-sharing might lead to a settlement. In 1939, when another waterfront strike blockaded the port, Governor Olson appointed George Sehlmeyer, at that time a state harbor commissioner, to a special committee to investigate the strike. It was Sehlmeyer's opinion that the public interest was greater than that of either labor or industry; that both groups were equally at fault; that arbitration must be accepted; and that legislation should be passed to give the state authority to intercede in any future port tie-up. This committee did not, however, play a significant part in the settlement of the strike.[11]

Since farm organizations had failed to stop the union practices of "hot cargo" and secondary boycott, either through publicity or through direct action, they turned to political action for possible relief. After renewed union activity in 1937 and 1938, employer groups, both urban and rural, decided to sponsor an initiative proposition calling for legal restrictions upon labor activity. Farm employer groups were especially anxious to secure protection against the use of secondary boycott and "hot cargo" by urban labor groups.[12]

A special organization, the California Committee for Peace in Employment Relations, was formed to sponsor this initiative proposition, which became Proposition Number 1 in the elections in the fall of 1938. Senator Sanborn Young was selected as chairman of this committee. The California Farm Bureau Federation, the Associated Farmers, the Agricultural Council of California, and the Farmers' Union, together with numerous industrial associations, endorsed the proposal and actively supported the committee's campaign. The formal argument in favor of Proposition Number 1, printed in the handbook distributed to all voters by the Secretary of State, was signed by Sanborn Young, by Alberta Gude Lynch, president of the Business Women's Legislative Council, and by Alex Johnson, secretary-treasurer of the C.F.B.F. The Farm Bureau was not, however, unanimous in its support of this initiative proposition. Some Farm Bureau members feared that their organization, by sponsoring the proposition, would alienate organized labor, whose support was essential to help defeat Proposition Number 20, a "single tax" proposal.[13] Others were indifferent or adopted a neutral position.

The terms of the initiative proposition were so long, involved, and ambiguous that they could be interpreted in many different ways. Certain provisions were clear, however: picketing in labor disputes involving the issue of union recognition was to be severely restricted; picketing in "legitimate" disputes involving wages, hours, and conditions of labor was to be permitted if "peaceful" and if limited to one picket at each entrance to the firm involved in the dispute; the secondary boycott was to be forbidden; and the union practice of labeling commodities produced or transported by nonunion labor as "hot cargo" and refusing to handle them was to be outlawed. Although many of the provisions seemed harmless enough, it was apparent to many that a popular endorsement of this initiative proposition would seriously curtail union activity and greatly weaken the labor movement in California.

Proponents of the plan argued that it would protect the general public against the excesses of labor activities but would in no way interfere with "legitimate" union measures. Holmes Bishop, president of the Associated Farmers, set the tone in a radio address.

... Some of the men who oppose Number One are not fooling around. Stop and think—who are they? What is their stake in California? What do they want? I'll tell you, and I'm speaking for thousands of farmers who sweat for the dollars they make. Many of the fellows who want to defeat Proposition Number One are so-called labor leaders who have a snap. Every worker pays for their support. Every worker has to kick in to be told what to do by those boys. And if Proposition Number One wins, those fellows won't have any pay for agitating trouble; they won't have cars to ride around in; they won't have rough neck shock troopers and goon squads hired, at fancy prices to beat workers into submission.... I say, we've got to drive 'em out.[14]

Labor unions campaigned against this proposition with all the money and energy at their disposal. And supporting them was the California State Grange. Charles O. Busick, attorney for the California State Grange, wrote in the *California Grange News:*

Today, we are asked to adopt on November 8, Initiative Proposition No. 1 on the Ballot, sponsored by Phillip Bancroft, candidate for United States Senator, and the Associated Farmers (an association composed largely of the agencies of banks and public utility corporations) which Initiative, if adopted, will deprive the people of California of each and all of these cherished rights so guaranteed by every Federal and State Constitution in our land....
Said by its proponents to be needed legislation for industrial peace, this initiative proposition would really take away the constitutional rights of labor; it is dangerous because the layman does not recognize the fascistic provisions hidden within the proposal....

This Initiative Amendment No. 1 is the most un-American, most vicious and most outrageous measure ever submitted to the American people.[15]

The Grange did not, however, participate actively in the campaign against the proposition, for it was devoting its time and energy to securing support for another proposition on the ballot, one that called for public ownership of electric power.

The proponents of Proposition Number 1 admittedly spent over a third of a million dollars in support of their proposal, but organized labor, with the support of progressives generally and with the backing of the successful Democratic candidate for governor, Culbert Olson, proved too strong. The proposition was defeated by a vote of 1,476,379 to 1,067,229.[16]

Employer groups in the state felt strong enough in 1941 to bring up the "hot cargo" issue again. The annual convention of the Farm Bureau in November, 1940, had resolved that there was need for legislation that would "insure to all labor its right to work without fear of coercion or intimidation as well as protect both labor and employer from picketing and secondary boycotts where no controversy exists as to wages or hours."[17] This resolution formed the basis for a bill, sponsored by the Farm Bureau and written in part by I. H. Pfaffenberger, general counsel for the Farm Bureau, providing for the outlawing of "hot cargo" and secondary boycott for the duration of the national emergency and providing injunctive relief for anyone injured by violation of the act. This bill (S.B. 877) was introduced in the senate by three rural Republicans: Frank L. Gordon, W. P. Rich, and Ray Hays. In the assembly the bill was introduced by John Phillips, friend of the Associated Farmers, and Seth Millington, anti-Olson Democrat from Butte County. The campaign to secure its adoption was led by the Farm Bureau, with the support of the Associated Farmers, the Agricultural Council, and the Farmers' Union. Von T. Ellsworth, research director for the Farm Bureau, provided for introduction of the bill and directed the campaign for its approval.

Edward Vandeleur, secretary of the State Federation of Labor, in testifying against the bill, presented the basis of agricultural labor's opposition to it when he said that farm laborers, because of the "compulsion of hunger," were without bargaining power, that they needed the help of their urban brothers, and that this bill would prohibit the use of those methods through which such aid could be extended. In other words, if the bill were passed urban unions could no longer force farm employers to hire union labor by refusing to handle farm commodities packed, processed, or transported by nonunion labor.[18]

By early May of 1941 it was apparent that both houses would endorse the bill. It seemed likely that Olson would veto the bill, but its supporters hoped that sufficient popular pressure might be exerted upon the Governor to secure his signature. The Farm Bureau advised its members to write to Governor Olson urging him to sign the bill. Farm Bureau President Ray Wiser sent to all local Farm Bureaus a special plea that read:

Labor is attempting to make a trade with Governor Olson on the basis that they will not attempt to organize field workers this year if the Governor will veto Senate Bill 877. In almost the next breath labor representatives say they are really going to organize all farm labor next year. Just as sure as this bill is vetoed, labor organizers, racketeers and foreign propagandists will be in the field immediately organizing field workers....

If "Hot Cargo" and "Secondary Boycott" are not outlawed even we, as farmers, and our families, may have to join the unions in order to work in our own fields, and in order to harvest and deliver our crops.[19]

But on May 27, 1941, Governor Olson did veto the bill on the grounds that it was unconstitutional. He held that the right to boycott and picket could not be denied by legislative enactment. Then began the struggle to secure sufficient votes to override his veto. In the senate, Jack Shelley, San Francisco labor leader, could get only four of his colleagues to vote against the bill. (One of these was the Grange-inclined senator from Stanislaus County, J. C. Garrison.) The assembly went into an all-night session on June 6, 1941, and finally at 4:02 A.M. the fifty-fourth "yea" vote was gathered in. Labor filed referendum petitions so that the law would not go into effect until the electorate had passed on it again. At the general elections in the fall of 1942, however, the bill was upheld by a vote of 1,124,624 to 909,061. The law remained in force until President Truman declared the national emergency at an end. At that time the state legislature repassed it as a permanent peacetime measure, but the state supreme court soon found this latter act unconstitutional.[20]

The Grange, though it did not join the other farm organizations in sponsoring and endorsing this bill in 1941, did not actively oppose it either. Rather, Sehlmeyer supported the Heisinger bill, which limited the application of the provisions concerning the secondary boycott and "hot cargo" to agricultural commodities only. Sehlmeyer probably thought that such a bill would be signed by the governor and that it would not be challenged by a referendum. In supporting the Heisinger bill, which had little chance of success, and refusing to take a definite stand one way or the other on the main bill (S.B. 877), Sehlmeyer again took the middle road and, in so doing, isolated his group from the other farm groups.[21]

12. CRIMINAL SYNDICALISM TRIAL AND LABOR LEGISLATION

One of the first steps taken by the Associated Farmers of California was to seek elimination of radical agitators from agricultural unions by securing prosecution of Communist leaders under the California Criminal Syndicalism Act. On July 20, 1934, police raided Communist headquarters in Sacramento and seized numerous pamphlets and other materials with which they hoped to prove that such radicals as Pat Chambers and Carolyn Decker were guilty of committing "crime, sabotage, violence, or unlawful methods of terrorism with intent to approve, advocate or further the doctrine of criminal syndicalism." Seventeen members of the Communist party were indicted under the terms of this law. When their cases were brought up for trial, two of the indictments were dismissed; the other fifteen leaders were prosecuted.

The Associated Farmers invested much time and money in aiding the prosecution in this case. Guernsey Frazer, a member of the Executive Committee of the Associated Farmers, lent his secretary to Sacramento County District Attorney McAllister. The Associated Farmers persuaded Elmer W. Heald, District Attorney of Imperial County, to assist McAllister, who had had little experience with this type of trial. Heald's expenses during his stay in Sacramento were paid for by the Associated Farmers. The A.F. further helped the government prosecution by hiring Captain William Hynes of the Los Angeles Police Intelligence to assist in the case; the A.F. paid him over $3,700 for his work as an operator from March 1 to April 3, 1935, in connection with the trial. In all, the Associated Farmers spent $13,780.59 to help secure conviction of the defendants.[1]

The money was not spent in vain. Eight of the fifteen were

found guilty and sentenced to prison for various terms. Although they were later released upon appeal to the Supreme Court, the immediate effect was to force the most experienced and most militant agricultural union leaders out of the field. With the key leadership gone, the migratory workers were not capable of organizing successfully, and relative peace returned to rural California.

After this trial, and in accordance with the new Communist party line directing loyal members to work within well-established trade unions rather than through separate unions of their own, left-wing trade-unionists began to conceal their connections with the Communist party. Consequently, it became more difficult for employers to prove that strike leaders were really Communist party members. On the other hand, in this situation it was easy for farm employer groups to declare that all agricultural union leaders were "Communists" and so to rationalize their refusal to deal with labor leaders. This was the theme played on constantly by the Associated Farmers: "Our members have shown a willingness at all times to meet with their employees and discuss wages and working conditions with them. We will not deal, however, with any Communist or other radical."[2] It was a simple matter for the A.F. to take the next step of insisting that all who did not agree with its program were radicals.

The Farm Bureau also blamed much of the labor unrest in agriculture on Communist agitation. The Farm Bureau convention in November, 1933, passed a resolution placing the blame for labor disturbances upon radicals and pledging itself to a battle against the Communist party. A resolution in 1935 advised the State Bar Association to disbar all lawyers who were Communists or who defended Communists. The next year the Farm Bureau recommended the deportation of all subversive aliens.[3]

When a bill providing for the repeal of the Criminal Syndicalism Act was proposed in the State Legislature in 1935, the Statewide Agricultural Committee of the State Chamber of Commerce called together a meeting of farm leaders to secure the defeat of that measure. To this meeting, held on February 28, 1935, came Alex Johnson, Ralph Taylor, R. V. Garrod, S.

Parker Frisselle, John Phillips, and Guernsey Frazer, among others. The stand taken by farm leaders at this meeting was in part responsible for the failure of the proposed repeal bill to pass.[4] The Grange was less active in this field, although its annual convention in 1934 did come out in favor of deporting alien radicals who were found guilty of violating the laws of the state.[5]

Local ordinances that curbed the activities of unions engaged in strikes were another instrument used by farm employers during the 1930's to resist the demands of agricultural labor. In the spring of 1934, when Edson Abel of the Farm Bureau and R. N. Wilson of the Chamber of Commerce traveled through the rural counties of California to organize local Citizens' Committees, the passage of county antipicketing ordinances was one by-product of their trip. Pressure from the Farm Bureau, the Chambers of Commerce, and the new units of the Associated Farmers helped secure the passage of such ordinances. In the years from 1936 to 1939 additional ordinances were passed. By 1939, antipicketing ordinances had been passed in thirty-four counties and in nineteen municipalities in the state of California.[6]

The terms of San Joaquin County Ordinance Number 414, passed March 6, 1934, illustrate the drastic nature of these ordinances. This ordinance prohibited the use of language or remarks that tended to provoke a breach of peace; it prohibited any person from loitering on any road or sidewalk in such a manner as to obstruct passage or to annoy persons passing by; it forbade the picketing of the premises of a business for purposes of inducing the employees of that business to quit work. It further stated that it was "unlawful for any person to utter ... any derogatory, indecent, opprobrious epithets or language, or to make any loud or unusual noise or to speak in a loud or unusual tone, or to cry out or proclaim, or to use any gesture ..." for the purpose of inducing any person to refrain from working or from patronizing or negotiating with any particular business.[7]

A Mendocino County Ordinance, Number 265, passed June 14, 1938, provided for general restrictions on strike activity and further declared that any person wishing to form a labor union had to make a written application to the board of supervisors. This application had to be published once a week for four weeks before the date of hearing. Then the board of supervisors was to determine if the union organizers were of "good moral character"; if it decided they were, a license would be granted upon payment of a $10 fee. This license would run for three months and was revocable at any time at the discretion of the supervisors.[8] That such ordinances tended to restrict normal strike activities is obvious.

State Grange opposition to these ordinances was expressed in a resolution, passed at its annual meeting in October, 1934, asserting that such ordinances were "plainly unconstitutional." The resolution declared, somewhat irrelevantly, that the State Chamber of Commerce was the motivating force behind the passage of these ordinances and that the Chamber "is indefatigueable [sic] in its efforts to deflate and depreciate our Country's Agricultural Standards, so that it is but a question of time until the status of the American Farmer will be on par with that of European peasantry, and thus become easy prey for international Big Business."[9]

In 1939 and 1940 some of these ordinances, and similar ones in other parts of the country, were held to be unconstitutional. The decisions were based on the belief that these ordinances violated the Fourteenth Amendment, since they denied the liberty of a citizen to publicize the facts of a labor dispute, a liberty of communications that, it was held, is secured against abridgment by a state.[10] These ordinances were, however, in full force during the 1930's, and they operated to aid agricultural employers in their attempts to break union and strike activities.

Farm organizations were also active in supporting and opposing labor bills presented before the state legislature in Sacramento. In 1937 Democratic legislators introduced several bills to protect the rights of labor and to strengthen the bargaining power of unions. Of these the most important was the Yorty "Little Wagner" bill. This bill guaranteed the right of collective bargaining to employees engaged in intrastate commerce and outlawed certain unfair labor practices. It followed, in outline, the terms of a New York State bill, which in turn had been based on the federal Wagner Labor Relations Act. Although it specifically excluded agricultural labor from its terms, it was opposed by the California Farm Bureau, by the Associated Farmers, and by the Agricultural Council of California. After the bill had passed the assembly by a vote of fifty-seven to nine, these farm organizations went to work to ensure its defeat in the senate. Philip Bancroft, chairman of the Deciduous Fruit Department of the Farm Bureau and lobbyist for the Associated Farmers, called upon farmers to work for its defeat because it would force the unionization of all farm labor and because "There is no use of our raising bumper crops if through labor legislation or labor racketeering we are to be prevented from harvesting them."[11] Hank Strobel of the Associated Farmers was also in Sacramento to work for defeat of the bill. These forces, in conjunction with urban employer groups, won the round when a motion by Senator Culbert Olson to bring the bill out of senate committee failed by a vote of 6 to 28.[12]

These same farm organizations, again in coöperation with other employer groups, were able to block passage of other prolabor bills in the 1937 legislative session: a wages and hours bill, several bills making it a felony to transport strikebreakers from one county to another, several bills to broaden workmen's compensation laws, and legislation to provide a system of mediation or voluntary arbitration of labor strikes. These bills exempted agricultural labor from their provisions, but they were, nevertheless, opposed by the Farm Bureau and the Associated Farmers because it was believed that these exemptions could be too easily removed by subsequent legislation. The farm employers also believed that it was to their interest to take a stand with industry, for, if industry submitted to governmental labor regulations, agriculture would be left to fight its battles alone.[13]

The issue came up again during the 1939 session of the state legislature. This time the farm employer groups, and the urban employer groups with which they were allied, found themselves on the defensive. But they built a strong defense and succeeded in blocking much of the Olson program. Among the many administration bills defeated, in part as a result of political pressure exerted by the Farm Bureau and the Associated Farmers, were a bill to establish a state labor relations board, a minimum wages and maximum hours bill, a bill outlawing labor injunctions, a bill creating a state commission to mediate and arbitrate labor disputes, a bill to prohibit the transportation of strikebreakers across county lines, and a bill to regulate farm camps.[14]

Also of interest to farm employers were the various bills dealing with agricultural labor that came within the scope of general social legislation. The California Farm Bureau Federation and the Associated Farmers both favored the exemption of agricultural labor from the terms of the federal Wages and Hours Act, National Labor Relations Act, and Social Security Act. Both organizations urged further that "agricultural labor" be defined to include all labor engaged in processing, packing, canning, and transporting agricultural commodities. The C.F.B.F. also wished the definition of "agricultural labor" to include "all employees of producer-owned and/or controlled coöperatives." Federal social and labor legislation did exempt agricultural labor and defined that term broadly.[15]

Success did not come so easily in the field of California state social legislation.[16] The California Unemployment Insurance Act of 1935 imposed a 3 per cent wage tax upon the employer. The act exempted "agricultural labor," but nowhere in the act was this term clearly defined. Until 1940, state officials accepted the broad definitions contained in federal legislation. During the Olson administration, however, the California Employment Commission narrowed the definition so that some employees previously exempt were now covered by the law. For example, the new definition no longer exempted workers engaged in the washing, grading, and packing of fruits and vegetables. This redefinition struck at the interests of the various coöperative marketing associations in the state, which were now required to pay the wage tax.

During the special session of the state legislature meeting in May, 1940, the Farm Bureau sponsored Assembly Concurrent Resolution Number 21, which criticized the California Employment Commission for its narrow definition of "agricultural labor" and requested that the definition be changed to conform with the definitions in the federal Social Security Act of 1939. This resolution was also supported by the Agricultural Council of California, the Associated Farmers, the California State Chamber of Commerce, and the Agricultural Producers Labor Committee. The Farm Bureau maintained that uniformity with federal legislation was desirable from an administrative viewpoint. It also insisted that California farmers should not be burdened with costs that their competitors in Florida and Texas did not have to bear. Farm Bureau leaders argued that, since agricultural employment in California was highly seasonal, it was ill-adapted to application of any unemployment insurance scheme. The resolution was released from committee but was not acted upon by the assembly. During the 1941 session of the state legislature several bills were introduced for amendment of the California Unemployment Insurance Act to make it consistent with the federal Social Security Act of 1939. This legislation was passed by the senate but turned down by the assembly. The Farm Bureau was, for the time, defeated on this issue.

The Farm Bureau won on another similar measure, however. California had had on its books since 1893 a law providing for "one day of rest in seven," a law that precluded employment of any person for more than six days out of seven except in case of "emergency." The emergency clause was interpreted to allow employers to employ a man more than six days out of seven if no other help could be secured and granting the worker his "one day of rest in seven" would mean loss of property. The new State Labor Commissioner for the Olson administration announced that the law would be applied in the future more rigorously than it had been in the past. During the 1941 session, however, the legislature passed a bill, sponsored by the Farm Bureau, that amended the law to authorize a workman to agree to work more than six consecutive days provided that he were assured that the lost days of rest would be granted later. Similarly, the Farm Bureau and other organizations were able to secure legislation relaxing regulations for the employment of child labor."

13. TAX REFORM AND THE RILEY-STEWART AMENDMENT

Property owners and taxpayers throughout the country suffered severe economic disabilities during the depression years. Not only did property values collapse, but income with which real estate taxes could be paid declined from month to month though costs of government continued to mount ever higher. Farmers were hard hit, since most of the costs of local government were paid for by taxation on real estate, buildings and improvements, and personal property. This high and increasing tax burden constituted a fixed cash cost to the farm operator, a cost that became ever harder to bear as prices plunged and net returns vanished. Tax delinquency and mortgage foreclosure plagued every rural community in the country. The farmers of California did not escape.

The costs of operating county government in California increased nearly threefold from 1919 to 1932 (from $43,395,449 to $111,800,457), but expenditures per capita did not quite double (increasing from $29.10 per capita in 1919 to $52.02 per capita in 1932).[1] The largest increases were in interest on indebtedness and in charity payments. Costs of education and costs of upkeep on county roads also increased greatly. Statistics indicate that from 1911 to 1929, a period in which the total cost of government in California increased by 482 per cent and total bonded indebtedness of all government units increased by 732 per cent, the population of California had but doubled and the assessed valuation of all property in California had but trebled. Expenditures on education and roads accounted for more than 60 per cent of total county disbursements, and these costs could not easily be cut without undermining the most essential functions of local government.[2]

Tax Reform: Riley-Stewart Amendment

Taxation to meet the total costs of government in the state of California in 1930 rested primarily upon real property. The *ad valorem* property tax paid for more than 75 per cent of total government expenditures in the state in that year. Real estate was taxed much more heavily than personal property. Many intangible forms of property evaded assessment entirely, but the land, buildings, and livestock of the farmer rarely escaped the eye of the assessor. In some parts of the state it was the practice to overassess rural property as compared with urban property and to overassess small rural holdings as compared with larger farms, and this tended to aggravate the tax inequities under which the farmer of California suffered.[3]

Tax delinquency became widespread as government costs continued to increase, as more and more people became dependent upon local relief, as farm prices tumbled, and as net farm income dwindled. Consequently, government in several California counties came near collapse. The tax problem was ably and dramatically summarized by Frank T. Swett, chairman of the Section on Agriculture of the San Francisco Commonwealth Club, when he declared before that group in January, 1932:

> So many farmers find they can't pay boom taxes when the income has disappeared that bank foreclosures are no longer news: they are looked upon as matters of daily routine.
> Families that have successfully farmed the same land for two or three generations are in many cases being forced off the lands their grandfathers or fathers operated....
> Unless changes are made in our tax system, further foreclosures will be multiplied to an extent as to throw thousands of acres out of cultivation; thousands of present farmers into the ranks of the unemployed; and bring about the decadence of a once prosperous agriculture based on American standards of living, into uncertain tenantry and undesirable peasantry.[4]

Both the Farm Bureau and the State Grange recognized the crisis in taxation as one of the most fundamental economic problems that farmers had to solve. As early as 1927 a new service department, the Tax Research Department, was created within the Farm Bureau to investigate the tax situation and work out a program for reform.[5] Farm Bureau demands for tax reform from 1929 to 1933 included attacks upon the

Tax Reform: Riley-Stewart Amendment

overreliance of government upon the general property tax as a source of revenue. The very first bulletin distributed by the newly created Tax Research Department dealt with this subject.

... The farmer, like other members of society, can pay a tax when he makes a net income but when his income is nil or his year's operations actually result in a deficit, the same tax in the absolute, which in years of prosperity would be borne unnoticed, becomes burdensome, and if adversity continues unbearable inevitably results in insolvency.⁶

The Farm Bureau demanded reduction in government costs, heavier taxation upon intangible forms of property, uniform assessment of all properties, taxation of publicly owned utilities, prevention of tax evasion, increased state aid to county governments (especially to reduce local expenditures for schools and roads), and taxation of personal income on the principle that "Income—not inventory—is the true measure of ability to pay."⁷

The Grange, although it rarely made such detailed studies as those Von T. Ellsworth wrote for the Farm Bureau, arrived at similar conclusions. Sehlmeyer and the Grange favored tax revisions that would, to a large extent, substitute new taxes for the general property tax. At various times, the Grange demanded a broadly based income tax, a limited sales tax on luxuries, and a heavier inheritance tax.⁸

During the 1931 session of the state legislature the Grange and the Farm Bureau coöperated in an attempt to secure tax reforms that would relieve the burden upon property.⁹ Assemblyman Percy West of Sacramento County introduced a bill, sponsored and written by the Grange, that proposed a graduated net income tax beginning at rates of 1 per cent on incomes up to $5,000 and increasing to rates of 5 per cent on incomes over $50,000. The Farm Bureau introduced its own income tax bill, which provided for rates at one-third of those in the federal income tax schedule. Both the Grange and the Farm Bureau proposals provided that the income tax would replace the local school tax on real property. The two farm organizations agreed to combine their proposals; the body and title of the Grange bill were kept, and the provisions of the Farm Bureau bill were incorporated into it.

Sehlmeyer appeared before legislative committees to support the compromise bill, as did Von T. Ellsworth and Alex Johnson, among others, for the Farm Bureau. The Farm Bureau also exerted pressure upon state legislators through local Farm Bureau centers. Decision on the bill was postponed, however, when an interim legislative committee was appointed to make a detailed investigation of the tax situation in California for the purpose of drafting a program for the reform of the entire tax structure. The interim committee recommended the creation of a tax research bureau within the State Board of Equalization and agreed to suggest no major alterations in the tax system until that bureau had made its report. Both farm organizations regretted that reform would be delayed until the next regular session of the state legislature, but they believed that the fight they had made in 1931 would strengthen their position in influencing any reforms that might be suggested in the future.

As economic conditions continued to deteriorate throughout 1931 and 1932, members of the Grange and the Farm Bureau became convinced that tax reform should not be postponed until 1933.[10] They decided to attempt to secure tax relief by sponsorship of an initiative proposition, in the form of an amendment to the state constitution, so that the voters could pass on tax reform in the general elections in 1932. Preliminary meetings to discuss tax reform were held in San Bernardino on July 13, 1931, and in San Francisco on July 27, 1931. A follow-up meeting, called by the California Farm Bureau Federation, was held in Berkeley on September 16, 1931. To this meeting came representatives of the California State Grange, the California Real Estate Association, the California County Tax Equalization Association, the County Supervisors' Association, and of course, the Farm Bureau itself. The delegates at this meeting organized a tax committee, to which one member from each of the groups present was appointed. It was decided that each organization should work out its own program for tax reform and that the committee should then try to formulate a single proposal that would be satisfactory to all the groups.

Tax Reform: Riley-Stewart Amendment

The Grange then called a meeting for January 20, 1932, at Sacramento for the purpose of reorganizing the tax committee formed at the Berkeley meeting into a larger State Coördinating Tax Committee, which, it was hoped, would enjoy wider appeal and broader membership. Such a larger committee was established and, headed by its permanent chairman George Sehlmeyer, met February 18, 1932. At that time the final form of the proposed initiative measure, the Property Tax Relief Amendment (which later became Initiative Proposition Number 9 on the state ballot), was agreed upon. It was endorsed by the California State Grange, the California Farm Bureau Federation, the California County Auditors' Association, the California Property Owners' Division, the California Real Estate Association, the California State Department of Education, the California County Tax Equalization Association, the California Teachers' Association, and the State Building Owners and Managers' Association. These groups had several things in common: many of them represented tax-burdened property owners; all of them wished the county governments to remain solvent; and all of them wanted the schools of the state to be adequately financed.

The proposed amendment to the state constitution included the following provisions: 1) that State aid to education be increased by approximately $50,000,000 a year, this increase to be financed by a state personal income tax and a state selective sales tax; 2) that a state equalization fund for education be created and apportioned in such a way as to equalize burdens among the counties and school districts and to afford maximum tax relief to property; 3) that counties be permitted to supplement state funds if they wished, but that the mandatory county school tax requirement in the state constitution be abolished; and 4) that the administration of all schools remain in local hands. The farm organizations, the property owner associations, the organizations representing local government officials, and the teachers' groups all coöperated closely in the campaign to secure ratification of their proposition. George Sehlmeyer, representing the Grange, and R. L. Miller, representing the Farm Bureau, appeared together at various mass meetings to urge support for Proposition Number 9.

The Farm Bureau declared in its publicity campaign that education was of statewide concern, that it affected every citizen of the community whether he owned property or not, and that the costs of education should, therefore, be borne by all citizens rather than by property owners alone. Spokesmen for the Farm Bureau maintained that ratification would be a step toward relieving the inequitable tax burden on property and that it would guarantee a uniform base of school expenditures for every child in the state while at the same time allowing any community to provide better school facilities if it chose to raise the extra revenues from within its own district. The income tax was defended on the grounds that it was based upon the ability to pay, it could not be shifted to others, it was elastic, and it could be efficiently and inexpensively collected. The Farm Bureau estimated that about $11,500,000 could be raised by the levy of a personal income tax at one-third of the federal rates and that an additional $43,500,000 could be raised by a selective sales tax on tobacco, candy, jewelry, cosmetics, entertainment, and other luxury items. Sehlmeyer, speaking for the Grange, said that, though the proposition was not perfect, it did constitute a step in the right direction and would lead eventually to the complete revision of the tax structure. He maintained that a selective sales tax and a personal income tax would reach individuals who did not already contribute to the expenditures of government from which the entire community benefited.

Substantial groups in California opposed the proposition, including the real estate interests of San Francisco, the public utility companies, and all the miscellaneous groups that demanded a reduction in government costs rather than a reallocation of burdens. These groups insisted that the school equalization fund would become a fixed charge upon the general funds of the state, that the ambiguity of the clause authorizing a selective sales tax would open the way for a general sales tax, and that, since the state already faced a deficit, a deficiency *ad valorem* tax on property would be a certainty in any event. They also pointed out that the state would contribute the money but would exercise little supervision over the expenditure of the funds, and they contended that extravagance always resulted when public funds were collected by one agency and expended by another. Among those who opposed Proposition Number 9 were A. C. Hardison and A. Ahlf, both former presidents of the California Farm Bureau Federation; George Harrison, Master of the State Grange from 1921 to 1929; R. V. Garrod, president of the Farmers' Union; and S. S. Knight, a self-appointed tax expert and an active member of the Grange and the Farmers' Union in the 1920's. The Ventura County Farm Bureau, led by E. C. Kimball (later vice-president of the C.F.B.F.), also went on record as opposed to the proposal.

Opponents of the proposition spent $30,000 to ensure its defeat, and its proponents spent but $7,500 to secure its ratification. These figures suggest at least one reason for its rejection by the voters in the fall of 1932. Other factors contributing to the failure of the proposition included these: its opponents succeeded in convincing the electorate that the measure was a proposal to increase school expenditures during times of financial depression rather than one to transfer the tax burden from local to state government; not enough time was allowed for public education; many members of the Farm Bureau and the Grange feared the use that might possibly be made of the sales-tax clause, and both organizations were therefore somewhat lukewarm in their campaign for adoption of the measure; and, finally, there were many voters in the state who preferred to wait for the regular session of the state legislature in the spring of 1933 to work out a more comprehensive plan of tax reform.

When the state legislature assembled in January, 1933, it soon became apparent that there were as many tax proposals as there were legislators and lobbyists. The task at once became that of working out some comprehensive, compromise plan that would be acceptable to enough politicians and pressure groups to permit its passage by the legislature and its ratification by the voters of the state. Accepted as a working basis for reform was a plan submitted by Ray L. Riley, State Comptroller, and Fred E. Stewart, member of the State Board of Equalization. As worked out in its preliminary form the Riley-Stewart plan provided: 1) that State Constitutional

Tax Reform: Riley-Stewart Amendment

Amendment Number 1 (which had been ratified in 1910 and had set up a dual system of taxation under which the state possessed sole power to tax the property of public utilities whereas all other property was left for county taxation) be repealed, and that all property of public utilities be returned to local tax rolls; 2) that expenditures of state government be permitted to increase no more than 5 per cent over any two-year period except by a two-thirds vote of the legislature, and that expenditures of local government be similarly restricted unless permitted to increase more rapidly by the State Board of Equalization; 3) that the constitutional provision for a mandatory local school tax be repealed; 4) that the state government contribute to the financial support of local schools in proportion to student enrollment; and 5) that a state transactions tax be levied upon the gross receipts of every person, firm, or corporation to raise the revenue for state aid to education.[11]

The proposal for a gross receipts tax stirred up great opposition from all quarters. The Farm Bureau joined in the attack upon this form of taxation, insisting that a gross receipts tax was just another "poor man's tax," that it would force out-of-state purchase of semifinished products to the detriment of the California economy as a whole, and that it was a regressive turnover tax that would pyramid every time a commodity changed hands. Sehlmeyer of the Grange also attacked this aspect of the Riley-Stewart tax plan, using similar arguments, and added that, if the plan were to be passed as it stood, the public utilities still would not be paying their fair share of the state's tax burden. It was obvious that the plan could not possibly pass the legislature without drastic revision in view of the opposition of the Grange and the Farm Bureau in addition to the criticisms and complaints of other pressure groups in the state. For several months discussion of tax reform occupied state legislators and all groups that had a vital interest in taxation policies. After long and arduous labor a compromise plan, a much-amended version of the original proposal, was presented. This plan met with the general approval of most groups and was incorporated as Senate Constitutional Amendment Number 30, which passed both houses and was then presented to the people for ratification or rejection in a special election in June, 1933.[12]

The Riley-Stewart plan in its final form contained the following provisions: 1) that State Constitutional Amendment Number 1 be repealed, and the operative property of public utilities be returned to county tax rolls; 2) that state and local government expenditures be permitted to increase no more than 5 per cent in the next two years except by special authorization; 3) that the mandatory local school tax be repealed; 4) that school costs be transferred from local units of government to the state, and state aid be granted to the schools in proportion to average daily attendance; 5) that the legislature be authorized to raise the funds for state support of education by income, sales, or severance taxes; 6) that counties be permitted to raise no more than 50 per cent of their total revenue from real estate taxes; and 7) that, in lieu of the prevailing deficiency state property tax, a state *ad valorem* tax on property be permitted, but its use be limited to the raising of funds equivalent to 25 per cent or less of total state appropriations.

The Grange and the Farm Bureau coöperated with many other groups in the campaign to secure ratification of this amendment. They pointed out that the proposed amendment offered a way to balance the state budget without increasing the burden upon common property. The Farm Bureau rejoiced that it had been able to secure substantial revision of the original plan, which it had been forced to oppose, and urged all its members to vote in favor of the modified proposal. The Farm Bureau asserted that the proposed amendment would reduce property taxation, restrict public expenditures at all levels, and permit the budget to be balanced. George Sehlmeyer urged all Grange members to vote in favor of the plan.

The advantages of the Riley Plan may be enumerated as follows: it limits the expenses of the state and municipalities, thereby setting up a budgetary control; it limits the amount of taxes which can be levied against common property; it relieves common property of the matching requirements now borne by the counties for school purposes; and it widens the tax base.

While there are some objectionable features in this amendment, we feel it is the only plan offered to the electors which will relieve common property of some of its burden of taxation and at the same time raise funds enough to balance the budget.[13]

The proposition was not without its opponents. Some insisted that the increased demand upon state funds would make necessary an *ad valorem* tax or a general sales tax. Others said that it proposed to aid rural counties at the expense of urban counties, that it provided relief for only the larger owner of property, or that it unwisely gave preference to education over all other state government services. But the coalition of farm, labor, and school organizations working together for the adoption of the amendment proved too strong for the opposition. The voters ratified it at a special election held on June 27, 1933.

The Grange and the Farm Bureau found it possible to coöperate throughout 1931, 1932, and 1933 on the issue of tax reform legislation, as has been shown. But this coöperation proved to be of short duration. In a matter of months the two farm organizations split apart during the debate over the enactment of a sales or income tax.

FARM ORGANIZATION
TAX POLICIES
14.
1933–1941

After the ratification of the Riley-Stewart tax proposal in June, 1933, the state legislature reconvened to work out the tax reform legislation authorized by the new amendment. The state budget was unbalanced, and the deficit was increasing; the legislators had to solve the state's fiscal problems by finding new sources of revenue. The Riley-Stewart amendment had shifted about $40,000,000 in annual school expenditures from the counties to the state. In addition, the state had lost about $30,000,000 in annual tax receipts through the return of public utility property to local tax rolls. The new amendment thus confronted the state with the problem of raising approximately $70,000,000 in new revenue—and this at a time when the state government was constantly finding it necessary to increase its expenditures to meet emergency needs created by the depression.[1]

The legislature, in the summer of 1935, considered two methods of raising this $70,000,000, a sales tax and an income tax. It had been tacitly understood by most groups working for ratification of the Riley-Stewart amendment that the additional revenue would come from these two sources. But some politicians had other ideas. No sooner had the amendment been ratified than its two authors began to work for the rejection of an income tax and the passage of a heavy retail sales tax, and this approach was adopted as the official position of Governor Rolph's administration. This program was opposed by twenty-five Democrats in the assembly, who held a caucus in mid-July and agreed not to support a sales tax unless it was accompanied by a personal income tax. In this stand they had the support of both the Grange and the Farm Bureau and of many of the other groups that had helped secure popular approval for the Riley-Stewart plan.²

The senate passed a flat 3 per cent sales tax in mid-July, 1933. An amendment, proposed by Senator H. C. Jones, progressive Republican from Santa Clara County, that would have exempted foodstuffs from the sales tax and incorporated an income tax in the bill to make up the difference failed of passage. So did a similar bill offered by a Grange senator, Chris N. Jespersen of San Luis Obispo County. These attempts to incorporate an income tax into the sales tax bill were motivated by a well-founded suspicion that if the two were passed as separate measures the governor would veto the income tax proposal and sign the sales tax bill. George Sehlmeyer was one of those working for a joint tax measure.³

The assembly soon passed its own sales tax measure, which provided for a flat rate of 2 per cent. Compromise between the senate and assembly bills was easily secured; a retail sales tax of 2½ per cent was passed by both houses. This rate was to drop automatically to 2 per cent in June, 1935.⁴ The Grange reluctantly agreed to the passage of this sales tax. In a letter to Senator Herbert C. Jones, dated July 26, 1933, George Sehlmeyer stated that the Grange favored an income tax but opposed a sales tax, which it felt would be but another burden upon the poor. The letter concluded, however:

> We supported a selective sales tax on luxuries on Amendment No. 9 on the ballot last year, and have not opposed a reasonable sales tax this year, owing to the serious financial condition of the State, but we feel it should be recognized wholly as an emergency measure.⁵

Assemblyman F. C. Clowdsley introduced the Farm Bureau's income tax bill, which set rates at one-third of federal levies for every income group. It was anticipated that this measure would raise approximately $15,000,000 over the two-year period. The bill had to be forced out of committee by an assembly petition, and on the floor the bill was amended to make its impact on the higher income groups proportionately lighter. In this form it was sent to Governor Rolph. Governor's Rolph's political supporters immediately began to put pressure on him to veto it. Of this group Will Rogers spoke when he advised Governor Rolph: "... there will be an exodus of people from the state in Rolls Royces, Lincolns and Cadillacs if you sign the bill."⁶ Rolph did what his friends expected and his enemies feared: he vetoed the income tax bill and signed the sales tax bill.⁷

The Grange was irate. Grange leaders and members felt that they had been betrayed by some of those with whom they had coöperated to secure passage of the Riley-Stewart amendment. After the ratification of that amendment in June, Grange policy had called for a substantial income tax and a sales tax on nonessentials. Before the legislature met in July, 1933, Grange members had read in their official newspaper:

> This country is never going to be stabilized until we decentralize wealth. I make this a flat statement of truth. The sooner we awaken to the fact that wealth is of no value to the nation unless it circulates, the sooner we will be free of the menace of further depressions and hard times. . . . The legislature meets on July 17 to enact tax laws in accordance with the mandate of the people. These laws, however, must be a protection to the poor and not the rich. . . . The Grange should prepare and sponsor an income tax and every Grange should get behind the move to protect the people from being sold out by destructive sales taxes, under the guise of "painless taxes."⁸

During the session the Grange had vigorously supported Senators Jones and Jespersen in their attempts to incorporate the income tax into the sales tax bill and to exempt food purchases from the sales tax. In all this they had failed.

At the annual convention of the State Grange in October, 1933, the delegates pledged themselves to work for the repeal of the sales tax and for the enactment of an income tax, proclaiming that "the chief beneficiaries of our economic system have succeeded in escaping a just and equitable proportion of the tax burden."⁹ To the Grange this problem was essentially a moral issue. One Grange member showed this moral concern when, looking back upon the outcome of the Riley-Stewart amendment, he wrote:

> A net income tax never was responsible for a hungry child, a destroyed home, or made a nation bankrupt. Its proponents have been termed visionary, and impractical, even though they would turn back a part of the stream of wealth diverted by the exploiter to freshen the hope of tomorrow. The sales tax constantly operates to dry the springs of human endeavor at their source.¹⁰

This ethical approach, the approach taken by the Grange on almost all economic and political matters, cannot be minimized if the Grange program is to be understood fully.

To the Farm Bureau, on the other hand, the tax problem was always one of hard, cold facts, of dollars and cents. The Farm Bureau had worked with the Grange for passage of an income tax and a sales tax on nonessentials. When its income tax bill was vetoed, the organization immediately set out to ensure acceptance of such a measure at a later date. When the general retail sales tax was passed, however, the Bureau at once declared that its "chief virtue" was "productivity" and on this basis vigorously defended it.[11] The reasons given for Farm Bureau support of the general sales tax were neatly summarized in the annual report of the Ventura County Farm Bureau, which stated: "It is not only a very definite measure for property relief, but it is making the people tax conscious, which is in itself a very needed thing."[12]

The disagreement of the Farm Bureau and the Grange over tax policy in the summer of 1933 was but another reflection of the basic difference in outlook of the two organizations. Farm Bureau acceptance of the general sales tax as a necessary evil was a practical move that the Grange could not comprehend and would not countenance. In subsequent years the two organizations were able to conduct parallel campaigns in favor of an income tax, or in opposition to various "single tax" proposals, but never again did they coöperate actively for acceptance of a common program.

The tax problem arose again, inevitably, in the 1935 session of the state legislature. Here again the battles centered around sales tax and income tax proposals. The Grange favored amendment of the sales tax to make it applicable to nonessential items only or, at the least, to exempt the purchase of foodstuffs from the tax. It also favored the passage of an income tax high enough to yield substantial revenue, not just high enough to establish a principle. The Farm Bureau, on the other hand, worked for retention of the sales tax and for an income tax at one-third the federal rate. The Grange considered the Farm Bureau's suggestions woefully inadequate.[13]

When the assembly proposed to increase the general sales

tax to a rate of 3 per cent but to exempt food purchases, the Farm Bureau opposed the exemption on the basis that it "will exempt many who should pay, will increase evasions and will increase cost of administration."[14] The Farm Bureau was forced into a position of supporting the proposal, however, in order to forestall attempts to repeal the sales tax entirely. The bill raising the rate to 3 per cent and exempting food was passed by the legislature, largely through the efforts of Senator Culbert Olson of Los Angeles County, and was signed by Governor Merriam. It was, to be sure, a compromise measure, but on the whole it came closer to meeting the demands of the Grange than those of the Farm Bureau.[15]

On the matter of an income tax, however, the Farm Bureau saw its own desires more nearly fulfilled. Senator Andrew Schottky of Merced County introduced the Farm Bureau's bill, which provided for a tax at one-third of the federal rates. It was expected that the returns from this tax would be approximately $20,000,000 every two years. In the assembly Frank Chatters of Tulare County introduced a similar bill, which was endorsed by the Merriam administration and based generally upon the Farm Bureau program. In opposition to these bills was one introduced by the new Democratic senator from Los Angeles County, Culbert Olson, which called for heavier rates in the higher income brackets and was designed to raise at least $45,000,000 every two years. This bill was more in line with what the Grange desired. But it was the Chatters bill that passed the legislature, and, despite renewed pressure against the enactment of any income tax, Governor Merriam gave it his signature.[16]

Both the Farm Bureau and the Grange vigorously opposed an attempt, in 1936, to repeal the income tax through popular initiative procedure. The Farm Bureau joined with other groups, including the California Teachers' Association, the State Supervisors' Association, and the State Department of Education, in this campaign, but the Grange chose to conduct its efforts independently of other groups and to confine its appeal to its own membership. Farm Bureau publicity stated that the graduated rates of the 1935 Income Tax Act were fair and equitable, that the act was productive of revenue, and that it was economical to administer. The argument used by the proponents of the repeal initiative, that the income tax was driving Californians to Florida, was not taken seriously by the electorate, and the initiative proposition was voted down by a substantial majority.[17]

Three times in this decade attempts were made to link repeal of the state sales tax to the enactment of a "single tax." Three times proponents of the "single tax" used the initiative procedure in attempts to secure ratification of their proposals, and three times they were defeated, though not without the expenditure of considerable time, money, and energy by those who would have suffered from the imposition of Henry George's panacea. Both the Grange and the Farm Bureau opposed the "single tax," but after 1933 the Grange consistently refused to coöperate with other groups in matters of tax policy. Sehlmeyer might, on occasion, agree with policies of the Farm Bureau, but he would under no circumstances unite with that group to achieve common goals.

In the spring of 1934, "single-taxers" in the state united with the tax committee of the State Federation of Labor to circulate initiative petitions for putting on the ballot a proposition that would repeal the sales tax of 1933 and cancel the clause of the Riley-Stewart amendment that limited use of the state *ad valorem* tax to 25 per cent of the state budget. Endorsement of this proposition would have opened the way to the imposition of the "single tax" on land. While the petitions were being circulated, the official journals of the Farm Bureau and of the State Grange warned farmers of the drastic consequences that the imposition of such a tax would have for agricultural interests. Although enough signatures were secured to qualify the proposition, it was ruled off the ballot because of a technical error in its wording.[18]

Two years later, in 1936, the "single tax" proponents were back again with an initiative proposition to link the repeal of the sales tax of 1935 with the enactment of a "single tax." This time the Farm Bureau coöperated with such groups as the State Supervisors' Association, the State Department of Education, and the California County Tax Equalization Association in a joint campaign aimed at defeating both the proposal for repeal of the sales tax, Proposition Number 1 on the ballot, and the proposal for repeal of the income tax, Proposition Number 2. The Farm Bureau said that these two propositions, if adopted, would deprive the state of large amounts of revenue, would increase the state deficit, and would shift the burden of taxation back upon the farmer. Grange publicity pointed to the dangers inherent in the "single tax" proposition but expressed regret that the repeal of the sales tax had been tied to this nefarious scheme to destroy property. The "single tax" was voted down by the electorate, as was the proposition to repeal the income tax.[19]

Nothing daunted, the advocates of the "single tax" made a third attempt in 1938 to smuggle it in under the guise of a sales tax repeal measure. To oppose the new initiative proposition, which was similar in most respects to the abortive 1934 and 1936 proposals, a State-Wide Council against the Single Tax was formed. The group was headed by C. C. Teague, president of the California Fruit Growers' Exchange. Among the farm organizations that joined the council were the Farm Bureau, the Associated Farmers, the Agricultural Council of California, and the Farmers' Union of California. In addition, such groups as the California Teachers' Association, the California Federation of Women's Clubs, the California League of Women Voters, the State Chamber of Commerce, and many others joined in the campaign to defeat the "single tax" once more. The Grange again restricted its campaign to influencing its own membership. Once again the "single tax" was defeated, but not without the expenditure of much time and money.[20]

As already pointed out, the Grange and the Farm Bureau, after 1933, found it difficult to agree on a tax program and absolutely impossible to coöperate for the realization of such a program even when the two groups were in basic agreement. Grange tax policy was based largely upon moral preconceptions of what it considered to be right and wrong in the economic world. Its program for a high income tax and a luxury sales tax did not win widespread support during the decade of the 1930's. The Farm Bureau's fiscal program was based on more practical considerations: property had to be relieved of an inequitable tax burden; this, it was thought, could best be achieved through the imposition of a moderate income tax and a general retail sales tax. The Farm Bureau program, which was supported by detailed, laborious, and technical tax studies and modified by practical political considerations, closely paralleled actual fiscal enactments by the state legislature. The position of the Grange was greatly weakened by the refusal of Sehlmeyer to allow his organization to work in coordination with other groups in the state; the Farm Bureau, on the other hand, was constantly strengthened in the execution of its policies by close coöperation with any and every group with which it could agree.

15. THE AGRICULTURAL PRORATE ACT

When the depression hit California in 1929 and farm prices tumbled, surpluses of farm commodities piled up, and farm profits disappeared, organized farmers began to seek measures through which their economic interests could be protected. Farm employers attempted to control wage costs by resisting the unionization of agricultural labor. Farm groups worked to shift the tax burden from owners of real property by the imposition of a personal net income tax and a general retail sales tax. Finally, in an attempt to raise prices of agricultural commodities, the farmers of the state evolved an agricultural marketing proration scheme. They hoped that this plan would raise price levels indirectly through control of surpluses and through the establishment of orderly marketing procedures. This program paralleled very closely the several New Deal agricultural adjustment acts, which attempted to achieve similar ends by similar means.

On this issue, as on others, California farm organizations were split. The Prorate Act was written, sponsored, supported, and indirectly administered by the Farm Bureau. It was fought at every step of the way by the California State Grange, and its amendment was finally secured largely through the efforts of that organization.

California's perishable crops were peculiarly sensitive to the erratic, often unpredictable functioning of supply and demand on the market. Temporary local gluts often resulted in prices so low that farmers in a particular area, growing a particular crop, found themselves operating at a loss. Cash operating costs in the production of these crops were fixed at such a high level that a slight drop in consumer price for a very short time could wipe out net gains. To meet this situation California farmers had, for many years, marketed their crops coöperatively in an attempt to exert effective control over price by regulating the

The Agricultural Prorate Act

size and timing of marketing operations. The success of the California Fruit Growers' Exchange in the citrus fruit industry had encouraged many other commodity groups to organize their own coöperative marketing associations.

In the first three decades of the twentieth century most of these coöperatives had enjoyed phenomenal success, but this success was based largely on a constantly expanding demand for the specialty crops that California had to offer. As national income and effective purchasing power rose in these years, and as consumer tastes turned to lighter and more balanced diets that included more fruits and vegetables, California farmers enjoyed relative prosperity. But when consuming power was slashed by mass unemployment in the early years of the great depression, prices of California's specialty crops fell faster and farther than those of more basic agricultural commodities.

Under these conditions, voluntary plans for coöperative market control broke down. As prices continued to fall in spite of the regulation of supply that marketing associations could exercise, thousands of producers began to market their own crops independently and haphazardly, with the result that the market was even further demoralized. Voluntary proration plans, operated by the various coöperatives in lemons, oranges, grapes, lettuce, apples, and nuts, to mention but a few, collapsed completely. Agreements that had operated for years with the voluntary participation of a great part of the growers were suddenly undermined by the increasing stress of surpluses and by the increasing tendency toward independent marketing. Many growers felt that their own production was but a small part of total production and had no significant effect upon market price.

To meet this crisis various legislative proposals for compulsory marketing proration were developed. E. A. Stokdyk, the agricultural economist who did the technical research that led to the formulation of the proration plan, summarized the need for compulsory proration as follows:

During the year 1932 a considerable volume of several specialty crops was unharvested because prices at the point of production were so low that it would not pay to harvest them. In fact, producers of several crops found themselves indebted to transporta-

The Agricultural Prorate Act

tion agencies at the end of the marketing season because their products did not sell for enough in the terminal markets to pay the freight. The uncertainty caused by such a situation probably resulted in both a larger physical and economic waste than would have occurred if definite steps had been taken to market limited quantities during each week of the shipping season and prorate such marketing among all producers.[1]

It was logical that the California Farm Bureau Federation, which had always maintained close contact with the coöperative marketing associations of the state and in which the more progressive and business-minded farmers furnished active leadership, should take the lead in working out the details of a plan for marketing proration. At least as early as 1928, leaders of the Farm Bureau were giving serious thought and discussion to the adaptation of the Australian plan for compulsory proration to California's special problems. But real interest was stimulated by the depression. In November, 1931, the delegates to the annual Farm Bureau convention passed a resolution insisting that all growers of a given commodity share the responsibilities and the costs of the disposal of surpluses of that commodity. Throughout 1932 sentiment favorable to compulsory marketing increased. County Farm Bureaus passed resolutions requesting legislation to establish compulsory marketing proration. At the annual convention in 1932, the delegates asked that a study be made of the problem of controlled marketing. On the basis of this resolution, and with the coöperation of the California State Chamber of Commerce, the Farm Bureau asked the Giannini Foundation of the College of Agriculture of the University of California to make such a study. The project was assigned to E. A. Stokdyk, who turned in his report early in January, 1933.[2]

On the basis of this report, Stokdyk and Edson Abel, legal counsel for the Farm Bureau, with the help of C. Thorp of the Walnut Growers' Association and Roy M. Pike of the Coöperative Dairyman's League, worked out an agricultural prorate bill. After modification by the Agricultural Legislative Committee, the bill was introduced into the senate by Ray Hays of Fresno and into the assembly by M. S. Meeker of Fresno County, Hubert B. Scudder of Sonoma, F. C. Clowdsley of San Joaquin, C. Ray Robinson of Imperial, John H. O'Donnell of Yolo, and E. H. Zion of Stanislaus County. It passed the assembly with but five dissenting votes, and it passed the senate with but one negative vote, that of Senator Harry A. Perry of Humboldt County, who was generally considered to have Grange sympathies.[2]

The Agricultural Prorate Act provided for the appointment by the governor of a Prorate Commission composed of four representatives of the growers (from the vegetable, dairy, citrus fruit, and deciduous fruit industries), two representatives of the consumers, one representative of the processors, one experienced commercial handler of agricultural products, and one experienced coöperative marketing executive. A definite procedure for a marketing proration program was established. First, growers of a given commodity in a given area were authorized to draw up a program incorporating a statement of need, a definition of the geographic area to be included in the zone, and an outline of procedure. This plan required the endorsement of two-thirds of the growers representing two-thirds of the production units (usually acres). The proposed program was then to be presented to the Agricultural Prorate Commission, which would determine whether it met the legal requirements of the act. The commission had first to ascertain whether the program had been legally ratified. If it found the ratification valid, the commission then had to decide whether the economic stability of that particular agricultural industry was indeed imperiled by market conditions, whether a program would advance the general public welfare without hurting the interests of any producer, and whether the program would operate in such a manner that no producer would receive unreasonable profits. If the commission were convinced, after the hearings, that all these qualifications and requirements were met, it would then declare the program in effect.

The Prorate Commission was to appoint local committees to administer the programs. Growers could nominate members to these local committees, and these suggestions were to be considered by the commission in making its appointments. The committees were to be composed of five members representing the producers and two members representing the handlers. If any marketing association controlled more than 20 per cent of the total production of a commodity, it was authorized to name producer members in proportion to its share in the control of total production, although it could in no case select more than three of these committee members.

The program committees were empowered to make surveys of the quantity of the prorated commodity that the market could absorb and of the level of production of that commodity in the prorate zone. On the basis of these studies, they were to compute how much total production might be expected to exceed total consumption. The committees were then to assign to each producer the proportion of his total production that he would be allowed to market. Each producer was to be granted a primary certificate that would show the total volume the grower could market for the entire season. Against this primary certificate would be issued secondary certificates, which had to accompany the commodity as it entered the channels of trade. Such programs were legally binding upon all growers within the commodity zone under penalty of a $500 fine. Administrative costs were to be paid for by a small fee on the certificates. All programs, in all their phases, were to be under the general supervision of the Prorate Commission, and any change in the programs had to be approved by the commission following further hearings. The operation of any program could be stopped by presentation of a petition signed by over 40 per cent of the producers or by decree of the Prorate Commission if it found that the prerequisites for the establishment of a program no longer existed.[4]

Such were the terms of the bill that was written and sponsored by the Farm Bureau. The opposition to the bill throughout the 1933 session of the legislature was led by the California State Grange. Some have said that Sehlmeyer led the opposition to the act because it was strictly a Farm Bureau measure and the Grange had not been asked to participate in preliminary discussions. Although there is probably a large element of truth in this charge, there were other reasons as well for the action of Sehlmeyer and the Grange. One basis of Grange opposition lay in the moral outlook of Grange leaders; it seemed sinful to restrict the production or marketing of food products at a time when people were in want of more and better food. The California Grange expressed this attitude in its opposition to the enactment of the federal Agricultural Adjustment Administration agreements as well as in its resistance to the formulation of the California Agricultural Prorate Act.

Paradoxically, the State Grange developed its own program for marketing controls. A resolution passed by the Grange convention in October, 1932, called for controlled marketing when two-thirds of the growers in a given industry voted to institute such a program. But the Grange wanted this marketing control in the form of a law compelling all growers to join existing coöperative marketing associations when two-thirds of the growers so desired. During the 1933 session of the legislature the Grange sponsored a bill incorporating this idea. But the Grange's proposal was not seriously considered at that time, for it was neither as carefully drafted nor as legally sound as the Farm Bureau bill.[5]

The Grange, realizing that its own plan for compulsory marketing agreements had no chance of passing, directed its efforts toward defeating the Farm Bureau's bill. Sehlmeyer said that the powers to be given the proposed Prorate Commission were too far-reaching and too arbitrary, that the proposed bill would work to the detriment of small farmers, and that the administration of any such plan should be directly controlled by the growers. The Grange Master wrote:

We do not feel that this bill should be supported. In the first place, the business of agriculture should be conducted by farmers themselves, and not by a commission. Further, an attempt to restrict production in California would have no beneficial effect whatsoever. We feel that a far better plan is that the producers of any one commodity in the industry should set up a coöperative agreement which would control that commodity.[6]

Grange opposition had little effect upon the opinions of the legislators, who, as already mentioned, almost unanimously endorsed the Farm Bureau bill.

To assist Governor Rolph in the selection of personnel for the Prorate Commission, the Farm Bureau sent letters to all county units and to the heads of all coöperative marketing associations in the state inviting suggestions. The Farm Bureau then asked A. P. Miller, the chairman of the State Board of Agriculture, C. C. Teague, the president of the California Fruit Growers' Exchange, and Alex Johnson, the secretary of the C.F.B.F., to review these nominations. Guided by these recommendations the governor appointed a Prorate Commission dominated by representatives of the larger growers, the large coöperatives and processors, and the Farm Bureau itself. The commission, in turn, selected Edson Abel, legal counsel for the Farm Bureau, to act as its executive secretary. He was released from his position with the Farm Bureau to administer the prorate programs. The Farm Bureau was active at every level: it drew up proposed proration programs, secured signatures on proration petitions, testified at proration hearings, helped in the selection of personnel for the local program committees, and gave favorable publicity to the program throughout the state and among all commodity groups.[7]

Farmers, processors, distributors, and economic experts have not been able to agree on the relative success or failure of the proration program as a whole. Proponents of proration have cited many examples of price increases and larger gross returns for the growers under the operation of a particular program. Opponents of proration have been able to point to many cases in which prices fell and gross returns declined during the operation of a program. Neither side, however, has been able to prove conclusively that the price increases or decreases cited were the direct result of the operation of a program and not merely the consequence of many intangible, extraneous supply and demand forces that lay beyond the power of proration to control. It is likely that programs were most effective when the prorated commodity was highly perishable and where it had a limited area of production or a limited market area. Under such conditions proration probably resulted in more orderly marketing and in higher and more stable market prices.[8]

Opposition to proration came from many sources and took many forms. Some of the adverse criticism came from such experts as C. B. Hutchison, dean of the College of Agriculture of the University of California, who pointed out that requirements for the establishment of proration programs were indefinite and ambiguous, that administration by an unpaid commission often resulted in inefficiency, that to finance the programs by the sale of certificates made the commission dependent for its income upon those whom it was supposed to be regulating, and that the procedure for modifying the programs was clumsy.[9]

Opposition to the organization and procedure of the proration program was expressed in the testimony of several farmers appearing before a Joint Committee on Agriculture of the state legislature in February, 1939. These farmers charged that growers had been rushed into signing petitions without proper notice, that they had been unduly influenced by threats that they would be unable to sell any of their crop without proration, that coöperative associations had often illegally signed up their members without specific authorization, and that the operation of the law had often brought a lower unit price and a far lower total return. Charges concerning the relationship of processors, canners, and commercial distributors to the program are difficult to assess, for it was stated that these groups sabotaged the program by domination of the committees and that they secretly worked for its repeal.[10]

There were always substantial minorities opposed to proration within every agricultural industry. In the manner of disaffected minorities, these groups often gave an exaggerated impression of their own size and influence. One group within the lemon industry, dominated by a few small coöperatives in competition with the California Fruit Growers' Exchange, brought court action to have the prorate act declared unconstitutional. Reversing an adverse decision in the lower courts, the state supreme court upheld all phases of the act and definitely established its full constitutionality.[11]

Of greater significance, however, was the opposition of many of the smaller farmers of the state, often unorganized but more often working through the State Grange. These farmers frequently complained that proration brought lower prices and decreased gross revenue. They charged that big growers often controlled the local program committees and were therefore able to juggle marketing permits to their own benefit. The red tape involved in marketing small quantities of farm products with proration certificates tended to irritate the small grower, and attempts to exempt small acreages from proration programs were not always successful.[12]

One economic basis for the complaints of the small farmers—increased underemployment—was rarely mentioned by opponents of proration. Yet it was probably true that in many cases the small farmer, who depended almost completely on his own labor and that of his family, found that the restrictions tended to increase underemployment on his farm whereas the unused family labor constituted a constant overhead cost.[13] Proration, however, was but one of several factors contributing to widespread underemployment on many small farms. C. B. Hutchison, dean of the University of California College of Agriculture, summarized this and other economic troubles of the small farmer as follows:

... Most marketing programs entail burdens as well as confer benefits. Neither the benefits nor the burdens are necessarily distributed equitably. Some growers may receive large gains, others may suffer actual loss. The most obvious source of inequities among growers has to do with inaccuracies in the estimates of production which in many programs constitute the prorate bases.

A less obvious source of inequity and one about which we know very little, arises from the differences in size of farm operations. There is some evidence that large operators gain relatively more from proration programs than do small operators even though the price increases apply equally well to both. In some cases the allotment which a small grower receives during a given proration period is so little that the costs per unit of harvesting and marketing it are substantially increased. Also, in some cases where a portion of the crop is left unharvested, the small farmer may lose some of the revenue which he would otherwise derive from the labor of himself and family, whereas the large operator may merely hire fewer laborers.[14]

The Farm Bureau defended proration and worked for its extension and perfection, but the Grange attacked the program and worked for its amendment or outright repeal. The first battle came during the 1935 session of the state legislature. The Grange sponsored an amendment that would have destroyed the Prorate Commission and placed all marketing agreements under the State Department of Agriculture. Some Subordinate Granges supported this amendment by attacking the appointed commission, which they claimed supported large shippers and growers at the expense of the smaller ones. The Executive Committee of the Grange Canning Peach Growers' Association also supported the proposed amendment and warned of the dangers of bureaucratic regulations. In the assembly the proposed amendment was supported by Ellis E. Patterson (later lieutenant governor under Culbert Olson) and opposed by John Phillips from Riverside County. The amendment met defeat by a vote of 37 to 40.[15]

The Farm Bureau, in the same year, sponsored two amendments, both of which were passed. These amendments authorized the local program committees to institute pooling of surpluses and to conduct campaigns of group advertising. Appearing before the legislature in support of these amendments, and in defense of the Prorate Act as a whole, were Edson Abel, Alex Johnson, Ray Wiser, Von T. Ellsworth, and Tom Robinson—all representing the Farm Bureau. The Agricultural Council of California was also influential in securing support for the amendments.[16]

The Farm Bureau sponsored further amendments in 1937 to strengthen the prorate program. The amendments passed the legislature, but in the last-minute rush of bills that piled up on his desk Governor Merriam overlooked these amendments, which failed to reach the statute books for lack of his signature. To conciliate the Farm Bureau, Merriam included amendment of the Agricultural Prorate Act among the subjects to be discussed by the special session of the state legislature called in the spring of 1938. John H. O'Donnell of Yolo County introduced the Farm Bureau amendments. His bill empowered local program committees to raise funds for advertising and for merchandising of prorated crops and to establish proration programs by grade, quality, and size as well as by quantity. It also authorized coöperative associations to sign prorate petitions for their members if expressly authorized by the membership to do so. These amendments were passed and signed by the governor. A Grange-sponsored bill, introduced by Assemblyman Michael J. Burns of Humboldt County, which would have eliminated the Prorate Commission and transferred its functions to the State Department of Agriculture, passed the assembly but died in senate committee.[17]

In 1939, Grange determination to repeal the Prorate Act or to amend it drastically was strengthened by the political influence that Sehlmeyer enjoyed in the Olson administration. Hundreds of letters and petitions urging drastic revision of the prorate system flooded the office of the governor. These, added to the counsel of Sehlmeyer, who had played an active role in the election of Olson in 1938, persuaded the administration to work for that end.

The campaign to secure repeal of the Prorate Act was launched in October, 1938, when Sehlmeyer, in his annual address before the State Grange convention, lashed out at the folly of the theory of economic scarcity. The convention backed up the State Master with a resolution calling for outright repeal of the Prorate Act. When the legislature convened in January, 1939, Senator Chris N. Jespersen, progressive Republican from San Luis Obispo County and a prominent Grange member, introduced a bill calling for outright repeal. The proponents of repeal knew that this extreme step stood little chance of legislative enactment; it was, nevertheless, introduced in order to give the Grange bargaining power in achieving a satisfactory compromise. What the Grange really had in mind was disclosed in a radio program on January 13, 1939, during which Senator Jespersen, a guest speaker, attacked the Prorate Commission as dominated by corporation farmers and called for the impartial administration of the program under the State Department of Agriculture. A bill providing for such a transfer of administration and for the abolishment of the Prorate Commission was sponsored by the Grange and introduced by George M. Biggar.[18]

The campaign picked up momentum on February 13 at a hearing of the Joint Agricultural Committee, before which many small farmers, some of them representing the Grange, testified against the act. One witness, Mrs. Ida Jensen of Winton Grange in Merced County, the owner of a fifteen-acre grape ranch, pled:

> Seventy-five per cent of us growers signed a petition to repeal the prorate act, but it was declared illegal. They said a T wasn't crossed

or an I wasn't dotted, or something. We collected dimes and half dollars to hire a lawyer to represent us, but the prorate commission put our case in a Los Angeles court, where we couldn't send anybody.

You have heard figures and statements from men who hire stenographers. We fell for them—I hope you don't. We don't know what will become of us—maybe we'll be migratory workers or serfs—but we know we can't go on like this under prorate.[19]

Her emotional testimony, much of which unwittingly jumbled the facts, was typical of that of many small bewildered farmers. Many blamed the operation of the Prorate Act for economic disabilities that were traceable to other factors. Commenting on the testimony presented at the hearing, the editor of the *Grange News* proclaimed in a front-page editorial:

... It was a story of their very life blood and it was not hard to see that the dirt farmer was speaking the truth as he related how the prorate had worked intolerable hardships for him.

And it is no wonder this unwanted measure has wrought great oppression among our agricultural population. It is the scheme of large business interests, drafted for their own benefit, not for the farmer's; and it was railroaded through by clever manipulating, misleading propaganda and the frightening effects of a "fear" campaign.[20]

At this hearing, spokesmen for the Farm Bureau were on the defensive. They argued that the act should be kept for those industries it had benefited. They maintained that the low farm prices in 1938 were not attributable to the proration programs and that prices would probably have been even lower had it not been for proration.[21]

In order to exert further popular pressure upon the legislature, the State Grange called a mass meeting in Sacramento for March 28. At this meeting, to which over three hundred farmers came, Governor Olson spoke in opposition to the prorate program as then constituted. He said:

There is too much influence by processing interests and not enough by dirt farmers themselves. The dirt farmer has been badly neglected in the administration of agricultural laws of the State. ... It is our aim to aid the farmer to realize cost of production plus a decent margin.[22]

The governor praised Sehlmeyer's leadership and thanked him for his aid and advice. Sehlmeyer also spoke, advocating that all marketing programs be put under the supervision of the State Director of Agriculture.[23]

The Farm Bureau, in the face of this opposition, presented its own bill to amend the Agricultural Prorate Act. This bill provided for administration of prorate programs entirely by the growers. The Farm Bureau contended that the growers should maintain control of the administration of the act rather than permit it to be turned over to a department of government. Ray Wiser, testifying before the Senate Committee on Agriculture, pointed out that proration would always attract a great deal of criticism, some of it justified and much of it bitter, and that such criticism, if directed entirely against the State Department of Agriculture, would tend to discredit the department as a whole and thus hurt the farmers indirectly. The Farm Bureau's bill was released from committee but failed to pass.[24]

To resolve the conflict between the Grange and the Farm Bureau on this issue, Senators Jespersen, Phillips, Biggar, and Crittenden worked out a compromise bill that they urged both organizations to support. This bill, which was accepted as a suitable compromise by the Grange but never received sincere Farm Bureau support, was subsequently enacted. Its provisions included these: 1) the Prorate Commission was abolished; 2) a new Agricultural Prorate Advisory Commission was created; 3) the entire administration of prorate programs was placed in the hands of the State Department of Agriculture; 4) some specific crops, including canning figs and grapes in the coastal dry-wine counties, were exempted from the terms of the act. Other aspects of the original act were kept unchanged. The passage of these amendments represented a substantial victory for the Grange and for the Olson administration. Subsequent attempts of the Grange in 1940 and 1941 to secure outright repeal of the act met with failure.[25]

Like many other California agricultural problems in the 1930's, agricultural marketing proration had its roots in economic depression and disappeared, for the time at least, when the war forced a reversal of economic trends. The struggle between the Farm Bureau and the Grange over agricultural proration, which reached its climax in 1939, was soon made meaningless by a wartime economy in which increased effective purchasing power raised farm prices and in which the basic problem of agriculture became the production of ever greater quantities of food in support of the war effort rather than the restriction of production and marketing.

16.

THE ISSUE OF
WATER AND POWER
1919–1933

California has an abundance of warm sunshine and a great variety of fertile soils. In the parts of California that receive sufficient rainfall during the winter months, the natural combination of sun, soil, and water makes the farms highly productive. But in many parts of the San Joaquin Valley and southern California natural rainfall provides insufficient moisture to allow intensive cultivation of crops. In these areas of rainfall deficiency the farmer must find his water elsewhere, dry-farm his land, or use it as range land. In areas suited to the intensive production of crops he may construct expensive gravity-flow irrigation systems, which carry the water from dams high in the Sierra Mountains down to the thirsty land, or pump the underground water that lies beneath his farm. Water pumps are operated by electric power, which can be manufactured as a by-product at the dams that store the water for irrigation. Charges for water and electricity constitute high cash operating costs for thousands of farmers in California, and cheap water and cheap power mean higher net profits. Water is useless without the power to lift it and move it about; in California, power can best be generated from falling water. Water and power are thus inextricably linked together.

The complex problem of securing sufficient inexpensive water and power has many diverse aspects—engineering, economic, political, and social. Few men have claimed to understand the problem in its entirety, and engineers, politicians, farmers, and scholars have compounded confusion by analyses that have been only partly valid. Passionate argumentation has begun where understanding has left off, and nearly everyone in public life has taken some stand on the problem. Because the problem has been, in one important aspect, agricultural, farm leaders have inevitably entered into the debate.

It is not surprising, in view of the other conflicts between the Grange and the Farm Bureau, that these two groups have rarely regarded this problem in the same light. It would be convenient to explain these differences entirely upon the basis of conflicting economic interest, but in reality the interests of the members of the two organizations have often been identical. One reason for such differences lies in the very complexity of the problem itself; on the water and power issue, many farm groups sincerely trying to improve the economic and social status of their membership have occasionally adopted policies that might well have operated to depress rather than to improve that status.

The great Central Valley Project has so captured the imagination of California citizens that other aspects of the water and power problem have often been overlooked. It is true that the Central Valley Project was the most important single development in the 1930's, but before that and continuing throughout the 1930's the farmers' struggles for adequate and cheap water and power took other forms as well. The policies and actions of the Farm Bureau and the Grange in relation to the Central Valley Project were based, in part at least, upon the attitudes of the two organizations toward public utilities in general—their regulation, taxation, and methods of establishing rates.[1]

Attempts of farmers to achieve equitable rates for electricity, upon which they depended for power to pump irrigation water, involved the great electrical public utilities in California. For most farmers in the rich, warm valleys of California, stretching from the Oregon border in the north to the Tehachapi Mountains in the south, there was but one such utility, the Pacific Gas and Electric (P. G. and E.) Company, with its various subsidiaries. In this area, with the exception of a very few districts in which electric utilities were publicly owned, P. G. and E. held a virtual monopoly of electric power.

Almost from its inception the Farm Bureau faced this problem. In April, 1921, the C.F.B.F. created a Law and Utilities

Department, headed at first by Judge F. S. Brittain and soon thereafter by J. J. Deuel. To this service department was delegated the task of representing the Farm Bureau before the State Railroad Commission, which was authorized by the Utility Act of 1911 to regulate rates and services of the public utilities. Members of the Utilities Department of the Farm Bureau collected information on technical and legal aspects of utility regulation, appeared before the Railroad Commission in cases involving rates for power used in agriculture, and dealt directly with the utility companies to secure better service at fairer rates.

In the first case the department handled, in the spring of 1921, Judge Brittain convinced the Railroad Commission that rates charged by the San Joaquin Light and Power Company should be lowered substantially for heavy consumers of power, the farmers who used electric pumps to irrigate their lands. Hundreds of changes in agricultural rates were secured by the department, and thousands of individual complaints of incorrect charges were adjusted without litigation through its intercession. The savings resulting to farmers from these actions undoubtedly ran into thousands of dollars. These substantial benefits accrued to all farmers and to all consumers of electricity, whether they were members of the Farm Bureau or not.[2]

In the early years of the depression, however, such actions proved inadequate. Electric power rates, based upon a "fair" return on capital investment, tended to remain at a uniform level, while farm prices and farm income decreased steadily. Furthermore, a sequence of dry years and the long-continued pumping of underground waters resulted in a constant lowering of the water table. As a result, it became necessary to sink ever deeper wells and, therefore, to use more and more electricity. Farm Bureau centers complained of these high fixed costs and demanded that the Utilities Department evolve legislation that would change the legal basis of rate determination. In response to these pleas the Farm Bureau decided to urge an amendment to the Public Utilities Act that would authorize the Railroad Commission to take into account the value of electrical service to the consumer in the setting of rates.[3]

In the 1933 session of the state legislature the Farm Bureau sponsored three bills to provide relief for farm consumers of electricity. The first, introduced by Senators Inman, Schottky, and Jespersen, proposed to prohibit charging utility rates in excess of the value of these services to the consumers. Another bill empowered the Railroad Commission to restrict electric rates to such levels as would yield to the utilities only that rate of return earned generally by businesses operating in the same area and bearing similar risks. These two bills were killed in committee. A third bill proposed a flat discount of 20 per cent on electric and gas bills for the following year. This bill received wide support until it was amended to death by C. C. Cottrell of San Jose, who succeeded in adding provisions to include telephone, water, and transportation rates in the 20 per cent cut.[4]

The Farm Bureau tried again, in 1935, to secure a change in the basis of rate-setting by sponsoring a bill that authorized the Railroad Commission to allow lower rates for agricultural consumption than for domestic consumption and that directed the commission to so limit rates that utilities would not earn a return in excess of that being enjoyed by business generally in the state. J. J. Deuel, testifying before a senate committee, pointed out that public utilities were earning 8 per cent on their investments while other businesses were making only about 5 per cent at best. The bill was killed in committee by a vote of seven to four. Voting to send the bill to the floor were Senators Metzger, Garrison, Olson, and Scollan; voting to block its consideration were Senators Duval, Hulse, Parkman, Reindollar, Snyder, Tickle, and Biggar.[5]

Another aspect of the electric utility problem involved the taxation of publicly owned utilities. These utilities were exempted from the gross receipts tax that was levied on privately owned utilities in 1911 and that continued in effect until the Riley-Stewart plan repealed this tax and returned the properties of the utilities to the county tax rolls. Farm leaders frequently observed that failure to tax publicly owned utilities meant that domestic consumers in cities—for most publicly owned utilities were municipal projects—enjoyed a lower electric rate than did rural consumers, who received their power from privately owned utilities, which passed on the gross receipts tax in the form of higher rates. Farm leaders also pointed out that urban consumers, by avoiding the burden of this tax, deprived the government of revenue, with the result that taxpayers generally had to pay higher taxes in other forms to make up for this loss.

Throughout the 1920's the Farm Bureau and the State Grange coöperated in campaigns to impose the gross receipts tax upon publicly owned utilities. Proponents of the public ownership of power accused the two farm organizations of acting as "dupes and cat's-paws" for the vested interests. Although it is true that the imposition of this tax would have inhibited the development of the public ownership movement, there is no reason to believe that either farm organization was improperly influenced by the private utility interests. All attempts to force the gross receipts tax upon publicly owned utilities by use of the initiative procedure failed, and the Riley-Stewart plan in 1933 put an end to such demands.[6]

George Sehlmeyer's predecessor as Master of the State Grange, George Harrison, had worked with the Farm Bureau and with other groups for the imposition of the gross-receipts tax on publicly owned utilities, but Sehlmeyer had other ideas on the subject. A long-time advocate of the public ownership of utilities and a close associate of J. M. Inman of Sacramento, H. C. Jones of San Jose, and Franklin Hichborn of Santa Clara, all of whom supported public ownership, Sehlmeyer led the Grange in a constant struggle against the private utilities.

The reversal of Grange opinion after Sehlmeyer's election as Master in 1929 was clearly indicated in the debate over the Clowdsley-Inman bill during the 1933 session of the state legislature. This bill, introduced before the final compromise on the Riley-Stewart plan was achieved, proposed the imposition of a special tax upon privately owned gas and electric utilities. Its passage would have increased the taxes paid by the private utilities by about $5,800,000 a year. This bill had strong Grange backing and was supported in legislative debate by Senators Inman, Jones, and Jespersen. They argued that privately owned utilities were not paying their full share of the state's taxes, that their rates and profits had been exorbitant, that the proposed tax could be paid by reducing the absurdly high salaries of top utility officials, and that passage of the bill would tend to relieve the tax burden upon property.

The Farm Bureau, on the other hand, opposed the proposal. J. J. Deuel observed that utilities enjoyed the right of including state taxes in their statements of operating costs and that, therefore, the proposed taxes would not come from net profits but would be passed on to the consumer in the form of higher rates. Deuel insisted that in this respect the utilities were not taxpaying institutions but tax collecting agencies for the state. Alex Johnson, speaking for the Farm Bureau, said: "If the utilities are making large profits, let them reduce the rates to the consumer."[7]

The bill passed the assembly by a vote of 54 to 26, but the rural-dominated senate turned it down by a vote of 18 to 22. In a bitter speech, Senator Inman blamed the Farm Bureau for its defeat. Some rural senators probably were influenced by the official stand of the Farm Bureau; others probably saw little sense in adopting this measure in view of the fact that the Riley-Stewart tax proposal was assured of passage; some may have cast a negative vote because of pressure, direct and indirect, exerted by the utility lobby. At any rate, the Farm Bureau was not acting as a "front" for the power trust, as some asserted.[8] The defeat of this bill and the enactment of the Riley-Stewart tax reform plan brought to an end all movements for increasing taxes on either privately or publicly owned utilities. Beginning in 1933 the water and power problem and debate took on new aspects, centering around the creation and operation, ownership, and control of the Central Valley Project.

Plans for the construction of a coördinated, statewide water and power project had been under consideration for many years. The basic engineering problem had long been recognized: to construct a series of storage reservoirs and canal systems in the Sacramento Valley to carry the surplus water of that region southward into the San Joaquin Valley where it was needed. About two-thirds of the water supply of the Central Valley lay in the Sacramento Valley, whereas approximately two-thirds of the arable land lay in the San Joaquin Valley. Colonel Robert B. Marshall of the United States Geological Survey concluded an investigation of the water problem in California with the presentation in 1919 of a detailed report to the governor of the state. From 1921 to 1923, the state government coöperated with private groups to draw up a coördinated water and power plan for the Central Valley. This plan provided for a project that would transfer water from the north to the south, impound flood waters, maintain the summer flow of the Sacramento River to permit year-round navigation, control the encroachment of salt water on the delta lands of the San Joaquin and Sacramento rivers, and manufacture electricity.[9]

The first step taken to secure legal authorization for this project came in 1922, when a state water and power measure was submitted to the electorate as an initiative proposition. This measure proposed to reserve unappropriated water and power sites in the public domain for the use and benefit of the people of the state. In the ensuing campaign began the great debate between the proponents of public ownership of utilities and the private utilities, who wished to maintain their virtual monopoly of the state's power resources. Gifford Pinchot stated the position of those supporting public ownership when he accused the private power companies of having failed to supply enough power at reasonable rates. He warned the voters of California: "... you have no coal, your oil some day will be gone, and only waterpower will be left. And he who controls a monopoly of power, will soon control all."[10]

Division of opinion within the Farm Bureau prevented that organization from taking a definite stand. Articles expressing approval of the proposition occasionally appeared in the California *Farm Bureau Monthly,* but the C.F.B.F. Executive Committee and the delegates to the annual conventions of the Farm Bureau refused to commit themselves.[11]

The Grange had, in October, 1921, passed a resolution, drawn up by George Sehlmeyer among others, that endorsed the proposed water and power plan on the basis that power was being monopolized by capitalists and speculators to the detriment of the consumer and the agricultural and industrial interests of the state. The Grange convention in October, 1922, however, refused to endorse the stand taken the previous year. The convention sponsored a debate on the initiative proposition, with Mayor Louis Bartlett of Berkeley speaking for the affirmative and Allison B. Ware of Chico for the negative. The formal debate set off a prolonged and heated discussion from the floor that ended in deadlock when resolutions pertaining to the initiative proposition were withdrawn "in the interest of harmony in the Grange."[12]

The 1922 proposition was defeated at the polls, but in 1924 another water and power initiative was on the ballot. This proposition provided for the establishment of a board of five members with power to direct construction and operation of dams, reservoirs, canals, and transmission lines for the conservation of water and the generation of electric energy. It authorized the issuance of $500,000,000 in state bonds to finance the acquisition of property and the construction and maintenance of the project. Once more the Farm Bureau was unable to reach a decision that all its members and leaders could endorse. Articles in the *Farm Bureau Monthly* presented arguments on both sides and advised readers to vote as they felt right. The Grange also evaded the issue, declaring that, although there was a need for a comprehensive water and power plan, the expenditure of huge sums of money to bring additional acreage into production was not advisable at that time. The initiative measure was defeated in the general election. A similar measure was introduced in 1926, and this also went down to defeat. As in 1922 and 1924, neither the Farm Bureau nor the Grange could reach a decision to support or oppose the proposition.[13]

Specific proposals for a coördinated water and power project for the great Central Valley were voted down, but the need for such a plan could not be denied so easily. By 1933 continued dry weather and continued overpumping of underground water reservoirs had lowered the water table to a dangerous level in many parts of the state. Many farms were abandoned when pumps began to spew up foul, brackish water or yielded no water at all. Salt water continued to encroach upon the fabulously rich delta lands, turning the soil sour and unproductive. Rivers, swollen by spring rains, flooded the farm lands of the rich valleys.

Planning for a coördinated water and power project did not cease with the defeat of the three initiative propositions in the 1920's. Engineers, agronomists, geologists, economists, and politicians continued to study the problem, to formulate plans, and to work out ideas for financing their projects. By 1931, State Engineer Edward Hyatt and his colleagues had worked out a detailed plan for a Central Valley Project. The plan provided for conservation of water in the north and its transfer to the south, flood control, improvement of navigation, control of the encroachment of salt water upon the delta lands, manufacture of electrical power to help operate the other features of the project, and sale of electricity to help finance the construction of the project. It was estimated that construction would cost $170,000,000.

George Sehlmeyer persuaded the Grange to lend its full support to this plan. The Grange insisted that irrigation and power be the primary aspects of the project and that it be owned and controlled by the people. Time and again, from 1929 to 1931, Grange leaders and delegates to the annual convention of the State Grange warned against the danger of letting private monopolies gain control of the water and power resources of the state. The Grange asked that the government be authorized to build its own power transmission lines so that it could retail the power generated at its dams and so that revenue from the sale of the power could be used to defray the costs of other features of the project. Sehlmeyer proposed that, until such time as the electricity was ready for sale, a heavy severance tax be levied upon the exploitation of natural resources of the state. Public ownership and control of the proposed Central Valley Project was the one cause that Sehlmeyer and the Grange worked for above all others.[14]

The Farm Bureau was also vitally concerned with the development of a coördinated water and power program for the Central Valley. With influential membership centered in the San Joaquin Valley, the Bureau viewed the plan primarily as one designed to bring water to parched lands of the valley. The farmers of the San Joaquin Valley regarded the generation of electric power as clearly secondary to and contributory to the water aspects of the proposed project.[15]

In the 1933 session of the state legislature a bill was introduced to authorize the construction of the Central Valley Project. In its technical aspects, this bill was based upon the state water plan of 1931. It provided for the creation of a Water Project Authority, which was to be governed by a five-man ex-officio board composed of the following state officials: the Director of Finance, the Director of Public Works, the Attorney General, the Comptroller, and the Treasurer. The Authority was to be granted the power to issue $170,000,000 in revenue bonds to finance construction of the project. The bonds were to be retired with the income received by the Authority from the operation of the water and power aspects of the program after its completion. The Authority was to be authorized to enter into contracts for the sale of water and electricity. If any federal aid was given to the project, the $170,000,000 authorization was to be reduced by the amount of the federal contribution. The purposes of the proposed project were stated to be: provision of supplemental irrigation water, salinity control, power generation, flood control, storage of water for industrial and domestic purposes, and navigation improvement.[16] The bill, in this form, was passed during the regular session of the legislature in 1933.

When the legislature reconvened in July, 1933, to pass remedial tax legislation, amendments to the Central Valley Project Act were submitted for consideration. The original act had made no provision for the sale of electric power to any agencies other than privately owned public utilities. Attempts by progressive Republicans, such as Senators J. M. Inman and H. C. Jones, to amend the law in the spring had been unsuccessful. But during the recess of the legislature the proponents of public ownership of power had worked out plans to secure the desired amendments in July. Suggestions from the New Deal administration in Washington, implying that no loans would be extended by the federal government unless the interests of the people were protected, greatly strengthened the position of those seeking amendment.

The Issue of Water and Power

Senators Inman and Jones, supported by Franklin Hichborn and George Sehlmeyer and others, secured the enactment of amendments which provided: 1) that in awarding contracts for sale of electric power, preference be given to state and nonprofit agencies over private companies; 2) that the Water Project Authority be authorized to construct its own electric transmission lines from Kennett (later Shasta) Dam to a point near Antioch; 3) that publicly owned utilities be permitted to secure power from the project in the future, even though private utilities had already contracted for purchase of the power; 4) that all existing water rights be protected.[17]

Following the enactment of these amendments, the Pacific Gas and Electric Company and allied groups postponed operation of the act by the filing of referendum petitions. The governor authorized a special election on December 19, 1933 to decide the fate of the Central Valley Project. In the campaign that followed, P. G. and E. naturally took the lead in urging rejection of the act. On the other side, the Grange was one of many groups working for its popular endorsement. A State Water Plan Association was established to coördinate the campaign of the organizations working for approval of the act. Senator Bradford Crittenden from San Joaquin County served as president of the association, Senator J. M. Inman from Sacramento as vice-president, and Senator John McColl of Shasta County as finance director. Inman represented the progressive forces in California that had for years been working for public ownership of power, but Crittenden represented the groups that were interested primarily in the irrigation phases of the project.

In advertisements carried in California farm journals, paid for by the State Water Plan Association, the California State Grange was the only farm organization whose name appeared in endorsement of the act.[18] In October, 1933, the State Grange passed a lengthy resolution that began by declaring:

> Whereas, no acceptable reason or excuse exists for allowing private individuals or corporations to become enormously rich and arrogant by monopolizing to themselves, said public resources to the debasement and enslavement of all the rest of our people.... The Grange reaffirms ... its adherence to the principle of Public Ownership of all our great natural resources.[19]

The resolution stated that the Grange endorsed the Central Valley Project because it would produce cheap electricity, provide flood control, raise the water table of the Central Valley, give employment to thousands of citizens of California, and release millions of dollars into the state's economy.[20]

The Farm Bureau divided along regional lines on the Central Valley Project referendum. Farmers of southern California, who had no direct stake in the water supply of the Central Valley and no chance of benefiting from the manufacture of electrical energy, were lukewarm at best toward a project whose cost, they assumed, would be paid by all but whose benefits would accrue to northern Californians alone. There was some opposition to the project in northern California also. Some Farm Bureau votes may have been influenced by the speeches that Senator Gordon of Napa County gave before Farm Bureau centers of that county in opposition to the act. In San Joaquin County a Farm Bureau member appeared before the Board of Directors to argue that the project would drown out his farms in the delta lands.[21] Farm Bureaus in other northern counties, however, supported the act vigorously. The December, 1933, issue of the Tulare County edition of the *Farm Bureau Monthly* carried a special editorial, set entirely in italics, that called for endorsement of the Central Valley Project.

Last Call! Vote for the Water Plan.

... An affirmative vote on the water plan will mean an immediate increase in Tulare county land values as well as in all real property. It will encourage thousands of farmers to hang on for the better day. It will mean the saving of thousands of farm homes that may otherwise shortly close their doors and be abandoned.

This is the supreme hour in the life of Tulare county. If we succeed on December 19th our future as an agricultural region is fairly sure. If we fail—but—We Must Not Fail![22]

The state organization was in an embarrassing position. Large and influential Farm Bureaus in the counties of the upper San Joaquin Valley were insisting that the Central Valley Project be endorsed. Large and influential Farm Bureaus in counties south of the Tehachapi were either lukewarm or opposed to the project. There was only one thing the state organization could do when it met in annual convention in November, 1933—straddle the issue. The official statement of policy on the coming referendum was couched in general and ambiguous terms: "We believe in and endorse a program which will conserve and develop the natural water resources of California, and recommend that these projects should be developed in a manner in accord with the needs of the State and its ability to economically carry them out."[23]

On December 19, 1933, the voters of the state endorsed the act by a popular vote of 459,712 to 426,109. Southern California voted against the act by a vote of nearly two to one. The San Joaquin Valley voted affirmatively by a vote of five to one, and the Sacramento Valley returned a little over three affirmative votes for every negative one. Tulare, Kings, Kern, and Madera counties voted over 90 per cent in favor of the project. The farmers of the Central Valley rejoiced. The Grange claimed a large share of credit for its own labors in behalf of the measure, which it regarded as a great victory over the vested interests of the state. But the water and power issue was far from being settled; the struggle for control of the project had just begun.[24]

17. STRUGGLE FOR CONTROL OF THE CENTRAL VALLEY PROJECT

The inauguration of the Central Valley Project created a multitude of controversial problems—technical, economic, and political. Many questions had to be answered. In this multiple-purpose project, what proportion of the total cost should be allocated to recipients of benefits from irrigation, flood control, navigation improvement, salinity control, and electric power? By whom should the facilities be constructed—the Bureau of Reclamation, the Army Engineers, or the State of California? How should the project be financed? Should the 160-acre limitation of reclamation law be applied? How should the project's electric power be distributed to the consumer? Many of these questions did not receive a definitive answer in the 1930's, and a few are still the center of heated political debate. From 1933 to 1941 the most significant dispute centered around the question of whether the state government and local publicly owned utilities or the Pacific Gas and Electric Company and other private utilities should distribute the electric power generated at the project dams. The debate took many forms at different times, but, no matter what the particular issue was, the Grange and the Farm Bureau were always on opposite sides.[1]

The original Central Valley Project Act, passed in 1933 and ratified by popular vote in December of that year, provided that the project was to be financed by the sale of $170,000,000 of state revenue bonds but that this sum was to be reduced by the amount of any federal aid that might be given to the project. In the depths of the depression few Californians seriously believed that the state could finance this huge project without federal assistance. It was the knowledge that state financial resources were insufficient for the task that persuaded the

Central Valley Project

legislature to amend the act in July, 1933. It was the hope that federal funds would flow into the state, and the belief that this money would help to restore mass purchasing power, that persuaded many people to endorse the plan even though they had no direct interest in the water or power aspects of the project. Immediately following the popular endorsement of the act, therefore, state officials, with the active support of many groups, began to seek federal assistance.

With unity of policy and purpose within California, and with a generous administration in Washington eager to restore the economy of the country by "priming the pump," federal aid was soon forthcoming. The Rivers and Harbors Act, passed in August, 1935, provided for a direct federal contribution of $12,000,000 for the construction of Kennett (later Shasta) Dam. In the fall of 1935 the Federal Emergency Relief Administration allocated an emergency grant of $4,200,000 for the Central Valley Project. In December, 1935, President Roosevelt approved the feasibility report for the construction of the project, and in 1937 Congress adopted it as a project of the Reclamation Bureau. Thus the federal government assumed full responsibility for a project that had originally been conceived as a state water and power plan.

As progress was made on the construction of Shasta Dam and other features of the project, the great debate over the method of distributing the electric power from the project began. Under federal law, that part of the total expenditures allocated for the construction of power facilities was to be repaid to the federal government at an interest rate of 3 per cent; funds expended on irrigation projects were to be repaid with no interest charge; and costs chargeable to flood control, navigation improvement, and salinity control were to be carried by the federal government with no repayment obligations whatsoever. Farmers of the upper San Joaquin Valley, interested primarily in securing supplementary water, hoped that revenue from the sale of electric power would be used to help finance the construction of irrigation facilities, thus making water rates lower. Farmers of the Sacramento Valley, on the other hand, were interested primarily in the distribution of power by government agencies at low rates.

There were two possible methods of distributing power: it could be sold to the Pacific Gas and Electric Company for distribution through facilities already built and owned by that company or the government could build its own transmission lines and sell the power directly to local publicly owned utilities. It was thought by some that the former method would result in higher power rates but lower water rates and that the latter method would bring lower power rates but higher water rates. Those who favored the sale of power to private utilities pointed out that the duplication of existing distribution facilities by the construction of competing government-owned transmission facilities would be uneconomic and that utility rates could be maintained at a "fair" level through the control exercised by the State Railroad Commission. Those who favored government distribution replied that approximately a third of the project's power would be needed to carry Shasta Dam water into the San Joaquin Valley and that another third would be used by farmers to pump ground water; therefore, this group insisted, cheap power meant low water rates.[2]

In this debate the California Grange, with its membership centered in the Sacramento Valley and in northern California generally, took the side of those who insisted on public ownership of electric distribution facilities. To the Grange the issue was one of whether the public would get the power generated at government dams at cost or whether the consumers would have to pay tribute in the form of high, legally guaranteed profits to privately owned utilities. The Grange favored legislation that would make it easy for local districts to organize publicly owned utilities. It also supported legislative proposals that would empower the government to build its own transmission lines for carrying electricity from the project dams to these utility districts.[3]

The Farm Bureau, on the other hand, took its stand with those who favored the sale of power from the project to P. G. and E. in the belief that the execution of this policy would result in lower water rates and would also prevent the uneconomic construction of duplicating, competitive facilities by the government. To the Grange, which led the crusade for public ownership and against the influence of private vested interests, the Farm Bureau's support of the private utilities appeared corrupt or, at best, misguided. To the Farm Bureau the Grange position seemed economically unsound, unrealistic, visionary, and radical.

The battle for ownership and control of electric power began in the 1935 session of the state legislature with the introduction of the first of a series of revenue bond bills by Senator J. C. Garrison, Grange leader from Stanislaus County.[4] Garrison, a long-time advocate of public ownership, was elected in 1934 to the senatorial seat previously held by David F. Bush, who had voted against the amendments to the Central Valley Project Act in July, 1933. Sponsoring the revenue bond legislation with Garrison was Senator Chris N. Jespersen from San Luis Obispo County, a progressive Republican and a prominent Grange member. Their bill provided that any political subdivision in the state could organize a public utilities commission, which would be empowered to issue revenue bonds for the construction of a public utility upon a majority vote of the people in the proposed district. These districts could purchase government power from Shasta Dam when it became available. A similar bill, which applied only to water and power projects, was introduced by Assemblyman Nielsen.

Opponents of the Garrison bill introduced amendments requiring a two-thirds vote of the people for the authorization of revenue bonds rather than a simple majority vote as provided in the original bill. They argued that a two-thirds vote was necessary to prevent the creation of unsound districts. Proponents of public power asserted, on the other hand, that provision for a simple majority vote was essential because private power interests would always be able, through the expenditure of huge sums of money, to convince at least one-third of the electorate to vote negatively no matter how sound the proposed project. They also maintained that revenue bonds would never be purchased unless the proposed district was indisputably sound and assured of sufficient revenue to pay off the indebtedness.

Opposition to public power in 1935 was led by Senator Ray Hays of Fresno County, who introduced the "two-thirds" amendment, and by Senators Duval of Ventura County and Difani of Riverside County. The proponents of public power, Garrison, Jespersen, and Nielsen, were joined in their resistance to the Hays amendment by Senators Culbert Olson and Jack Metzger and by Assemblymen H. Dewey Anderson and Ellis E. Patterson. The Garrison-Jespersen bill and the Nielsen bill passed both houses by substantial majorities and without crippling amendments. The private utilities and their friends, however, persuaded Governor Merriam to veto them. In justifying his vetoes the governor said that a two-thirds vote of the people was desirable in the acquiring of public indebtedness. Attempts to override the veto of the Nielsen bill failed when the affirmative vote in the assembly fell seven votes short of the fifty-four required to repass the bill. Further efforts to enact revenue bond legislation were delayed until 1937.

Before the legislature convened in 1937, the Grange began a campaign to win popular support for legislation designed to promote public ownership of utilities. At the annual convention of the Grange in 1935, Louis Bartlett, former mayor of Berkeley and long-time advocate of public ownership of power, addressed the Grange in support of revenue bond legislation. His arguments and those of Grange leaders, among whom the foremost was George Sehlmeyer, won the day in a resolution that endorsed these principles:

1. Public ownership and operation of all public utilities.
2. Public utilities shall be financed by the sale of bonds based upon the revenue derived from the project and shall in no wise be a lien upon the property of the property owners of that district.
3. Revenue bonds shall be financed upon a simple majority vote of the voters of that district.[5]

Again in 1936 the Grange convention endorsed revenue bond legislation and pledged the organization to sponsor and work for such legislation in 1937.[6]

A special Senate Committee on Public Utilities had been chosen in 1935 to investigate the problem of control of electric power from the Central Valley Project. This committee, composed of J. L. Seawell, Leonard J. Difani, J. C. Garrison, Walter H. Duval, and Chris N. Jespersen, conducted hearings throughout the state. At these hearings local Grange leaders testified in support of public ownership. The majority report, signed by Seawell, Garrison, and Jespersen, endorsed revenue bond legislation.⁷

On December 21, 1936, the California State Grange called a convention in San Francisco to coördinate the efforts of the groups that were working for the passage of revenue bond legislation. Another Grange-sponsored strategy meeting, held January 7, 1937, was attended by Senators Garrison, Jespersen, Olson, Gordon, Biggar, Metzger, and Westover and by Assemblymen Heisinger, Donnelly, Clark, Lore, and Yorty. After these meetings, two bills were drawn up on the basis of the information gathered by the Special Committee on Public Utilities: the Garrison bill, which provided that political subdivisions be granted authority to issue revenue bonds, upon a majority vote of the people, for the financing of water, power, communications, transportation, gas, irrigation, and harbor projects; and the Nielsen bill, in which the provisions were limited to water and power projects.

In the debate on these bills the arguments put forth in 1935 were repeated. The opponents of public power again proposed amendments that would have required a two-thirds affirmative vote in revenue bond elections, and again these amendments were voted down. The Garrison bill passed the senate by a vote of 38 to 0 and the assembly by a vote of 65 to 10. The Nielsen bill passed the senate by a comfortable margin but failed to get through the assembly.

Throughout the spring of 1937 the Grange was influential in winning support for the Garrison bill. After the bill had passed the legislature, while it was awaiting the Governor's signature, the Executive Committee of the State Grange wrote a letter to Governor Merriam stating its case for support of revenue bond legislation as follows:

> The California State Grange is interested in measures of this kind for several reasons. First, we believe it is unfair that where publicly-owned districts are formed the obligation should rest on the property within the district; it should be carried by the utility. Further, we believe the issuance of revenue bonds will have a tendency to prevent the formation of districts which are financially unsound, because it will be necessary for the proponents to prove to the investors that the district is sound before the bonds can be sold.⁸

It is doubtful if this letter had much influence on the decision of Governor Merriam to sign the Garrison bill. It is more likely that Merriam realized that a veto would be easily overridden and chose to sign it rather than face a hostile legislature. At any rate, the bill was endorsed by the governor. But referendum petitions were soon filed that made the terms of the act inoperative until the voters rendered a final decision in the 1938 general election.

The Garrison Act referendum, Proposition Number 13 on the ballot, was but one of several important issues in 1938.[9] The voters had to make up their minds not only on revenue bond legislation but also on the antiunion initiative measure and on a proposition for old age pensions. In addition they were confronted with the senatorial race between Sheridan Downey and Philip Bancroft and the gubernatorial contest between Frank Merriam and Culbert Olson.

The Garrison Act was supported by the Democratic slate of candidates led by Culbert Olson, the McClatchy chain of newspapers, the *San Francisco News,* the Irrigation Districts Association of California, the League of California Municipalities, the California State Federation of Labor, the Railroad Brotherhoods, the California State Grange, and other groups of lesser importance. The act was opposed by almost all the newspapers of the state (with the two major exceptions noted above), the State Chamber of Commerce, the California Taxpayers' Association, the California State Federation of Women's Clubs, the Agricultural Council of California, the California Farm Bureau Federation, and several lesser groups.

To coördinate the campaign against revenue bond legislation a State Association against the Garrison Bond Act was formed. The Farm Bureau affiliated itself with this organization. The association centered its attack upon revenue bond legislation in general and upon the majority vote provision of the Garrison Act in particular. In a pamphlet entitled "Halt this Plunge into Squandermania," the association declared that all public bonds constituted private mortgages against property and that today's debts were tomorrow's taxes. This leaflet asserted that the Garrison Act opened the way for the creation of "hundreds of new boards and commissions, with dictatorial powers and arbitrary control over the expenditure of borrowed money."[10] It charged further that the act endangered school funds by removing taxable property from the tax rolls. Other publicity distributed by the association said that the Garrison Act was "a ruinous and radical scheme which would plaster every California farm with a new load of debt."[11]

Since the annual convention of the Farm Bureau would not meet until after the November elections, the Board of Directors of the state organization made the decision to oppose the act. The board declared that it opposed the act because it was too broad in scope, because it created too many new governmental agencies, and because it would repeal the sound custom of requiring a two-thirds vote for ratification of bond issues. In the campaign of 1938, however, the Farm Bureau devoted more time and money to urging popular ratification of the antiunion initiative proposition than it did to urging the rejection of the Garrison Revenue Bond Act.[12]

The State Grange campaigned vigorously in support of the act, although it was handicapped by inadequate financing and by the illness of Sehlmeyer during the concluding months of the campaign. The Grange devoted much of its publicity to defending the principle of revenue bond legislation. The affirmative argument, printed in the official voters' guide, was signed by Sehlmeyer, Senator Garrison, and Walter D. Wagner, the executive secretary of the Irrigation Districts Association of California. It stated that the act "merely gives communities, that have authority to acquire revenue producing projects, the right, by a majority vote, to finance them out of the revenues from the project itself instead of out of taxes."[13] The argument also pointed out that revenue bonds were in general use throughout the nation to finance public improvements without recourse to taxation.

The issue, as the Grange saw it, was clearly stated in the following article by Franklin Hichborn:

> The policy of the power companies is to oppose any water development which may threaten their monopoly of power production. Failing to prevent the water development, their next step is to block if possible the production of the by-product of the development, hydro-electric power. Failing there the power companies

plan to get control of the power, the development of which public funds have made possible....

To issue general obligation bonds a two-thirds vote is required. By misrepresentation, intimidation, appeal to prejudice and use of unlimited sums of money the power companies can often prevent the necessary two-thirds affirmative vote being cast. This means defeat of the bonds, failure to establish a publicly-owned distributing system for handling the Shasta power and leaves the power companies the only agency in the field to take the power over....

Revenue bonds on the other hand, requiring a majority vote for authorization take the two-thirds vote club out of power company hands. Reckless use of money may prevent a two-thirds affirmative vote; seldom, when the proposed public-ownership enterprise is sound can it prevent a majority affirmative vote.[14]

In the closing days of the campaign the Grange probably knew that the Garrison Act had little chance, that adverse publicity in a generally hostile press and high-pressure propaganda financed by the private power interests would prove too much for the meager resources of the Grange and the labor groups. The Grange was bitter. An editorial in the *Grange News* charged that there were only two reasons why some groups were supporting the private utility side of the argument: "1. The party is receiving filthy lucre to do so; 2. They are too stupid to realize what they are doing."[15]

Grange fears of defeat were realized in the fall when the voters overwhelmed the Garrison Act by a vote of 511,305 to 1,350,861. There were many reasons why the Garrison Act was rejected, but perhaps the most important is found in a comparison of funds expended by the two sides. The type of financing used by the Grange may be seen in an article in the *Grange News* telling of a meeting of Castle Grange No. 455 on October 21, 1938. This meeting, according to the newspaper account, unanimously passed a resolution to select one of the Grange members to campaign throughout Siskiyou County in support of the Garrison Act and to contribute five dollars "toward a fund for the education of the public in favor of this Act."[16] The only expenditure in support of the act reported to the Secretary of State was a sum of $510.15 spent by the State Grange.[17] The Pacific Gas and Electric Company admittedly expended $63,826.61 on its campaign to defeat the act.[18]

Central Valley Project

The Garrison Act was defeated, but the Democratic slate, led by Culbert Olson, a strong advocate of public ownership of electric power, won the election. Because of the voters' repudiation of revenue bond legislation, the new administration turned to other forms of legislation to accomplish the same purpose. The original Central Valley Project Act of 1933 had provided that the $170,000,000 bond authorization be reduced by the amount of any funds spent by the federal government in the construction of the project. This sum was frozen by adoption of the project by the Reclamation Bureau in 1937. To free any part of the original bond authorization, therefore, would require an amendment to the original act.[19]

The Olson administration proposed such an amendment in the Pierovich bill, which provided that the State Water Project Authority be authorized to issue revenue bonds for the purpose of acquiring or constructing power transmission and distribution facilities for use in connection with the project. The funds could be used directly for these purposes or could be lent to lesser political units which would take charge of the work. The intention of the bill was stated by Governor Olson in a special message to the senate in which he said:

> In order that the farmers may obtain water from the project at reasonable cost, revenues from electric power must bear a major portion of the financial burden of the project. To assure obtaining the necessary maximum power revenue for this purpose, and at the same time, provide for the delivery of electric power to the ultimate consumer at a reasonable price, it is essential that public agencies in addition to those already existing be organized which will be in a position to purchase and distribute the electric power to the people.[20]

This was a bill that the Grange could endorse wholeheartedly, since that organization had always contended that the transmission and distribution of electric power by publicly owned facilities would bring maximum revenue and the lowest possible rates.

The State Farm Bureau took no formal position on the Pierovich bill, though at least two of the strongest county Farm Bureaus vigorously opposed it. The Madera County Farm Bureau Board of Directors stated its opposition to the bill on the grounds that it would make $170,000,000 available for expenditure without first securing the approval of the voters of the state and that it would delay the completion of the project with federal funds. The San Joaquin County Farm Bureau Board of Directors opposed the bill on the grounds that it would put the state directly into the business of distributing electric power, that it would force municipalities to adopt public ownership, and that the whole movement "would in the end react to agricultural users of power in that very likely municipalities in setting up their districts would not include agriculture, and if agriculture is left out by itself, it will, of necessity, cause an increase in power rates."[21]

Neither the Grange nor the Farm Bureau, however, played a key role in the legislative battle over the bill. The struggle was essentially one of the Olson administration and all those who favored public ownership of power against the private power interests and groups allied to the utilities by financial or ideological considerations. The private utility lobbyists exerted tremendous pressure in the closing days of the session to secure a negative vote. These efforts were not without effect, for, although the Pierovich bill passed the senate by a vote of 24 to 15, it failed to gain a majority in the assembly.

Nothing daunted, Governor Olson decided to include the matter of public power legislation in his call for a special session of the state legislature to meet in January, 1940.[22] The administration's proposal was sponsored by Senators Garrison, Jespersen, Hollister, Kenny, Powers, and Shelley. It called for the "unfreezing" of $50,000,000 of the $170,000,000 originally authorized in 1933. These funds were to be used by the state for the construction of electric transmission and distribution facilities so that the state government would be in a position to contract with the federal government for the purchase and distribution of Shasta Dam power.

Once again the state organization of the Farm Bureau took no official position. Several county Farm Bureaus, however, including the Farm Bureaus of Merced, Kern, and Tulare counties, took firm stands against the proposed legislation. These Farm Bureaus stressed the importance of the Central Valley Project as a flood control and irrigation project and expressed fear that if funds were diverted to the construction of electrical distribution facilities the project as a whole might suffer. This opposition came from counties that needed water desperately but were little concerned with cheap power.

The State Grange once more supported the administration. It observed that, unless there were some agency in the field to compete with the Pacific Gas and Electric Company for the purchase of Shasta Dam power, private monopoly would be able to purchase the power on its own terms and sell it back to the public at a large profit. On January 22, 1940, over two hundred farmers, many of them Grangers, appeared at an open hearing of the Water Project Authority. In their testimony, many Grange members from the Sacramento Valley insisted that, since surplus water from the Sacramento Valley was to be diverted into the San Joaquin Valley, farmers in the northern valleys should at least receive cheap power in return. Sehlmeyer announced that the Grange would support any proposal to provide for public ownership of electric power and proclaimed that the Grange would fight any attempt to make the Central Valley Project "a water conservation plan that does not include the development and distribution of power."[23]

Once again, however, the proponents of public ownership, led by Sehlmeyer and Olson, were defeated. The administration's proposal to "unfreeze" $50,000,000 of Central Valley Project revenue bonds was blocked in committee by a coalition of Republicans and anti-Olson Democrats. These legislators, who had earlier formed an "economy bloc" to undermine the administration's unemployment relief policy, were now uniting to destroy other features of the Olson program as well.

Thus far the proponents of public ownership of power in California had been completely unsuccessful in their various attempts to secure this goal: revenue bond legislation had been vetoed in 1935, defeated by referendum vote in 1938, and tabled by legislative committee in 1939; proposals to "unfreeze" state bonds for the Central Valley Project had been blocked in the 1939 and 1940 sessions of the legislature. Late in 1940 it was decided, therefore, that another approach would have to be used. Frank Clark, the State Director of Public Works, and Governor Olson worked out a new idea, which received the strong endorsement of the California State Grange. The Olson administration suggested the creation of a federal regional authority, modeled after the Tennessee Valley Authority, that would assume complete control over all aspects of the Central Valley Project. The idea, however, met with such strong resistance that it was soon dropped. Harold Ickes refused to go along with any scheme that transferred control of the project from his own Department of the Interior. Then, too, most members of the California congressional delegation were decidedly cool toward the proposal. By the spring of 1941 the Olson administration had dropped its plan for a federal authority.[24]

But the proposal, once advanced, could not be so easily forgotten. The Grange, which had been influential in the formulation of the new approach, continued to publicize it, hoping that this plan might succeed where other plans had failed. The Grange continued to insist that there were thousands of farmers in the northern part of the state who would receive no benefit from the Central Valley Project unless it came in the form of cheap electrical energy. The Grange stated its support for the proposal in an editorial entitled "A California TVA Would Be Welcome."

Power and water should be provided at the lowest possible rate consistent with annual return sufficient to meet the amortization costs of the project. The cheaper power and water are obtainable when Central Valleys Project is completed, the more the people will benefit. The state legislature has refused to pass legislation which would make distribution of power from Shasta Dam by public ownership possible. If a federal set-up similar to the TVA, which has reduced rates materially in the Tennessee Valley, is necessary to bring the benefits of the Central Valley to the people, we are for it.[25]

The delegates to the annual convention of the State Grange in 1941 voted their endorsement of this view.[26]

The California Farm Bureau Federation aligned itself once more against the Grange. It continued to place primary emphasis upon the irrigation and flood control aspects of the project and to insist that power development remain a secondary phase. The Farm Bureau feared that a federal authority might sacrifice the water interests of the state to those of electric power. The Farm Bureau position was clearly stated in an article in its official publication.

... Our hopes and expectations were that the electric power developed would be used to pay a considerable portion of the cost of redistribution of water. It is now apparent that if the proposed policy of the Interior Department is carried out, no revenue may be expected from that source, and the burden on water will be so heavy as to make its use impractical to a large degree.[27]

A resolution passed by the delegates to the annual Farm Bureau convention in 1941 stated that the Farm Bureau was opposed to control by any federal authority that would deprive the state of jurisdiction over the waters within California. Another resolution declared that "the right to regulate, control and distribute the waters of all nonnavigable streams within the state is within the exclusive jurisdiction of the state" and urged that legislation be enacted to ensure that irrigation and flood control would continue to be the primary objectives of the project.[28]

The debate over the public power issue of the Central Valley Project from 1933 to 1941 was merely a prelude to longer, more violent, and more inclusive controversies over the project in all its phases in subsequent years. The struggle did not really begin in earnest until after 1941, and it has increased in intensity with each subsequent year as the construction of the physical plant of the project has drawn closer to completion.

18. STATE POLITICS AND REFORM

State politics in California during the 1930's were marked by corruption. Corruption of politics was certainly not unknown in other states, but in California the corruption was probably deeper and more widespread. Other states had their lobbies, legitimate and otherwise, but in California the power of the lobbyists was nearly supreme.

The strength of the lobbies, working honestly or corruptly, was in part due to the weakness of political parties in the state. The weakness of party organization, in turn, had many roots. The Progressive movement in the decade before the First World War had struck at "bossism" and, in so doing, had discredited the institution of government by party. Reforms enacted by the Progressives had weakened the influence of parties. Party labels had been eliminated from the ballot at local elections; provision for initiative, referendum, and recall had given impetus to the formation and strengthening of pressure groups; and the practice of cross-filing worked to confuse party lines, to elect minority candidates, and to destroy party discipline. A constitutional amendment ratified in 1934, which greatly extended the state civil service, virtually eliminated one important source of party patronage, one important method by which loyal party workers could be rewarded. Long-continued dominance of one party, the Republican, disrupted the unity of both the major parties. Finally, party discipline in California was weakened severely by the constant migration into the state of newcomers from other parts of the country. Party machines were difficult to organize and maintain when the voters within a particular district or precinct were a new group for nearly every election.

All these factors weakened the role played by the political party and enlarged the power of organized interest groups. In this atmosphere farm groups enjoyed political power rarely possessed by similar organizations in other states. Legislation affecting agriculture was rarely introduced as part of a party program; instead, it was usually written, sponsored, and steered through the legislative process to enactment by the Farm Bureau, the Grange, the Associated Farmers, the Agricultural Council, or the Agricultural Department of the State Chamber of Commerce.

The political power of the farm lobbies was enhanced by the passage of an amendment to the state constitution that gave rural counties predominant representation in the state senate.[1] Before 1928, representation in both houses of the legislature had been based upon "equal population" districts. The shift of population from northern to southern California and from rural to urban areas in the years 1910–1920 made rural legislators and politicians from northern California reluctant to enact reapportionment legislation that would surrender their traditional control of state politics to the new centers of population. It proved impossible to provide for reapportionment on the basis of "equal population" districts in the legislative sessions of 1921, 1923, and 1925. To break this deadlock, and to guarantee the continued dominance of rural and northern California, farmer organizations of the state, in coöperation with urban groups in northern California, drew up a constitutional amendment that was presented to the voters in the form of an initiative proposition in 1926. This proposal, called the "Federal Plan," provided that assembly districts would continue to be based upon population but that senatorial districts would be based on the counties, with not more than one senatorial district per county and with not more than three counties in any one district.

The Farm Bureau, the Grange, the Farmers' Union, and the Agricultural Legislative Committee coöperated with the San Francisco Chamber of Commerce to secure popular ratification of this proposal. The farm organizations declared that their plan was analogous to the provision of the federal constitution for equal political representation of the various states in the United States Senate. The farm groups also played on the well-grounded fear that, if their proposition failed, the corrupt city politicians of Los Angeles, San Francisco, and

Alameda counties would dominate both houses of the legislature. Further, they insisted that the farmer needed protective legislation to insure his prosperity and that prosperity for agriculture meant economic happiness for the entire state. The proposition was endorsed by a popular vote of approximately four to three. Representation in the state legislature was reapportioned in 1931 on the basis of the 1930 census and in accordance with the provisions of the "Federal Plan." Predominant representation of the "cow" or "landscape" counties in the senate was assured.

This did not always mean, however, that the farmers of the state controlled the senate, for the operation of the plan had consequences that were not anticipated when it was enacted. The plan was designed, in part, to secure strong representation for the agricultural interests of the state, but it actually resulted in underrepresentation for many of the most dominantly agricultural counties. For example, the counties of Los Angeles, Fresno, Santa Clara, Kern, and San Joaquin were among the ten counties having the largest total population, the largest rural population, and the highest annual value of agricultural production, but each of these counties was entitled to only one senator.[2]

Furthermore, private interests often found it easier to influence rural legislators than political representatives with urban constituencies. Rural senators were obliged to vote "correctly" on matters of purely local importance if they wished to secure reëlection, but often they were free to vote as they wished on many other matters, matters with which rural constituencies were not vitally concerned. This fact permitted corporate interests to influence votes on many important issues. However, next to the state and local Chambers of Commerce, probably the most powerful legitimate group influence upon legislators was that exercised by the county Farm Bureaus and the state Farm Bureau Federation. Of less influence was the Grange, which often was obliged to seek support for its program among urban legislators. It is not surprising, then, that the Farm Bureau stoutly defended the "Federal Plan" throughout the 1930's against all attempts to revise the constitution so as to make population the only basis for legislative representation, but the Grange occasionally participated in such attempts at revision.

In 1933 the state legislature placed on the ballot for the 1934 election a proposition calling for a constitutional convention. This proposition was endorsed by the slim margin of 705,915 to 668,080. It was the obligation of the next legislature, meeting in 1935, to provide the machinery for calling together the convention. But the 1935 legislature could not agree upon an acceptable plan for apportioning the delegates and, dominated by fear of the strength of radical sentiment, refused to take any action whatever. During the debate that year, the Board of Directors of the Farm Bureau insisted that representation in any convention must be based on existing assembly and senatorial districts. The Executive Committee of the State Grange, on the other hand, toyed with the idea of supporting a move for a unicameral legislature.[3]

Although no provision was made for the calling of a convention, the State Grange did join with other groups in advocating a unicameral legislature. In November, 1935, the delegates to the annual meeting of the State Grange endorsed the principle of unicameralism in a resolution stating that two houses were unsatisfactory and a burden upon the taxpayer and that a one-house legislature would be more efficient and progressive and would enact better laws with less political strife. George Sehlmeyer declared that the senate, which was supposed to represent the farmers, had often voted against the farmers' interests.[4] An editorial in the *California Grange News* stated Grange opposition to the existing political system.

... A few years ago we secured what is called the Federal Plan of Reapportionment. How did it work out? The rural sections were supposed to control the Senate, but they don't. In 1935 the Senate was 90% under the control of so-called big business. As far as the farmer is concerned the plan is about a 100% failure. The best support agriculture had came from the Senators from San Francisco and Los Angeles.[5]

Franklin Hichborn, writing in the Grange News, accused the senate of being a reactionary house "where the dirt farmers have found small comfort and little satisfaction.... The dirt farmers are progressive; the swivel chair farmers are at best the tools of reaction."[6]

When independent progressive politicians in the state drew up definite plans for a unicameral legislature based upon population alone, however, the Grange discovered that it could no longer go along with the movement. In 1937 the Grange passed a resolution stating that, though it favored unicameralism in principle, it could not support any proposal that would base representation on population alone, since a legislature so constructed could not possibly understand and appreciate the complex problems of diverse areas. This position remained the official policy of the Grange in subsequent years.[7]

The Farm Bureau never considered supporting any scheme for unicameralism, no matter what the proposed basis of representation. The annual conventions of that organization in 1935 and 1937 stated their opposition to any change in the existing system of representation. In 1937, the State Chamber of Commerce, fearful that an attempt to place on the ballot an initiative proposition calling for establishment of unicameralism might succeed, created a special Committee for California against the Unicameral Legislative Initiative. This committee was headed by C. C. Teague, president of the California Fruit Growers' Exchange, and included representatives from the Farm Bureau, the Associated Farmers, the Farmers' Union, and the Agricultural Council, in addition to representatives from such nonfarm groups as the American Legion, the California Real Estate Association, and the California Taxpayers' Association. These groups were spared an expensive campaign, for the unicameral proposition failed to qualify for a place on the ballot.[8]

The Associated Farmers defended the existing system of representation on the ground that it provided protection for the farmer against radical legislation sponsored by labor-dominated legislators from urban areas. After the stormy legislative session of 1937, during which the Associated Farmers in coöperation with the Farm Bureau and other conservative groups succeeded in blocking much progressive legislation, the Associated Farmers stated its official position.

... What would have resulted in the 1937 Legislature if the Senate had been nonexistent and the Assembly had been the sole legislative body?

The Assembly passed the lop-sided Yorty labor relations act which set up unfair practices for employers, but placed no restrictions whatever on labor unions or workers. The Senate killed it. The Assembly voted some $30,000,000 in special appropriations which were killed in the Senate. The Assembly voted a pardon for Tom Mooney; the Senate refused to concur. . . .

To the State of California, whether rural or urban, a One-House Legislature, during 1937, would have been little short of disastrous. The Senate is accused by proponents of the One-House scheme of having leaned to the side of conservatism. The Assembly, it can be said with greater truth, leaned to the side of radicalism. But out of the two came a "balance of power"—a middle-of-the-road program that was fair to city and country, liberal and conservative, relief recipient and taxpayer—and that after all, is representative government—the plan of democracy![9]

In the face of the opposition of most groups except labor, and with but lukewarm support from the Grange, all attempts to secure a unicameral legislature failed.

The Grange took the lead in another movement for political reform, a movement to secure legislation curbing political corruption through the regulation of lobbying activities. This crusade for clean politics began in 1935 with the introduction of a "purity-in-elections" bill by two Grange legislators, Senator J. C. Garrison and Assemblyman Hugh P. Donnelly, both of Stanislaus County. The proposed bill made it unlawful for any corporation to contribute to the political campaign of any candidate for public office. The Garrison-Donnelly bill was defeated, however, largely through the influence of the interests that it sought to regulate.[10]

After the Garrison Revenue Bond Act was rejected in the referendum of 1938, the Grange determined to accelerate its campaign for strict regulation of the activities of private lobbyists. This determination was deepened after the publication early in 1939 of the Philbrick report, which furnished documentary proof of widespread corruption in state politics. During the 1939 session of the legislature, Assemblyman Hugh Donnelly introduced a bill that required all lobbyists appearing before the state legislature to register with the government and to declare whom they represented and what they were being paid. This bill, like the Garrison-Donnelly bill, failed to pass the assembly despite vigorous Grange support. The Grange pointed out that the very refusal of the legislature to pass such reforms constituted additional evidence that they were sorely needed. In 1941 Assemblyman Donnelly introduced another "purity-in-elections" bill, which required each lobbyist to file data on the conditions and terms of his employment. By this time the anti-Olson "economy bloc" dominated the legislature, however, and the bill failed to receive even the slight attention the Garrison-Donnelly bill had received in 1939. There is no evidence that any farm organization other than the Grange lent active support to these proposals to curb political corruption through the regulation of lobbying activities.[11]

Farm organizations in California never openly entered political campaigns for the election or defeat of a particular candidate or party. Each organization insisted that it had nothing whatsoever to do with partisan politics. Yet farm groups inevitably became involved in politics. Each organization had its own program that it wished to see enacted into legislation. To secure favorable legislation, each group had to support those legislators who were friendly to its policies; conversely, to secure the votes of the members of farm organizations, each legislator had to grant favors to the group or groups most influential in his own district. Farm organizations did not formally endorse the candidacies of particular politicians; there were, however, other effective means by which farmers could reward their friends and punish their enemies.

During the depression decade, the Grange strongly supported certain legislators, and these legislators in return sponsored Grange legislation. The following progressive Republicans were usually on the Grange side of every problem: Senator H. C. Jones, Santa Clara County; Senator J. M. Inman, Sacramento County; Senator Chris N. Jespersen, San Luis Obispo County; Assemblyman Percy G. West, Sacramento County; and Assemblyman Michael Burns, Humboldt County. The following Democrats coöperated closely with the Grange: Senator J. C. Garrison, Stanislaus County; Senator Culbert L.

Olson, Los Angeles County; and Assemblyman Hugh Donnelly, Stanislaus County. Of these legislators the following were active Grange members and leaders: Burns, who was also a member of the Machinists' Union; Donnelly, who was a member of Turlock Grange; Jespersen, who was a delegate to several conventions of the State Grange; and Garrison, who was Master of Stanislaus Pomona Grange in 1934 and served as chairman of the Legislative Committee at the annual conventions of the Grange from 1934 through 1938. Both Garrison and Jespersen were also members of the Farm Bureau; the latter served, at one time, as president of the San Luis Obispo County Farm Bureau. Many of the legislators upon whom the Grange relied for support of its program came from counties where the Grange was either weak or nonexistent; among these were Jespersen, Olson, and Burns. In the early part of the decade the Grange program was usually sponsored by Republican legislators who belonged to the old progressive wing of the party, but in the later years of the period the Grange worked increasingly often through the Democratic party. Its alliance with the Democratic party was especially strong in the years 1939 to 1943, when the Grange supported Governor Olson's program and the administration in turn backed many Grange proposals.[12]

The Farm Bureau, on the other hand, usually worked with conservative Republicans and, in the later period, with the anti-Olson Democrats of the "economy bloc." These anti-Olson Democrats were led by Seth Millington of Butte County and Gordon Garland of Tulare County. The following Republicans frequently sponsored Farm Bureau legislation: Senator Frank L. Gordon, Napa County; Senator Ray Hays, Fresno County; Senator Bradford Crittenden, San Joaquin County; Senator Andrew R. Schottky, Merced County; Senator J. I. Wagy, Kern County; Senator Frank W. Mixter, Tulare County; Assemblyman John Phillips, Riverside County; Assemblyman M. S. Meeker, Fresno County; and Assemblyman George A. Clarke, Merced County. Unlike the Grange, the Farm Bureau exerted greatest influence over legislators from those counties in which the farm organization itself was large and powerful.

Throughout the 1930's George Sehlmeyer was the Grange as far as most legislators were concerned. Occasionally, as during consideration of the Jones Mortgage Moratorium Bill in 1935 or during the battle over the prorate amendment in 1939, Sehlmeyer called on Grange members to come to Sacramento to influence the course of legislation. Legal advice was furnished to Sehlmeyer by Charles Busick. These two men carried nearly the entire load of legislative work for the Grange.

In contrast, the Farm Bureau lobby was a large and smoothly functioning machine. In addition to the president of the Farm Bureau, who was usually in fairly constant residence in Sacramento during legislative sessions, the following executive officers were present at all times: the legal counsel (Edson Abel, later R. L. Miller, and then I. H. Pfaffenberger); the director of the Research Department, Von T. Ellsworth; and the director of the Law and Utilities Department, J. J. Deuel. In addition to this staff, the following representatives of the Farm Bureau were active in Sacramento during the 1935 session of the legislature: Alex Johnson, Col. Fred Robson, Tom Robertson, George Wilson, Mrs. Ahart, John Watson, and Ernest Vehlow.[13]

The lobbying methods of the Farm Bureau were thorough and painstaking. During the 1937 session of the legislature Von T. Ellsworth and R. L. Miller analyzed more than four thousand bills that might affect agriculture directly or remotely. On the basis of these analyses the Board of Directors of the Farm Bureau and the chairmen of the various commodity departments, meeting in the second week in March, agreed upon the official attitude of the Farm Bureau toward each one. In 1941 an even more detailed legislative analysis was made. Ellsworth surveyed more than four thousand bills and assigned those of interest to agriculture to the Farm Bureau officer best qualified to understand the terms of the proposed bill. Each bill was studied, and a brief report was made on each. On the basis of these studies the Board of Directors of the Farm Bureau, meeting from March 4 to 6, 1941, determined final policy.[14]

State Politics and Reform

The lobbying activities of the Farm Bureau did not stop with legislative analyses. Beginning in 1935, Von T. Ellsworth kept county Farm Bureaus informed of the progress of agricultural bills through the distribution of legislative news letters. Through this medium the mass support of local units could be rallied in support or opposition of a particular vital measure. The county Farm Bureaus maintained close relationships with local assemblymen and senators. Time after time, in every county in which the Bureau was influential, legislators were invited to attend meetings of the county Farm Bureaus. In the long run, these meetings were effective in gaining the legislators' support for Farm Bureau projects.[15] Von T. Ellsworth reported at the annual convention of the C.F.B.F. in November, 1937:

Many county farm bureaus now regularly follow the policy of periodically discussing farm bureau legislative program with their legislators or congressmen, as the case might be, and with the farm bureau legislative representative. Experience indicates that harmony and cooperation result from such joint conferences.[16]

The Associated Farmers was represented in Sacramento during legislative sessions from 1936 to 1939 by Philip Bancroft. Bancroft also served as chairman of the Deciduous Fruit Department of the California Farm Bureau and occasionally wrote articles on pending legislation for the Farm Bureau. The executive officers of the Associated Farmers also came to Sacramento from time to time to exert influence on legislation that the organization considered to be of special importance. The effectiveness of the Associated Farmers as a lobbying group, however, was hampered by its known connection with industrial and urban groups and by its record of violence in agricultural strikes.

In summary, in the field of politics the Grange worked congenially with progressive Republicans and with liberal Democrats; the Farm Bureau worked in harmony with conservative Republicans and with a few conservative Democrats; whereas the Associated Farmers coöperated only with the most conservative Republican legislators. The Farm Bureau and the

Associated Farmers were satisfied with the system of representation by county in the state senate and did not participate in any of the reform movements to regulate political corruption. The Grange, on the other hand, was active in all political reform movements. Of the three groups, the Farm Bureau had by far the most skillful, efficient, and effective lobby.

19.

FARM GROUPS IN POLITICS
1929–1941

In spite of their repeated assertions of nonpartisanship, farm organizations played an active and significant role in California state politics in the 1930's. Although farm organizations never endorsed political candidates for office, leaders of these groups worked for the election of candidates they believed would be sympathetic to their policies and programs. It is impossible, of course, to estimate the degree to which members of the organizations followed the advice of their leaders when it came to casting their votes.

When Governor James Rolph took office in 1931, George H. Hecke, who had been State Director of Agriculture since 1919, resigned and refused reappointment. His action was a blow to the Rolph administration, for Hecke had the confidence and support of all farm organizations and of the farm press. To succeed Hecke the State Board of Agriculture recommended the appointment of either A. A. Brock or Professor R. L. Adams, either of whom would have been acceptable to agricultural interests. Rolph ignored this advice and sentiment, however, and appointed Dudley Moulton, who had formerly been Agricultural Commissioner of the County of San Francisco and who was a personal friend of the new governor. Moulton was in trouble from the day he took office in July, 1931, until he was dismissed in February, 1933. He failed to work in coöperation with the State Board of Agriculture; his relations with the United States Department of Agriculture were never cordial; and there were constant rumors of corruption within his department. Charges and countercharges, resignations and dismissals, were daily occurrences.[1]

In the midst of this political turmoil, the State Grange met for its annual convention in October, 1932. There were strong rumors that the Grange would demand the recall of Governor Rolph, but Sehlmeyer insisted that, though several Subordinate Granges were asking for such action, the State Grange did not contemplate going to this extreme. From the convention came a resolution demanding a sweeping investigation of the departments of Finance, Agriculture, and Public Works, but Rolph was not mentioned by name nor was there any hint of a recall movement.

In December, 1932, Moulton took a step that thoroughly undermined the already sagging prestige of the Rolph administration: he arbitrarily fired George K. York, supervisor of the federal-state Market News Service for the State of California. Rolph and Nils A. Olsen of the United States Department of Agriculture forced the reinstatement of York, but friendly relations between the federal and state governments could not be restored.²

Soon after the legislature convened in January, 1933, Senator J. M. Inman, a close personal and political friend of Sehlmeyer, launched an investigation of the Rolph administration. On the basis of his committee's findings of maladministration and financial irregularities (if not full-fledged corruption), the Executive Committee of the State Grange decided to institute recall proceedings against Rolph as soon as the National Grange would sanction this move. The decision was announced publicly on January 23, 1933. Three days later Sehlmeyer announced that the National Grange had no opposition to recall action and that the State Grange would start the circulation of petitions charging the Rolph administration with maladministration, financial extravagance, and general incompetence.³

Opposition to the Grange's action soon developed. Vince Garrod, president of the Farmers' Union, accused Sehlmeyer of playing politics on the side of the Democratic Party; the Agricultural Legislative Committee declared it would have nothing to do with the movement; James M. Cremin, a Grange member from Marysville, claimed that Sehlmeyer had not consulted the membership in this matter; Thomas Mathews, president of the Yuba County Farm Bureau, declared that the whole affair was a "huge joke"; Senator John McColl observed that the movement was sponsored by "a few agitators who would rather raise hell than work on their own farms"; and even Senator Inman announced that he would take no part in the agitation. Opponents of Sehlmeyer's action pointed out that Rolph's term was nearly over and that recall proceedings would cost the state a half million dollars and asserted that in any event, if the facts were correct and the evidence sufficient, impeachment, not recall, was the proper and legal remedy. Early in February, Yreka Subordinate Grange threatened to institute recall proceedings against Sehlmeyer if he continued circulation of the petitions, and Joseph Holmes, Past Master of the State Grange, called on the National Grange to investigate the political activities of the Executive Committee of the California State Grange. Masters of all the Granges in Santa Clara County, representing over a thousand Grange members, voted to oppose the movement. In the face of this opposition, the State Grange decided to delay circulation of the petitions until the final conclusions of the Inman Committee's investigation were released.

The agitation had some effect on the governor, however. Rolph requested Moulton's resignation, and, when Moulton refused to resign, the governor dismissed him. On February 23, 1933, A. A. Brock, a candidate who was acceptable to all farm groups in the state, was appointed to the office of State Director of Agriculture. With the dismissal of Moulton the Grange lost its primary issue, and, with widespread opposition to the recall movement within the Grange threatening to disrupt that organization, the Executive Committee decided to drop the whole affair. The movement for recall collapsed completely, but not before it had forced the dismissal of Moulton.[4]

In the political maneuvering that preceded the 1934 campaign the Grange played an indirect role. Many Grange leaders and members were interested in the career of Sheridan Downey, a young Sacramento lawyer who had attracted some attention as chief counsel for the Inman Committee's investigation of the Rolph administration. The June and July issues of the *California Grange News* carried two long articles by Downey in which he presented his analysis of the economic crisis and his plan for ending depression. Downey maintained, in these articles, that the root of depression was the maldistribution of wealth; income and capital were concentrated in the hands of the wealthy few, and the masses suffered because of insufficient purchasing power. Some of the remedial measures Downey suggested included: currency inflation, government control of production, regulation of capital savings, limitation of income, and creation of a state corporation with power to purchase the products of farm and factory and to assure fair wages, prices, and income. Downey dramatically portrayed the contradictions of want in the midst of plenty.

Here still are the fertile farms, capable of giving to our people in generous abundance all the food that we could use, but their owners approach despair; and past these, too, flows the vast and somber multitude of the idle, seeking work they cannot find and food they are denied though, from its superabundance, it rots and decays in the land....
Our only problem is one of distributing increasing wealth and allocating increasing leisure. To accomplish this we must build a bridge from producer to consumer....[5]

At the annual convention of the State Grange in October, 1933, Downey was permitted to address the delegates. In his speech he announced his advocacy of government ownership of banks, artificial stimulation of workers' incomes, regulation of corporation surpluses, decentralization of great fortunes, unemployment insurance, and government guarantees of employment. On the following day, October 20, 1933, Downey announced his candidacy for the office of governor. Downey continued to address Grange meetings throughout the state during the winter and spring of 1933 and 1934.[6]

Sometime in May, however, Downey had a conversation with Upton Sinclair, candidate for nomination as governor on the Democratic ticket on an "End Poverty in California" (E.P.I.C.) platform. In this conversation Downey pointed out that he had the support of the Grange and the Railroad Brotherhoods and advised Sinclair that the E.P.I.C. program of "production for use" could never succeed in one state alone. By the conclusion of this meeting, however, Sinclair had persuaded Downey to surrender his own candidacy for governor and to run for lieutenant governor on the E.P.I.C. platform.[7]

Farm Groups in Politics

At the Grange convention held just before the general elections in 1934, all political resolutions were banned from consideration, and Downey, though present, was not permitted to speak.[8] The *Grange News* did, however, carry publicity favorable to the E.P.I.C. program. One article said:

> Well, he [Sinclair] proposes to repeal the sales tax. I'm for that. Then he proposes to levy an income tax that will whittle the greedy big-grabbers down to my size. That suits me. He's going to have us produce for use instead of profits. That means we'll have plenty of everything. I've got three boys coming out of school and no jobs for them. He's going to see that every person that wants a job can have it. When we produce too much, instead of being out of work—we'll take a vacation with pay. That sounds mighty good. I'm for Upton Sinclair.[9]

This article did not represent official Grange policy, since the Grange could not endorse any candidate, but it did reflect the opinions of Sehlmeyer, who controlled the official publication of the organization. It is reasonable to suppose that many Grangers cast their votes for E.P.I.C. candidates but that many others voted for the victorious Republican candidates, Merriam and Hatfield.

The Farm Bureau, on the other hand, though bound by the same self-imposed prohibition against official endorsement of any candidate, was unmistakably friendly to the campaign of Frank Merriam. A Merriam for Governor Farmers' Committee had the active support of the following Farm Bureau leaders: Roy K. Cole, Fred J. Hart, E. C. Kimball, Ben H. Schulte, Amon Swank, and U. B. Tyler. Also serving on this committee were Philip Bancroft, Holmes Bishop, and Forrest Frick of the Associated Farmers and George R. Harrison, Master of the State Grange from 1921 to 1929.[10] In the gubernatorial race that followed, Merriam won a plurality of the votes cast. Downey polled nearly two hundred thousand more votes than Sinclair on the same ticket and barely missed defeating the Republican candidate for lieutenant governor, George J. Hatfield.

The Farm Bureau worked in friendly coöperation with the Merriam administration from 1935 to 1939. It is true that the governor forgot to sign several routine bills sponsored by the Farm Bureau during the 1937 session of the legislature, but R. W. Blackburn, the president of the Farm Bureau at that time, talked to the governor and was assured that nothing of this sort would occur again. During the special session of the legislature in 1938, Merriam made up for his oversight by affixing his signature to the resubmitted routine bills. At the 1937 convention of the Farm Bureau, Merriam addressed the delegates on the subject of taxation and legislative reform and, it was said, made a "profound impression" on the large audience present.[11]

During these years the Grange chose to work with Culbert Olson, Democratic senator from Los Angeles. At the conclusion of the 1935 legislative session the Grange drew up a chart of legislative votes on fourteen measures that seemed to be of special importance to the Grange program. Senators and assemblymen were listed as voting "good" or "bad" on each of these key issues. Of all the senators in the legislature, Culbert Olson came off with the best voting record in the eyes of the Grange—fourteen "good" votes. Not even the Grange senators, Garrison and Jespersen, had done this well: Garrison was listed as having cast twelve "good" votes and two "bad" ones; Jespersen had cast eleven "good" votes and one "bad" one and had been absent on two occasions. Senators McGovern of San Francisco and Perry of Humboldt County were also included among those having excellent records. On this same chart, Senator Sanborn Young, conservative Republican and the chairman in 1938 of the special committee to support the antiunion initiative proposition sponsored by the Farm Bureau, was recorded by the Grange as having cast fourteen "bad" votes. Other senators listed as having completely "bad" records were Duval, McCormack, Snyder, and Stow.[12]

It is not surprising, in view of these facts, that in the 1938 gubernatorial contest the Grange supported Culbert Olson, whereas the Farm Bureau indirectly promoted the candidacy of the incumbent, Governor Merriam. Neither organization officially endorsed either candidate, but there could be little doubt of where the sympathies of the two groups lay. Olson campaigned vigorously against the antiunion initiative proposition and warmly defended the Garrison Revenue Bond Act.

In view of the nature of the Democratic campaign that year, it was inevitable that the Grange would hope and work for Olson's election and the Farm Bureau for his defeat.

Farmers of the state were also interested in the contest that year between Philip Bancroft and Sheridan Downey for United States Senator.[18] Philip Bancroft had served on the Executive Committee of the Associated Farmers from 1934 to 1938 and had been one of the vice-presidents of that organization in 1936 and again in 1938. He had also served as Chairman of the Deciduous Fruit Department of the California Farm Bureau Federation. Bancroft's platform stated these principles: 1) that labor unions be made responsible before the law; 2) that sit-down strikes be outlawed; 3) that the National Labor Relations Act be amended to prevent the National Labor Relations Board from turning the country over to the Communist-dominated C.I.O.; 4) that public and union offices be denied to Communists; 5) that aliens be purged from the relief rolls and that the entire relief setup be freed from the influence of "politics and sob-sisters"; 6) that five years' residence be required to qualify for county and state relief, and fifteen years' residence for old-age assistance; 7) that reciprocal trade agreement legislation be repealed; and 8) that such New Deal reforms as the Federal Deposit Insurance Corporation and the Securities Exchange Commission be supported. In addition to the personal, though not official, support of his friends in the Associated Farmers and the Farm Bureau, Bancroft had the backing of Senator Hiram Johnson, Herbert Hoover, former Governor George Pardee, Charles Real (a Bay Area official of the A.F. of L.), and the Republican newspapers of the state.

Downey had the unofficial support of many Grange leaders and members, of organized labor, of progressives generally, and of the "Ham-and-Egger's," whose old-age pension proposition he endorsed. Downey campaigned for public ownership and distribution of power, the Garrison Revenue Bond Act, conservation of natural resources, broad social security welfare measures, and the "thirty dollars every Thursday" pension scheme.

It was against Downey's connections with the "Ham-and-Egger's" that Bancroft directed most of his campaign oratory. Downey, in return, concentrated his fire upon the antilabor policies of Bancroft and especially upon his record of action as a leader of the Associated Farmers. One election pamphlet printed by Downey supporters said of Bancroft:

> Let us examine the professed doctrines of this millionaire walnut-grower from Contra Costa County. Beside him, Herbert Hoover, the Californian whom California rejected by half a million votes, is a mild royalist, a watery individualist.
> Mr. Bancroft is not a wolf in sheep's clothing; he is a ruthless wolf in wolf's gray skin, a wolf who runs with his pack and knows no law but the law of tooth and claw.[14]

In the general elections, Downey defeated Bancroft by over three hundred thousand votes; Olson beat his Republican opponent, Frank Merriam, by a substantial majority. The antiunion initiative proposition, the Garrison Revenue Bond Act, and the "Ham-and-Egg" proposition were all turned down by the voters.[15]

Immediately following Olson's election there were rumors that the incoming governor would appoint George Sehlmeyer to the post of State Director of Agriculture. The *Sacramento Bee*, in making public this rumor, pointed out that Sehlmeyer had been friendly to Olson's candidacy and that the two were in agreement on many issues.[16] Sehlmeyer, who was then recovering from a serious illness, denied that he had any ambitions to hold government office. He also advised the governor-elect that the Grange was perfectly satisfied with the Department of Agriculture as it had been administered by A. A. Brock. Three months after Olson took office, however, Brock resigned to make way for an Olson appointee, William B. Parker, one-time president of the powerful San Joaquin Farm Bureau. Parker brought with him as assistant director, Sidney G. Rubinow, the publicity director of the California Farm Bureau Federation from 1936 to 1939. Parker loyally supported Olson's program, especially during the battles for drastic amendment of the Agricultural Prorate Act and for enactment of the Pierovich Central Valley Project bill in 1939.[17]

Sehlmeyer and Olson remained on friendly terms throughout the latter's administration. Olson frequently called upon Sehlmeyer for advice on diverse economic and political issues. Sehlmeyer's suggestions were occasionally ignored, of course, or overridden by other political friends of the governor. But the Master of the State Grange and the governor agreed on policy for the Central Valley Project, labor relations, administration of unemployment relief, and agricultural marketing. Officials of the Olson administration were often guest speakers on the monthly Grange radio program. Sehlmeyer was appointed by Olson to the State Board of Harbor Commissioners, an appointment that was confirmed by the senate in April, 1939, with only three dissenting votes.[18]

Olson also tried to coöperate with leaders of the Farm Bureau: he frequently called Farm Bureau leaders in for conferences on agricultural policy; he consulted Ray Wiser on unemployment relief administration policy; and he attempted to give favorable consideration to routine Farm Bureau legislation. The attitude of Ray Wiser toward this last service was recorded in the minutes of the meeting of the Board of Directors of the Sacramento County Farm Bureau on February 20, 1940 as follows:

Mr. Wiser in mentioning the past Legislature at regular session, stated that this was the first administration in power in the State that had signed all bills passed, sponsored by the Farm Bureau, but one and the Farm Bureau had agreed that this would be better revised and presented at the next legislature.[19]

But except on routine matters the policies of the Farm Bureau and those of the Olson administration were diametrically opposed; there was little real basis for successful coöperation. With the Associated Farmers, Olson had even less of a basis for coöperation. Olson's outspoken attacks on that group, including his testimony before the La Follette Committee in 1939, and the parallel attacks of the Associated Farmers on Olson had aggravated basic mutual feelings of distrust and antagonism.

During the 1939 session of the legislature, the Farm Bureau and the Associated Farmers were on the defensive against the comprehensive program for reform proposed by Olson and supported by Sehlmeyer and the Grange. The Farm Bureau sponsored an absolute minimum of legislation of its own, to conserve its energies for blocking the "radical" Olson program. In its fight, the Farm Bureau had the support of the Associated Farmers and the Agricultural Council. The Grange-endorsed Olson program won substantial victories in drastic amendment of the Agricultural Prorate Act and in relief appropriations and policy, but it suffered defeat on legislative proposals relating to labor relations, social legislation, taxation, and public ownership of electric power in the Central Valley Project. In securing the defeat of a major part of the Olson program, the Farm Bureau worked closely with three Democratic assemblymen who, in 1940, were to form the core of the "economy bloc": Seth Millington, of Butte County; Gordon Garland, a citrus grower of Tulare County; and Clinton J. Fulcher, of Modoc County.[20]

The Associated Farmers claimed major credit for the defeat of Olson's program. Philip Bancroft, reporting to the annual convention of the Associated Farmers in December, 1939, declared that not one of the 140-odd bills opposed by the group had been passed and jubilantly announced:

> In conclusion we wish to call your attention to the fact that the Governor has more than once publicly stated that our organization was responsible for the defeat of his 1939 legislative program, and your Committee wishes to take this occasion to extend our sincere thanks to Governor Olson for having paid the Associated Farmers the highest compliment that a governor could possibly have paid to any group of men in the United States.[21]

In the fall of 1939 Governor Olson addressed the annual conventions of both the Grange and the Farm Bureau. The Grange was deeply disappointed over the defeat of the administration's measures. When Olson told the Grange delegates that he would continue to fight for public ownership of electric power and when he appealed to the Grangers for support in retiring those legislators who had blocked his program into a "nice, peaceful, private life," they applauded him vigorously.[22] In contrast with the warm reception the Grange gave him, Olson's reception by the delegates to the Farm Bureau convention was cold and hostile. In his speech before that group, the governor made no attempt to conciliate Farm Bureau leaders, who had played a major part in blocking his program. He reviewed his program for "production for use" to replace the cash dole, for generous old-age assistance, for sympathetic labor legislation, for cheap electric power and cheap water, for marketing legislation to protect the dirt farmer, and for major tax revision, and he sarcastically expressed mock surprise that Farm Bureau leaders should oppose such worthy measures.[23] In view of the content and tone of the speech, Governor Olson could hardly have expected any reception but the one he was given.

During the special legislative sessions in 1940 and throughout the regular 1941 session, the political alignments were the same. The Farm Bureau and the Associated Farmers united with other groups and politicians to limit relief appropriations, to destroy the State Relief Administration, and to prevent the passage of labor legislation, public power bills, tax reform measures, and legislation to regulate lobbying activities. The Farm Bureau and the Associated Farmers were generally pleased with the rout of Democratic forces; the Grange was disgusted. An editorial in the *Grange News* of June 20, 1941, attacked the state Legislature.

Servants of the People?

Resembling a circus more than a decorous law-making body, the California State Legislature early this week wound up its 54th biennial session and went home.

What with the political bickering and not enough time for serious consideration of vital issues at hand the legislature adjourned leaving approximately one hundred thousand persons in the state without means of support and left a state agency [the State Relief Administration] in the embarrassing position of not having enough funds to continue and having no authority nor funds to dissolve its operations and abide by state law in the payment of its employees.

It is sincerely to be hoped that California is in for better legislative days and that this important body can be improved to properly serve the public it represents.[24]

20. SUMMARY AND CONCLUSION

The attitudes and actions of California farm organizations from 1929 to 1941 were determined by economic depression and the peculiar structure of agriculture in the state. During the depression years farmers were caught between falling prices and relatively high and stable cash costs. The prolonged depression was attended by a myriad of new problems that had to be solved if the farmers of the state were to survive and continue production. In view of the complex economic and social structure of California agriculture, it is not surprising that various farm groups arrived at different answers and took divergent actions.

Because of the multiplicity of contradictory economic interests, California farmers did not constitute a homogeneous group. One factor that made for disunity was the great variation in the size of farms and the type of farm operation. A social pyramid existed. At the apex were a few large industrial farmers, cultivating thousands of acres and employing thousands of transient laborers. At the next level was a larger group composed of substantial commercial farmers, who had heavy investments in land, building, and equipment and who hired many migratory workers during the harvest season. The third and by far the largest single group was made up of small and part-time farmers, who often farmed on too small a scale to permit an adequate return on capital investment or to provide a decent family income. Forming the base of the pyramid were the thousands of farm laborers, often of alien race and culture, who could never hope to become an established part of the communities through which they drifted. Although these groups had many grievances in common, each had its own peculiar economic problems, social views, and political prejudices, which were often in conflict with those of the other groups.

Summary and Conclusion

California farmers were also divided by their specialization in greatly diverse crops, each with its own climatic, agronomic, technical, managerial, marketing, and labor requirements and problems. And, finally, the indisputable fact of regionalism separated farmers one from the other. The problems and needs of farmers in one section of the state often varied from those in another, and the great distances between them made common understanding difficult.

The attitudes, policies, and actions of the various farm organizations reflected these diversities and conflicts. The reaction of each group to the issues of the 1930's depended upon various factors: the size and type of farm operation represented by its membership, the geographic location of its membership, the character of its leadership, its organizational structure, and its historical development.

The California State Grange, founded in 1873, was the oldest farm group in the state. It enjoyed great influence during the turbulent decade of the 1870's, but it played a very small role in the historical development of the state during the next four or five decades. Gaining renewed strength in the years following the First World War, the Grange reverted to its old role of social protest during the 1930's, another decade of social upheaval. From 1929 to 1941, under the dynamic leadership of George Sehlmeyer, it increased its membership from about 8,000 to nearly 24,000. These members were, with few exceptions, the small and part-time farmers of the state. They lived in northern California—in the Sacramento Valley and in the counties of Santa Clara, Napa, Sonoma, Shasta, Siskiyou, and Modoc. By 1941 the Grange had extended its influence into the San Joaquin Valley and into the counties south of the Tehachapi, but these new centers of membership had little effect upon the formulation and execution of policy until a later time.

For many members the Grange was a community center for social activities, valued for the fraternal aspects of its program, but for many more it was a mechanism through which the small farmers could seek redress of their grievances. Few Grange members could afford to take an active part in the leadership of the state organization, since most of them had neither the time nor the money to leave their farms and attend conferences in distant parts of the state. As a consequence, the execution of Grange policy devolved upon a few executive officers, and the State Master, with the advice and counsel of a small executive committee, exercised broad powers. Delegates to the annual conventions of the state organization formulated general Grange policy. But these delegates, representing hundreds of Subordinate Granges, could be controlled by a Master who was skilled in the ways and techniques of a politician.

George Sehlmeyer was just such a Master. Of long experience in the Grange and sensitive to popular opinion, Sehlmeyer dominated every policy and action of the group he led. Although he was often politically to the left of the farmers he represented, Sehlmeyer never went so far as to isolate or alienate himself from Grange members. Sehlmeyer could lead the Grange only in ways that its members wished to go, and his recognition of this fact was one source of his continuing power and popularity. The fact that Sehlmeyer's position as Master of the State Grange was never seriously challenged is attributable in part to his own skill as a practical politician and in part to the fact that his policies and actions undoubtedly had the enthusiastic support of the small farmers who made up the bulk of the membership of the organization.

The California Farm Bureau Federation was a completely different type of farmer organization. Originally formed to furnish a base of coöperation with the Extension Service of the College of Agriculture of the University of California, the Farm Bureau continued to keep its educational program at the center of local activities. Just as farmers joined the Grange for its social and fraternal aspects, so farmers joined the Farm Bureau to take advantage of its educational programs for the promotion of better technical and managerial practices on the farm.

Total membership in the Farm Bureau from 1929 to 1941 remained at a little more than 20,000 families. The Farm Bureau had members in nearly every important agricultural county in the state, but its membership was largest in those areas that produced the greatest value of agricultural commodities, the counties of the San Joaquin Valley and of southern

Summary and Conclusion

California. The farmers who joined the Farm Bureau were among the more substantial, prosperous, and progressive agriculturists in the state.

Leadership was more widely distributed in the Farm Bureau than it was in the Grange. The several service and commodity departments on both the local and state level drew many farmers into active participation in Farm Bureau programs. Farmers who had sufficient leisure and money to travel to various parts of the state and attend time-consuming meetings were selected to serve on the Board of Directors and on the powerful statewide departments and committees. Inevitably, Farm Bureau policy was conservative and reflected the attitudes of the larger farmers of the state. Operating with a substantial budget, the state organization had sufficient funds to employ a large staff to carry on the routine administrative and political activities of the group. Although leadership was shared by many men rather than concentrated in a few hands, the same men were reëlected to official positions year after year. The Farm Bureau maintained close relations with the coöperative marketing associations and with other farm organizations in the state: the Agricultural Council, the Farmers' Union, the Agricultural Department of the Chamber of Commerce, and the Associated Farmers.

The Associated Farmers of California represented a third distinct type of farmer organization. This group, organized at the instigation of the Chamber of Commerce and the Farm Bureau following a series of costly and violent agricultural strikes in 1933 and 1934, and financed primarily by industrial and urban interests, reflected the reactionary attitudes of the large farm employers and of the nonfarming interests who paid its bills. Its single purpose was to resist the unionization of workers in the canneries, processing sheds, and fields of California.

The organization never enjoyed a wide base of permanent membership. Local units were organized quickly to meet the threat of agricultural strikes, only to disappear once the danger had passed. Its policy was determined by a small group of men who constituted the leadership of the state organization. It was incorporated in 1934 and reorganized on a broader base in

1937–1938, but its power was dissipated, for a time at least, by the revelations of the La Follette Committee in 1939 and 1940.

The Associated Farmers confined its activities to the field of labor relations. When union activities in field or city threatened the economic interests of farmers, the Associated Farmers took the lead in opposing the demands of labor. The organization was constantly vigilant against radical agitators. It assisted in the prosecution of Communists under the state's Criminal Syndicalism Act. It secured the passage of antilabor ordinances in agricultural counties, and it worked for the passage of restrictive labor legislation and for the defeat of proposals that would strengthen the position of organized labor. It occasionally formed local vigilante brigades to break agricultural unions by direct and drastic action.

The Farm Bureau allowed the Associated Farmers to handle labor disturbances by itself, but in the legislative sphere the two groups coöperated closely. Both groups worked constantly to support and reinforce the conservative unemployment relief policy of the State Relief Administration and to return the administration of relief to county officials. The Grange was not so directly involved in the field of labor relations, since its members, who for the most part employed relatively few migrant laborers, were not so directly threatened by union activities. In fact, the Grange was frequently sympathetic to the cause of labor. It opposed the passage of antilabor ordinances, condemned vigilante actions on the part of farmers, and sought the enactment of legislation that would protect the farmers through government mediation or arbitration of labor controversies. It also resisted the return of relief administration to the counties and supported liberal programs of social legislation.

There was greater unity among all farm organizations in relation to the taxation problem. The Grange and the Farm Bureau coöperated with other groups to secure drastic modification of the tax structure in 1933, but in subsequent years the two groups found it increasingly difficult to work together in this field, even though their policies were often identical. The Farm Bureau supported the general sales tax, but the

Summary and Conclusion

Grange preferred a selective sales tax on luxury items, with food exempted. The Farm Bureau was influential in securing the enactment of a moderate state income tax, whereas the Grange continually and unsuccessfully sought the passage of legislation that would provide for a much heavier tax upon personal income, especially in the higher income brackets. The Associated Farmers participated in several campaigns to defeat initiative propositions providing for the "single tax," and it worked for economy in government, efficient administration, and low taxation.

The Farm Bureau wrote, sponsored, and secured the enactment of the Agricultural Prorate Act in 1933 and indirectly helped to administer it. The Grange, on the other hand, insisted that the operation of the act injured the small farmer and sought to destroy the program of marketing proration or at least to weaken it by drastic amendment. The Grange was successful in this campaign in 1939, but by that time the need for proration had disappeared as the artificial stimulation of wartime economy had raised prices and increased levels of national food consumption. The Associated Farmers was not publicly interested in this program.

The dispute over ownership and control of the water and power features of the Central Valley Project drove the Farm Bureau and the Grange still further apart. The Grange, with its membership located chiefly in northern California and with a long history of opposition to the forces of private monopoly in any form, favored public ownership of the entire project, hoping that public ownership would bring lower rates for electric power and destroy the private power interests, which it considered an evil monopoly. The Farm Bureau, with its membership centered in the San Joaquin Valley and in southern California and with a traditionally conservative outlook, emphasized the irrigation aspects of the project and favored the distribution of electricity through the privately owned facilities already in existence, hoping that this method would bring lower water rates and greater over-all economy and efficiency. The Associated Farmers took no active part in this controversy.

Summary and Conclusion

All of the farm organizations professed to be aloof from partisan politics. It is true that none of them ever formally endorsed a slate of candidates, but actually each farm group took an active part in politics to secure the enactment of programs that it favored. The Grange worked with progressive Republicans and with liberal Democrats, whereas the Farm Bureau and the Associated Farmers coöperated with conservative and reactionary Republicans and with a few conservative Democrats. The Grange was sympathetic to the E.P.I.C. program in 1934 and to the candidacies of Sheridan Downey and Culbert Olson in 1938. The Farm Bureau and the Associated Farmers, on the other hand, worked with Frank Merriam during his term as governor and supported Philip Bancroft, a prominent leader in both farm groups, in his campaign for United States Senator in 1938. During the Olson administration, Sehlmeyer and the governor worked in friendly coöperation on all issues, whereas the other two farm groups were largely responsible for the creation of an anti-Olson coalition that grew in strength with each legislative session and that blocked much of the Grange-endorsed Olson program.

The peculiar economic and social structure of agriculture in California was to a large extent responsible for the fundamental differences between the various farm organizations. The depression created new problems, intensified old ones, and made more apparent the basic discrepancies between the various farm groups. Of the three organizations the California Grange was the farthest to the left on most issues. The Associated Farmers occupied a position on the extreme and often fanatical right, and the Farm Bureau stood in the conservative center. With the onset of war in 1941, many of the acute problems that California farmers had faced during the long years of the depression were brought to an end or at least temporarily alleviated or postponed. After Pearl Harbor California farm organizations had to adjust their programs and policies to meet the many new problems which arose out of the domestic war effort, and their activities consequently were much modified and changed in the years that followed.

Appendices

A. MEMBERSHIP OF THE CALIFORNIA STATE GRANGE 1873–1941

Year	Number of subordinate granges	Total membership	Year	Number of subordinate granges	Total membership
1873	104	3,168	1915	42	3,057
1874	231	14,910	1916	44	3,148
1875	264	15,193	1917	47	3,299
1876	...	7,660	1918	46	3,453
1877	235	6,761	1919	44	3,462
1878	98	5,467	1920	43	3,804
1879	71	3,262	1921	48	4,796
1880	29	1,276	1922	49	5,016
1881	33	1,612	1923	49	5,069
1882	51	2,171	1924	54	5,478
1883	47	2,034	1925	61	6,256
1884	44	2,289	1926	65	6,994
1885	54	2,863	1927	70	7,399
1886	...ᵃ	2,786	1928	81	8,710
1887	...	3,032	1929	82	8,335
1888	47	.....	1930	87	8,423
......	...	.....	1931	102	9,288
1905	43	2,666	1932	136	11,173
1906	43	2,460	1933	164	12,286
1907	37	2,255	1934	201	.....
1908	34	2,327	1935	245	19,886
1909	35	2,226	1936	264	21,285
1910	33	2,068	1937	280	21,647
1911	33	2,240	1938	288	22,575
1912	33	2,222	1939	289	22,783
1913	37	2,483	1940	298	23,238
1914	46	3,245	1941	304	23,492

SOURCE: California State Grange, *Journals of Proceedings of the Annual Sessions*, 1873–1888, 1905–1941, *passim*.

ᵃ Where no numbers are given the figures presented by the secretary were entirely unreliable.

B.

MEMBERSHIP OF THE CALIFORNIA STATE GRANGE 1929 AND 1932

County	Membership, 1929	Membership, 1932	County	Membership, 1929	Membership, 1932
Amador	...ᵃ	67	Sacramento	560	524
Butte	100	481	San Joaquin	.....	66
Contra Costa	113	112	San Luis Obispo	.....	70
El Dorado	...	532	San Mateo	161	202
Fresno	...	113	Santa Clara	1,048	1,006
Glenn	350	425	Santa Cruz	.....	72
Humboldt	...	106	Shasta	493	994
Lake	73	90	Siskiyou	791	852
Lassen	372	398	Sonoma	1,583	1,392
Mendocino	431	423	Stanislaus	55	67
Modoc	643	481	Sutter	.....	68
Monterey	370	553	Tehama	.....	538
Napa	557	435	Trinity	.....	119
Placer	50	170	Tulare	186	195
Plumas	121	394	Yolo	43	50

SOURCE: California State Grange, *Journals of Proceedings of the Annual Sessions*, 1929, 1932.
ᵃ Where no figures are given there was no Grange organization in that county in 1929. Statistics by counties are not available for years since 1932.

C.

MEMBERSHIP OF THE CALIFORNIA FARM BUREAU FEDERATION, 1920–1941

Year	Membership	Year	Membership
1920	10,794 [a]	1931	21,025
1921	17,712	1932	20,616
1922	23,774	1933	15,259
1923	26,041	1934	18,061
1924	20,953	1935	19,713
1925	20,267	1936	20,606
1926	19,958	1937	22,716
1927	19,431	1938	23,129
1928	20,507	1939	20,678
1929	18,939	1940	20,906
1930	20,421	1941	22,154

SOURCE: California Farm Bureau Federation, Minutes of the Annual Meetings, 1920–1941.

[a] These figures are for family membership. For comparison with statistics of the Grange, in which membership is based on the individual, these totals may be multiplied by 1.6.

D. MEMBERSHIP OF THE CALIFORNIA FARM BUREAU FEDERATION, 1929 AND 1941

County	Membership, 1929	Membership, 1941	County	Membership, 1929	Membership, 1941
Alameda	110	401	Placer	341	50
Butte	366	281	Riverside	750	649
Colusa	336	352	Sacramento	325	464
Contra Costa	123	420	San Benito	323	135
El Dorado	98	125	San Bernardino	455	866
Fresno	638	889	San Diego	214	480
Glenn	18	...	San Joaquin	1,216	1,299
Humboldt	1	...	San Luis Obispo	719	503
Imperial	515	728	Santa Barbara	549	681
Kern	506	600	Santa Clara	...	100
Kings	327	426	Santa Cruz	241	133
Lake	128	267	Shasta	...	107
Lassen	285	220	Siskiyou	...	36
Los Angeles	1,582	1,902	Solano	345	307
Madera	358	567	Sonoma	647	644
Marin	338	216	Stanislaus	425	672
Mendocino	466	559	Sutter	666	496
Merced	200	606	Tehama	212	490
Modoc	...	74	Tulare	1,412	1,714
Monterey	226	406	Ventura	824	800
Napa	370	347	Yolo	722	693
Nevada	66	63	Yuba	192	228
Orange	1,344	1,158			

SOURCE: California Farm Bureau Federation, Minutes of the Annual Meetings, November, 1929, and November, 1941.

E. LEADERSHIP OF THE CALIFORNIA STATE GRANGE 1929–1941

State Master:
George Sehlmeyer, 1929–

State Overseer:
W. J. Dorris, Modoc County, 1929–1931
A. M. Robsin, Yolo County, 1931–1932
Mark T. Hunt, Sacramento County, 1932–1933
F. A. Wells, Monterey County, 1933–1937
L. H. Valentine, Humboldt County, 1937–1942

State Lecturer:
Mrs. Ida M. Clendening, Santa Clara County, 1925–1931
Mrs. Alice Williams, Siskiyou County, 1931–1937
Margaret Kleaver, Siskiyou County, 1937–1939
Uriel Shields, Butte County, 1939–

Members of Executive Committee:
Roy I. Church, Sonoma County, 1923–1931
H. A. Craig, Siskiyou County, 1929–1932
John Hartley, Napa County, 1929–1939
Harry Barnes, Santa Clara County, 1931–
F. W. Loosley, Shasta County, 1932–1935
V. R. Parrish, Stanislaus County, 1935–1942
George A. Critchett, Butte County, 1939–

SOURCE: California State Grange, *Journal of Proceedings of the Annual Sessions*, 1929–1941.

F. LEADERSHIP OF THE CALIFORNIA FARM BUREAU FEDERATION, 1929–1941

President:
R. W. Blackburn, 1929–January, 1938
Ray B. Wiser, January, 1938–

Vice-President:
U. Butte Tyler, 1929–1931
Ray B. Wiser, 1931–January, 1938
E. C. Kimball, January, 1938–1941

Secretary:
Alex. Johnson, 1925–1941

Board of Directors:
Members from Region 1:
　J. A. Smiley, 1927–1932
　W. F. Eldridge, 1932–1939
　C. O. Hoober, 1939–1941
Members from Region 2:
　Roy K. Cole, 1928–1934
　E. C. Kimball, 1934–January, 1938
　J. P. Butler, January, 1938–
Members from Region 3:
　C. R. Swanson, 1929–1930
　M. W. Dula, 1930–1941
Members from Region 4:
　B. H. Schulte, 1925–1932
　L. E. McChesney, 1932–1934
　R. C. Maclachlan, 1934–1937
　T. F. Thwaits, 1937–1941
Members from Region 5:
　Leland C. Stoll, 1926–1930
　Amon Swank, 1930–1938
　A. J. Sturtevant, 1938–

Members from Region 6:
  Edwin Van Riper, 1929–1931
  C. J. Rolph, Jr., 1931–
Member from Region 7:
  J. E. Bandy, 1927–1941
Members from Region 8:
  J. C. Johnson, 1927–1932
  C. A. Benson, 1932–1936, 1938–
  N. B. Kinley, 1936–1938

SOURCE: California Farm Bureau Federation, Minutes of the Annual Meetings, 1929–1941.

G.

LEADERSHIP OF ASSOCIATED FARMERS OF CALIFORNIA 1934–1939

1934–1935

Officers:
S. Parker Frisselle, President
C. E. Hawley, Vice-President
Guernsey Frazer, Executive Secretary
R. N. Wilson, Temporary Secretary and Treasurer
Gilbert H. Parker, Publicity Director

Executive Committee:
S. Parker Frisselle
C. E. Hawley
Walter E. Garrison
L. W. Frick
Philip Bancroft
Holmes Bishop
Russell T. Robinson
A. N. Jack
Charles A. Worden
David S. Bell
Fred A. Stewart
Harry Sears

Board of Directors:
Ten members
SOURCE: La Follette Committee, *Hearings,* Part 60, pp. 22149–22152.

1936

Officers:
Walter E. Garrison, President
Philip Bancroft, Vice-President, North
C. E. Hawley, Vice-President, South
Fred Goodcell, Executive Secretary
John Phillips, Organizer
H. C. Morgan, Organizer

Executive Committee:
Walter E. Garrison
Philip Bancroft
C. E. Hawley
S. Parker Frisselle
Hugh T. Osborne
L. W. Frick
Russell T. Robinson
Charles S. Brooks
Henry L. Strobel
Holmes Bishop
David S. Bell
Fred C. Hogue
B. A. Schwartz

Board of Directors:
Twenty-one members
SOURCE: La Follette Committee, *Hearings*, Part 60, p. 22153.

1937

Officers:
W. E. Garrison, President
Holmes Bishop, Vice-President, South
H. L. Strobel, Vice-President, North
Fred Goodcell, Executive Secretary
Stuart Strathman, Field Secretary

Executive Committee:
Walter E. Garrison
Holmes Bishop
Henry L. Strobel
Philip Bancroft
S. Parker Frisselle
F. J. Palomares
Hugh T. Osborne
L. W. Frick
W. B. Camp
W. E. Spencer
Arthur E. Clark
Charles A. Brooks
Stuart Strathman
M. J. Bonham
J. K. Sano
R. J. McClain
Fred Hogue

Board of Directors:
Sixty-three members from thirty counties
SOURCE: La Follette Committee, *Hearings*, Part 60, p. 22155.

1938

Officers:
Holmes Bishop, President
Philip Bancroft, Vice-President, North, until May 28, 1938
Henry L. Strobel, Vice-President, North, after May 28, 1938
Hugh T. Osborne, Vice-President, South
W. B. Camp, Treasurer
Fred Goodcell, Executive Secretary until April
Henry L. Strobel, Temporary Secretary
Harper L. Knowles, Executive Secretary after June
Stuart Strathman, Field Secretary

Executive Committee:
Holmes Bishop, President
L. J. Shuman, District 1
B. A. Schwartz, District 2
Fred L. Hogue, District 3
J. Z. Anderson, District 4
L. W. Frick, District 5
W. E. Spencer, District 6
O. R. Patterson, District 7
Walter E. Garrison, Past President
S. Parker Frisselle, Past President
Philip Bancroft, Northern Representative at Large
Henry L. Strobel, Northern Representative at Large
Hugh T. Osborne, Southern Representative at Large
J. Z. Cannon, Southern Representative at Large

Board of Directors:
Eighty-six members from thirty-five counties

SOURCE: La Follette Committee, *Hearings,* Part 67, p. 24587; Part 60, pp. 22156–22157.

1939

Officers:
Holmes Bishop, President
John Watson, Vice-President, North
Ray E. Badger, Vice-President, South
W. B. Camp, Treasurer
H. E. Pomeroy, Executive Secretary
Stuart Strathman, Field Secretary
Robert Franklin, Publicity Director

Executive Committee:
Holmes Bishop
W. B. Camp, District 1
Philip Bancroft, District 2
H. A. Perry, District 3

H. Russell Robbins, District 4
Harold Angier, District 5
Henry L. Strobel, District 6
R. F. Schmeiser, District 7
John Watson, Northern Representative at Large
H. Schuyler, Northern Representative at Large
Ray E. Badger, Southern Representative at Large
Hugh T. Osborne, Southern Representative at Large
Walter E. Garrison, Past President
S. Parker Frisselle, Past President

Board of Directors:
Forty-two members from forty-two counties
SOURCE: La Follette Committee, *Hearings,* Part 60, pp. 22150–22151.

NOTES TO CHAPTERS

NOTES TO CHAPTER 1

[1] Many scholars have made valuable contributions to the study of the economic and social structure of California agriculture. Among the most important are R. L. Adams, M. R. Benedict, Alvin Carpenter, Marion Clawson, H. E. Erdman, Levi Varden Fuller, Claude B. Hutchison, Stuart M. Jamieson, Carey McWilliams, George M. Peterson, Paul S. Taylor, and R. G. Wagenet.

[2] United States Senate, Subcommittee of the Committee on Education and Labor, 74th Congress, Pursuant to Senate Resolution 266, A Resolution to Investigate Violations of the Right of Free Speech and Assembly and Interference with the Right of Labor to Organize and Bargain Collectively, Chairman, Robert M. La Follette, Jr. (hereafter referred to as La Follette Committee), *Reports*, Part III, p. 405.

[3] George M. Peterson, *Composition and Characteristics of the Agricultural Population in California, Bulletin 630* (University of California, College of Agriculture, June, 1939), pp. 39–41.

NOTES TO CHAPTER 2

[1] California State Grange, *Journals of Proceedings of the Annual Sessions*, Oct., 1873 (hereafter referred to as Grange, *Proceedings*); *California Grange News*, Oct. 5, 1937, p. 3, Nov. 5, 1938, p. 2; Ezra S. Carr, *The Patrons of Husbandry of the Pacific Coast* (San Francisco, 1875), pp. 76–103, 131–155, 220–280; Oliver H. Kelley, *Origins and Progress of the Patrons of Husbandry in the United States* (Philadelphia, 1875), *passim*.

[2] Solon J. Buck, *The Granger Movement, 1870–1880* (Harvard University Press, 1913), pp. 249–251; Carr, *op. cit.*, pp. 201–214.

[3] Grange, *Proceedings*, Oct., 1876, pp. 8, 10, Oct., 1879, p. 19, Oct., 1922, pp. 123–125; *California Grange News*, Nov. 5, 1938, p. 4; Buck, *op. cit.*, pp. 264, 271–272; Carr, *op. cit.*, pp. 161–172, 177–178, 181–183, 205–210.

[4] Grange, *Proceedings*, Oct., 1877, pp. 25, 46, Oct., 1878, pp. 21–23, 27–28.

[5] *Ibid.*, 1879–1889, 1891–1893, 1899, 1906–1920, *passim*.

[6] *Ibid.*, 1921–1929, *passim*.

[7] *Ibid.*, 1907–1929, *passim*.

[8] At the time of writing (1951), Sehlmeyer continues as State Master.

[9] Annual reports of secretary in Grange, *Proceedings*, 1929–1941, *passim*.

[10] *California Grange News*, Oct. 5, 1939, p. 6.

[11] Statistics on membership were published in Grange, *Proceedings*, 1929–1941, *passim*. Detailed figures compiled by writer from this source may be found in Appendix A and Appendix B. For many years membership was listed for each Subordinate and Pomona Grange in the state. Beginning in 1933, however, there was no geographic breakdown of membership figures. Requests for more detailed statements were politely but firmly refused by George Sehlmeyer. In comparing membership of the

Grange and the Farm Bureau, it should be kept in mind that Grange membership is held by the individual, whereas Farm Bureau membership is based on the family unit. Orville Merton Kile, in his official history, *The Farm Bureau Through Three Decades* (Baltimore, 1948), uses a conversian figure of 1.6 to compare membership of the two organizations. Grange statistics may be divided by 1.6 or Farm Bureau figures may be multiplied by 1.6 for purposes of comparison.

[12] Charles M. Gardner, *The Grange—Friend of the Farmer, 1867–1947* (Washington, D.C., 1949), p. 497.

[13] Grange, *Proceedings*, 1929–1941, *passim*.

[14] *California Grange News*, Oct., 1933, p. 1.

[15] Address of George Harrison, in State Department of Agriculture, *Monthly Bulletin*, Feb., 1929, pp. 86–87; speech of William P. Knight, *ibid.*, Jan., 1939, pp. 29–31; report of M. E. Williams, in Grange, *Proceedings*, Oct., 1933, pp. 76–78; address of George Sehlmeyer, *ibid.*, Oct., 1937, p. 28; statement of State Senator J. C. Garrison, *ibid.*, Oct., 1941, p. 96; interview with State Senator Chris N. Jespersen, in *California Grange News*, Jan. 20, 1939, p. 1; writer's interview with Franklin Hichborn, Feb. 2, 1950.

[16] *California Grange News*, Dec., 1933, p. 1.

[17] "The California Agricultural Problem: A Report by a Voluntary Committee," n.p., Oct. 23, 1938, p. 18.

[18] Grange, *Proceedings*, Oct., 1934, p. 141, Oct., 1936, p. 151, Oct., 1938, p. 150, Oct., 1940, pp. 179, 182–183, 185, 219; *California Grange News*, Aug. 5, 1939, p. 2, Mar. 20, 1941, p. 4.

NOTES TO CHAPTER 3

[1] E. D. Tetreau, *The Objectives and Activities of the California Farm Bureau, Bulletin No. 563* (University of California, College of Agriculture, Nov., 1933), p. 11; California Farm Bureau Federation, Minutes of the Annual Meetings of the California Farm Bureau Federation (hereafter referred to as C.F.B.F., Minutes), Nov., 1926, p. 127; California *Farm Bureau Monthly* (hereafter abbreviated *F.B. Monthly*), Solano County edition, Apr., 1921, p. 9, San Benito edition, May, 1923, pp. 13–14, Tulare edition, June, 1928, pp. 28, 30–31, July, 1928, p. 26, San Joaquin edition, June, 1938, pp. 16J–16L, Oct., 1939, p. 16C.

[2] The following discussion of the early history of the organizational structure of the Farm Bureau is based on *F.B. Monthly*, various county editions, 1921–1929, *passim*; C.F.B.F., Minutes, 1921–1929, *passim*.

[3] *F.B. Monthly*, Alameda edition, Sept., 1937, p. 9, July, 1938, p. 4.

[4] *Ibid.*, Alameda edition, Dec., 1929, pp. 28–31; C.F.B.F., Minutes, Nov., 1931, pp. 7–8, 15 ff.; Tetreau, *op. cit.*, p. 39; Dean E. McHenry, "The Third House—A Study of Organized Groups before the California Legislature" (Master's thesis, Stanford University, 1933), pp. 116–117.

[5] The *Farm Bureau Monthly* published one statewide master copy from which the various county editions incorporated material. Each county edition added its own news items and articles of local interest. These edi-

Notes to Chapters

tions often printed minutes of meetings of the board of directors of the county Farm Bureaus. The editions for Alameda, San Joaquin, and Tulare counties were especially complete and valuable.

[6] Annual reports of service departments in C.F.B.F., Minutes, 1921–1941, *passim;* Tetreau, *op. cit.,* pp. 42–48, 75–76.

[7] Annual reports of commodity departments in C.F.B.F., Minutes, 1921–1941, *passim;* Tetreau, *op. cit.,* pp. 40, 48–51.

[8] Tetreau, *op. cit.,* pp. 51–60, 65–71, 80–82. Tetreau was hired to make a survey of the business activities of the Farm Bureau in order to gather information on which future policy decisions of that organization could be based. Tetreau concluded that Farm Bureau business ventures had not been succesful enough to warrant their extension at that time. For evidence of the close relations of the Farm Bureau and the coöperative marketing associations, see Kile, *op. cit.,* pp. 385–386; C.F.B.F., Minutes, Nov., 1937, pp. 28–31; *F.B. Monthly,* San Joaquin edition, Feb., 1931, p. 7, Alameda edition, Aug., 1933, p. 10.

[9] Detailed membership statistics were printed annually in C.F.B.F., Minutes. Tetreau, *op. cit.,* pp. 12–19, may also be consulted. The writer's compilations are printed in Appendix C and Appendix D.

[10] Annual reports of the secretary treasurer in C.F.B.F., *Minutes.*

[11] *F.B. Monthly,* Alameda edition, Jan., 1930, p. 16, Feb., 1938, p. 4.

[12] *Ibid.,* Butte edition, Dec., 1931, p. 3, Alameda edition, Feb., 1938, pp. 4, 10, May, 1938, p. 12; *Pacific Rural Press,* March 22, 1941, pp. 214–215; *Who's Who in California, 1942–1943,* p. 998.

[13] *F.B. Monthly,* Alameda edition, Dec., 1929, p. 21, San Joaquin edition, Sept., 1931, pp. 27, 30.

[14] *Ibid.,* Alameda edition, Feb., 1938, pp. 4, 10, Ventura edition, Feb., 1938, p. 3.

[15] For observations on the nature of Farm Bureau membership, see Tetreau, *op. cit.,* pp. 24–27; C.F.B.F., Minutes, Nov., 1940, p. 16; reprint of editorial in *Livingston Chronicle* (Merced County) in *Sacramento Bee,* Jan. 31, 1940, p. 10; "The California Agricultural Problem," pp. 18, 46.

[16] Editorial observations in *Pacific Rural Press,* Nov. 26, 1938, p. 516. It is reproduced here exactly as published; the fragmentary sentences and punctuation are Pickett's, not the writer's.

NOTES TO CHAPTER 4

[1] See data presented in Robert F. Martin, *Income in Agriculture, 1929–1934* (National Industrial Conference Board, Study No. 232, 1936), pp. 19, 74, 88, 90.

[2] California State Chamber of Commerce, "Migrants, A National Problem and Its Impact on California" (n.p., 1940), pp. 10, 15; R. G. Wagenet, "Handbook on Farm Labor Placement in California" (n.p., 1941), p. 214; Paul S. Taylor, "Again the Covered Wagon," *Survey Graphic,* July, 1935, pp. 349–351.

[3] La Follette Committee, *Hearings,* Part 53, pp. 19467–19468.

Notes to Chapters

[4] Norman Lowenstein, "Strikes and Strike Tactics in California Agriculture: A History" (Master's thesis, University of California, 1940), pp. 72–73.

[5] Stuart M. Jamieson, "Labor Unionism in Agriculture" (Doctoral dissertation, University of California, 1943), p. 51.

[6] La Follette Committee, *Reports*, Part III, p. 212.

[7] Jamieson, *op. cit.*, pp. 51–53; Bureau of Agricultural Economics, *Backgrounds of the Farm Labor Problem* (Washington, D.C., 1942), pp. 143 ff.; La Follette Committee, *Reports*, Part III, pp. 210 ff.

[8] La Follette Committee, *Reports*, Part V, p. 737.

[9] *San Francisco Chronicle*, June 6, 7, 1936.

[10] Letter from Edward Vandeleur to William Green, quoted in *San Francisco Chronicle*, June 27, 1936.

[11] Jamieson, *op. cit.*, p. 380.

[12] Quoted in B.A.E., *op. cit.*, p. 149.

[13] Jamieson, *op. cit.*, p. 68.

[14] *Ibid.*, pp. 68 ff.; B.A.E., *op. cit.*, pp. 149 ff.

[15] Jamieson, *op. cit.*, p. 75.

[16] *Ibid.*, pp. 75, 426, 444; B.A.E., *op. cit.*, pp. 150–154.

[17] Jamieson, *op. cit.*, table 1, p. 42.

[18] *San Francisco Chronicle*, Sept. 1–Oct. 5, 1933.

[19] *Ibid.*, Oct. 1–Nov. 5, 1933; Jamieson, *op. cit.*, pp. 260–273; La Follette Committee, *Hearings*, Part 54, pp. 19899–20036; La Follette Committee, *Reports*, Part IV, pp. 506–514; clippings in file of Paul S. Taylor in Bancroft Library, University of California.

[20] *San Francisco Chronicle*, Jan. 9–24, 1934; La Follette Committee, *Hearings*, Part 54, pp. 20037–20065; John Phillips, C. B. Hutchison, and W. C. Jacobsen, "The Imperial Valley Farm Labor Situation" (n.p., April, 1934); Simon J. Lubin, J. L. Leonard, Will J. French, Report of the National Labor Board by Special Commission (mimeographed release no. 3325, n.p., n.d.); "Imperial Valley Mob," *New Republic*, Feb. 21, 1934, pp. 39–41; "It's Revolution, These Officials Report," *Pacific Rural Press*, April 28, 1934.

NOTES TO CHAPTER 5

[1] La Follette Committee, *Hearings*, Part 55, pp. 20075–20091, 20235–20236.

[2] *Ibid.*, pp. 20240–20241.

[3] *Walker's Directory of Directors, 1931–1932*, p. 490.

[4] La Follette Committee, *Hearings*, Part 55, p. 20078.

[5] *Ibid.*, p. 20242.

[6] Named to the Executive Committee of the new group were: S. Parker Frisselle (chairman); L. W. Frick, cotton grower and vice-president of the Agricultural Labor Bureau of the San Joaquin Valley; Alex Johnson, executive secretary of the C.F.B.F.; Guy R. Kinsey of the Pear Growers' Protective Association of San Jose; Fred A. Stewart, official of Anderson,

Notes to Chapters

Clayton Cotton Company; and Ray B. Wiser, vice-president of the C.F.B.F. R. N. Wilson, manager of the Agricultural Department of the State Chamber of Commerce, continued to act as secretary of the group. La Follette Committee, *Hearings*, Part 55, pp. 20080, 20242; La Follette Committee, *Reports*, Part IV, pp. 580–583.

[7] Speech by E. F. Loescher, in California State Chamber of Commerce, Agricultural Department, "Important Farm Labor Developments" (n.p., Oct. 28, 1937), p. 4.

[8] La Follette Committee, *Hearings*, Part 55, p. 20248. Also see letters written by Alex Johnson, *ibid.*, p. 20243.

[9] *Ibid.*, p. 20243; also see article by G. H. Parker in *California Journal of Development*, June, 1935, pp. 6, 19.

[10] La Follette Committee, *Hearings*, Part 68, p. 25009.

[11] Northern representatives named to the Executive Committee were L. W. Frick, W. E. Garrison, Ernst E. Behr, and Russell Robinson. Southern representatives were C. E. Hawley, John Phillips, A. N. Jack, and F. A. Stewart. The name of F. A. Stewart was not made public because of his connection with the Anderson, Clayton Company. He was later replaced by Guernsey Frazer, whose connections were more directly agricultural. Frick headed the California Cotton Coöperative Association, a ginning association of the San Joaquin Valley. Garrison was a grape grower and held a position with the California Wine Institute; it was Garrison who led resistance to workers in the Lodi grape strike in the fall of 1933. Robinson was a lettuce grower in the Salinas Valley. Hawley was an official of the California Fruit Growers' Exchange. Jack was a leader of the Western Growers' Protective Association. Phillips was state assemblyman from Riverside County. La Follette Committee, *Hearings*, Part 55, pp. 20252–20254.

[12] *Ibid.*, Part 49, p. 17917.

[13] *Ibid.*

[14] La Follette Committee, *Reports*, Part IV, p. 598.

[15] *Ibid.*, Part VIII, pp. 1157–1159.

[16] *Ibid.*, Part IV, pp. 601–605.

[17] La Follette Committee, *Hearings*, Part 69, pp. 25679–25680; La Follette Committee, *Reports*, Part IV, pp. 612–615.

[18] La Follette Committee, *Hearings*, Part 55, pp. 20119–20120; La Folletter Committee, *Reports*, Part IV, pp. 612–615.

[19] La Follette Committee, *Reports*, Part VIII, pp. 1152–1153.

[20] La Follette Committee, *Hearings*, Part 68, pp. 25025–25026.

NOTES TO CHAPTER 6

[1] La Follette Committee, *Hearings*, Part 60, p. 21989.

[2] *Ibid.*, Part 69, p. 25453. Horst, though never a Grange officer, was a prominent Grange member and often wrote articles and gave speeches for that organization.

[3] Roy M. Pike, "Californians—Wake Up!" *California Journal of Development*, Jan., 1936, pp. 12–13, 42–44.

Notes to Chapters

[4] La Follette Committee, *Reports,* Part V, p. 742.
[5] La Follette Committee, *Hearings,* Part 50, pp. 18270–18271.
[6] *Ibid.,* Part 58, p. 21335; see also Part 60, pp. 21973–21974.
[7] *Ibid.,* Part 60, pp. 22149—22152.
[8] *Ibid.,* p. 22153.
[9] *Ibid.,* p. 22154.
[10] *Ibid.,* Part 67, p. 24587, Part 60, pp. 22156–22157.
[11] *Ibid.,* Part 60, pp. 22150–22151.
[12] "Push California Land Labor Fight," *Business Week,* Aug. 12, 1939, p. 33. An unnamed Associated Farmers leader was quoted in the *San Francisco Chronicle,* Dec. 8, 1938, on this matter: "Like every other organization, we have had some bad boys. Some of their past actions have not done the association any good. It is regrettable and, therefore, important, that these things do not occur again. We must have our house in order.... The Associated Farmers have no quarrel with agricultural workers. They want to work, we want them to work, and we want to pay them as much as we can. Our quarrel is with their leadership—the radicals, the agitators, who don't want them to work."
[13] *San Francisco Chronicle,* Dec. 9, 1939.
[14] *Ibid.,* Dec. 2–3, 1940.
[15] See Appendix G for list of officers of the Associated Farmers.
[16] La Follette Committee, *Reports,* Part VIII, p. 1201.
[17] *Ibid.,* pp. 1193–1198, 1457.
[18] *The Associated Farmer,* April 15, 1940, pp. 3–4.
[19] La Follette Committee, *Reports,* Part VIII, pp. 1594–1596, 1600–1606; *San Francisco Chronicle,* Dec. 7, 1937, Oct. 21, 1938, Dec. 10, 1938; *Rural Observer,* July–August, 1938.

NOTES TO CHAPTER 7

[1] California State Chamber of Commerce, Agricultural Department, "Farm Labor Policies" (n.p., n.d., probably June, 1937).
[2] La Follette Committee, *Hearings,* Part 68, pp. 24857–24858.
[3] McHenry, *op. cit.,* pp. 122–127.
[4] Article by George H. Hecke in State Department of Agriculture, *Monthly Bulletin,* Nov., 1929, pp. 583–585.
[5] *Sacramento Bee,* Apr. 1, 1937, p. 20.
[6] "The California Agricultural Problem," pp. 18–19; *Pacific Rural Press,* Dec. 21, 1929, p. 675, Dec. 23, 1933, p. 499; *California Cultivator,* Oct. 11, 1930, p. 349, Feb. 15, 1930, p. 190, Jan. 4, 1936, p. 21.
[7] C.F.B.F., Minutes, Nov., 1940, p. 167; *F.B. Monthly,* San Joaquin edition, Feb. 1931, p. 16C, Monterey edition, Sept., 1931, pp. 3, 6, San Joaquin edition, March, 1931, p. 26, Napa edition, March, 1932, p. 27, San Joaquin edition, Sept., 1933, p. 16B; Grange, *Proceedings,* Oct., 1930, p. 107.
[8] *California Grange News,* June, 1932, pp. 3, 7.
[9] Grange, *Proceedings,* Oct., 1936, p. 166, Oct., 1931, pp. 92–93, Oct., 1932, p. 85; *California Grange News,* May, 1936, p. 8, Feb. 20, 1940, p. 1; *F.B. Monthly,* Alameda edition, Sept., 1936, p. 9.

¹⁰ *Sacramento Bee,* March 30, 1937, p. 18.
¹¹ *F.B. Monthly,* San Joaquin edition, March, 1937, pp. 16D–16G, Marin edition, March, 1937, p. 3, Monterey edition, Nov., 1937, p. 3, Napa edition, April, 1938, p. 6, Fresno edition, March, 1939, p. 3, Sacramento edition, Aug., 1939, p. 7, Tulare edition, April, 1941, pp. 3, 26; article by Don Goodcell, manager of the Associated Farmers of Ventura County in Ventura edition, Jan., 1938, pp. 3, 6.
¹² C.F.B.F., Minutes, Nov., 1934, p. 12, Nov., 1937, pp. 150, 152, Nov., 1938, p. 11; *Pacific Rural Press,* Dec. 11, 1937, p. 627.
¹³ Letter of Alex Johnson to S. Parker Frisselle dated May 6, 1937, in La Follette Committee, *Hearings,* Part 68, p. 24958.
¹⁴ Letter of S. Parker Frisselle to Alex Johnson dated May 7, 1937, *ibid.,* pp. 24958–24959.
¹⁵ Letter of Alex Johnson dated Jan. 19, 1938, *ibid.,* p. 24945.
¹⁶ Letter of Alex Johnson to E. C. Kimball dated Aug. 2, 1938, *ibid.,* pp. 24941–24942; letter of Kimball to Johnson dated Oct. 18, 1938, *ibid.,* p. 24962.
¹⁷ *F.B. Monthly,* San Joaquin edition, Feb., 1931, p. 16C; C.F.B.F., *Minutes,* Nov., 1941, p. 150.

NOTES TO CHAPTER 8

¹ *Transactions of the Commonwealth Club,* Dec. 22, 1936, pp. 244–245.
² The attitude of the Associated Farmers toward labor's demands for better conditions was reflected in a cartoon published in *The Associated Farmer,* Nov. 14, 1937, entitled "Possible Effects of Rural Labor Organization." It pictured two sullen-looking hogs picketing the front door of a small farm home, carrying signs which read: "We Demand Better Living Conditions."
³ La Follette Committee, *Hearings,* Part 49, p. 17946.
⁴ Minutes of meeting of the Associated Farmers on June 26, 1936, in La Follette Committee, *Reports,* Part VIII, p. 1256.
⁵ *San Francisco Chronicle,* Jan. 15, 1939.
⁶ Frank J. Taylor, "The Right to Harvest," *Country Gentleman,* Oct., 1937, p. 72.
⁷ La Follette Committee, *Hearings,* Part 53, pp. 19504–19505.
⁸ *Ibid.,* Part 69, p. 25271.
⁹ Philip Bancroft, *The Farmer and the Communists* (address delivered April 26, 1935, privately printed), pp. 4, 13.
¹⁰ *F.B. Monthly,* Alameda edition, Jan., 1928, pp. 10, 17, Yolo edition, Sept., 1923, p. 29, San Joaquin edition, March, 1924, p. 30, Tulare edition, March, 1926, p. 30.
¹¹ *Ibid.,* Yolo edition, Feb., 1928, pp. 3, 30–31, Alameda edition, Feb., 1928, p. 4, March, 1930, p. 12, Madera edition, March, 1930, p. 31; speech by Ralph H. Taylor, in C.F.B.F., Minutes, Nov., 1929, 16 unnumbered pages.
¹² *F.B. Monthly,* San Joaquin edition, Oct., 1936, pp. 8D, 28B.

[13] *Ibid.*, San Joaquin edition, Feb., 1937, p. 27.
[14] *Pacific Rural Press*, April 2, 1938, p. 392, April 9, 1938, p. 428, April 23, 1938, p. 481, May 14, 1938, p. 565.
[15] C.F.B.F., Minutes, Nov., 1936, p. 14.
[16] California State Chamber of Commerce, Agricultural Department, "Farm Labor Policies," pp. 1–2. Also see *California Cultivator*, July 31, 1937, p. 555; *Pacific Rural Press*, July 17, 1937, p. 62; *The Associated Farmer*, July 17, 1937, p. 1.
[17] Grange, *Proceedings*, Oct., 1930, p. 11. Sehlmeyer's estimate of 90 per cent was, of course, grossly exaggerated. Also see Grange, *Proceedings*, Oct., 1930, pp. 88–89, Oct., 1933, pp. 95–96.
[18] *California Grange News*, May, 1934, p. 5.
[19] Grange, *Proceedings*, Oct., 1937, pp. 158, 160.
[20] Report of Mrs. W. J. Dorris, Chaplain, in Grange, *Proceedings*, Oct., 1933, p. 25.
[21] *Ibid.*, Oct., 1937, p. 162.
[22] *Ibid.*, Oct., 1938, p. 140.
[23] *Ibid.*, pp. 139–140; *California Grange News*, Oct. 20, 1938, pp. 1, 4.

NOTES TO CHAPTER 9

[1] La Follette Committee, *Reports*, Part VIII, pp. 1307–1316.
[2] *Ibid.*
[3] *Ibid.*, pp. 1535–1537; *ibid.*, Part IV, pp. 549–550; *The Associated Farmer*, July 28, 1936, p. 3.
[4] La Follette Committee, *Hearings*, Part 50, pp. 18465–18466; La Follette Committee, *Reports*, Part VIII, pp. 1398–1405; *The Rural Observer*, Sept.–Oct., 1938; *San Francisco Chronicle*, Apr. 15–30, 1937; Institute for Propaganda Analysis, "The Associated Farmers," *Propaganda Analysis*, Aug. 1, 1939, pp. 8–9.
[5] *San Francisco Chronicle*, Oct. 20, 1938.
[6] *Ibid.*, Oct. 26, 1938.
[7] *Ibid.*, Sept.–Nov., 1938; Jamieson, *op. cit.*, pp. 438–441.
[8] *San Francisco Chronicle*, May, 1939; Jamieson, *op. cit.*, pp. 450–457.
[9] Jamieson, *op. cit.*, p. 451.
[10] Report of the Cotton Wage Hearing Board, 1939 (mimeographed report, in file of Paul S. Taylor in Bancroft Library).
[11] *San Francisco Chronicle*, Sept. 27, 1939.
[12] Report of the Cotton Wage Hearing Board, section signed by whole committee.
[13] *Ibid.*, majority report signed by William B. Parker, George Sehlmeyer, Ray B. Wiser, and R. L. Adams.
[14] *Ibid.*, minority report signed by H. C. Carrasco, Mrs. H. E. Erdman, and Carey McWilliams.
[15] *The Associated Farmer*, Oct. 15, 1939, p. 2.
[16] The following discussion is based on La Follette Committee, *Hearings*, Part 51, pp. 18633–18773; Jamieson, *op. cit.*, pp. 450–457; *San Francisco Chronicle*, Sept. 20–Nov. 18, 1939.

Notes to Chapters

[17] *San Francisco Chronicle,* Oct. 9, 1939.
[18] La Follette Committee, *Reports,* Part VIII, pp. 1513–1514.
[19] *San Francisco Chronicle,* Oct. 16, 1939.
[20] La Follette Committee, *Hearings,* Part 51, p. 18655.
[21] Undated, mimeographed leaflet issued by U.C.A.P.A.W.A., C.I.O. (probably mid-October, 1939, in Library of Bureau of Public Administration, University of California).
[22] *Ibid.*
[23] La Follette Committee, *Reports,* Part VIII, pp. 1518–1519; *San Francisco Chronicle,* Oct. 19–21, 1939.
[24] *San Francisco Chronicle,* Oct. 23, 1939; La Follette Committee, *Reports,* Part VIII, p. 1523.
[25] *The Associated Farmer,* Nov. 15, 1939, p. 4.
[26] Mimeographed leaflet distributed by the Committee to Aid Agricultural Workers (Bakersfield, Oct., 1939, in Library of Bureau of Public Administration, University of California).
[27] *San Francisco Chronicle,* Oct. 22, 1939.
[28] *Ibid.*
[29] *Ibid.,* Oct. 22–27, 1939.
[30] *Ibid.,* Nov. 2, 1939.

NOTES TO CHAPTER 10

[1] Stanley Paul Faustman, "Pressure Groups and the California State Relief Administration" (Master's thesis, University of California, 1942), pp. 173–174.
[2] *Ibid.,* pp. viii–ix, 175; Leigh Athearn, "Unemployment Relief in Labor Disputes—California's Experience," *Social Service Review,* Dec., 1940, pp. 629–630; Milton Chernin, "Unemployment Relief Administration" (Bureau of Public Administration, University of California, March 5, 1937), p. 3; Victor Jones, "Relief and Welfare Organization in California" (Bureau of Public Administration, University of California, April 24, 1939), pp. 6–7; Victor Jones, "Transients and Migrants" (Bureau of Public Administration, University of California, Feb. 27, 1939), pp. 10–14. Personnel in other state agencies were blanketed under civil service by a constitutional amendment ratified in 1934.
[3] Winston W. Crouch and Dean E. McHenry, *California Government, Politics and Administration* (Revised edition, Berkeley, 1949), p. 360; Faustman, *op. cit.,* pp. 175–188; Athearn, *op. cit.,* p. 641; La Follette Committee, *Hearings,* Part 68, pp. 24952–24953.
[4] *California Cultivator,* July 2, 1938, p. 418.
[5] California State Chamber of Commerce, Agricultural Department, "Important Farm Labor Developments during 1937," p. 3.
[6] *The Associated Farmer,* Dec. 14, 1937. Three years later Von Ellsworth, Research Director of the C.F.B.F., echoed this "No Work—No Eat" slogan when he called for recognition of the principle: "Those who will not work shall not eat." Quoted in C.F.B.F., Minutes, Nov., 1937, p. 55.

[7] C.F.B.F., Minutes, Nov., 1933, p. 12.
[8] *Ibid.,* Nov., 1935, p. 12.
[9] *Ibid.,* Nov., 1938, p. 17.
[10] *Ibid.,* Nov., 1935, p. 127.
[11] Article by Alex Johnson in *F.B. Monthly,* Alameda edition, June, 1935, pp. 9–12. Also see Alameda edition, July, 1935, p. 10, Tulare edition, June, 1935, p. 3.
[12] La Follette Committee, *Hearings,* Part 68, p. 24953.
[13] *California Grange News,* July, 1932, pp. 1, 6.
[14] *Ibid.,* Mar., 1933, p. 3. Note the similarity of this proposal to the basic scheme of Sinclair's "End Poverty in California" program.
[15] Grange, *Proceedings,* Oct., 1935, p. 144.
[16] *Ibid.,* Oct., 1937, p. 31.
[17] Quoted in Paul S. Taylor, "From the Ground Up," *Survey Graphic,* Sept., 1936, p. 529.
[18] Grange, *Proceedings,* Oct., 1936, pp. 145–146.
[19] *Ibid.,* Oct., 1937, pp. 175–176.
[20] *F.B. Monthly,* Kern edition, July, 1939, pp. 6–7; Faustman, *op. cit.,* p. 189; Athearn, *op. cit.,* p. 642; *Pacific Rural Press,* May 27, 1939, p. 487.
[21] Transcript of Conference on Farm Labor, Sacramento, June 12, 1939 (typewritten copy in Bureau of Public Administration, University of California), pp. 1–14.
[22] *Ibid.,* p. 6.
[23] Report of Conference on Farm Labor, Sacramento, June 27, 1939 (typewritten copy in Bureau of Public Administration, University of California), pp. 1–29.
[24] *Ibid.,* p. 10.
[25] *Ibid.,* pp. 20, 22, 26.
[26] For early demands of farm organizations for the return of relief to the counties, see: *F.B. Monthly,* Kern edition, June, 1936, p. 3, Merced edition, March, 1937, p. 7, Alameda edition, Sept., 1938, p. 12, Solano edition, June, 1939, p. 7, Faustman, *op. cit.,* pp. 146–147, 159–160; Jones, "Relief and Welfare Organization in California," p. 2; C.F.B.F., Analysis of Senate Constitutional Amendment #2, Bulletin 24 (Berkeley, Aug. 15, 1938), pp. 1–4; C.F.B.F., The Relief Situation in California, Bulletin 38 (Berkeley, July 24, 1941), p. 4.
[27] Letter of resignation of H. Dewey Anderson dated August 14, 1939, in *Senate Journal,* Jan. 30, 1940, pp. 34–41; address of Sidney G. Rubinow, in *Transactions of the Commonwealth Club,* Feb. 18, 1941, pp. 403–406, 420.
[28] C.F.B.F., Minutes, Nov., 1938, p. 19; *F.B. Monthly,* Alameda edition, Jan., 1939, p. 12.
[29] Grange, *Proceedings,* Oct., 1938, pp. 141–142.
[30] *California Grange News,* Feb. 20, 1939, pp. 1, 8.
[31] *F.B. Monthly,* Fresno edition, June, 1939, pp. 3, 7, Madera edition, June, 1939, p. 3, Tulare edition, May, 1939, p. 16B, Kern edition, July, 1939, p. 7; C.F.B.F., Minutes, Nov., 1939, pp. 16–17; *Pacific Rural Press,* June 17, 1939, p. 540.

Notes to Chapters

³² Grange, *Proceedings*, Oct., 1939, pp. 18–19, 169–170, 184.
³³ *F.B. Monthly*, Merced edition, Feb., 1940, pp. 6–7, Solano edition, Feb., 1940, p. 7, Ventura edition, Feb., 1940, p. 3, Marin edition, Feb., 1940, p. 3; San Joaquin edition, March, 1940, p. 16C.
³⁴ Reprint of editorial from the *Livingston Chronicle* in *Sacramento Bee*, Jan. 31, 1940, p. 10. E. G. Adams, editor of the *Livingston Chronicle*, was an old-line agrarian radical, a loyal Democrat, and a political friend of Governor Olson.
³⁵ *Sacramento Bee*, Feb. 17, 1940, p. 20.
³⁶ *California Grange News*, Feb. 20, 1940, p. 1, Jan. 5, 1940, p. 4, Feb. 5, 1940, p. 3.
³⁷ *Sacramento Bee*, Feb. 24, 1940, p. 1. Also see *F.B. Monthly*, Alameda edition, Jan., 1940, p. 12; C.F.B.F., Legislative News Letter, No. 1, Feb. 1, 1940, p. 1, No. 2, Feb. 20, 1940, p. 1.
³⁸ *Sacramento Bee*, May 13, 1940, pp. 1, 17, May 24, 1940, pp. 1, 23; *California Grange News*, May 20, 1940, pp. 1, 6; *F.B. Monthly*, San Joaquin edition, May, 1940, pp. 16G, 16H, Alameda edition, June, 1940, p. 16, Tulare edition, July, 1940, p. 3; C.F.B.F., Legislative News Letter, No. 3, May 10, 1940, p. 1; *Pacific Rural Press*, April 20, 1940, p. 295.
³⁹ *Sacramento Bee*, Sept. 13, 1940, pp. 1, 19, Sept. 14, 1940, pp. 1, 5; Sidney G. Rubinow, in *Transactions of the Commonwealth Club*, Feb. 18, 1941, pp. 403–406, 420.
⁴⁰ Grange, *Proceedings*, Oct., 1940, 10–11, 202, 206–207.
⁴¹ Resume of Sehlmeyer's speeches in *California Grange News*, Jan. 20, 1941, p. 4. Also see issues of Jan. 5, 1941, p. 1, Jan. 20, 1941, pp. 1, 12, April 5, 1941, pp. 1, 3; *Sacramento Bee*, April 1, 1941, p. 17.
⁴² Crouch and McHenry, *op. cit.*, p. 361; *Sacramento Bee*, March 17, 1941, p.1, April 25, 1941, pp. 1, 25, May 7, 1941, pp. 1, 4, June 17, 1941, pp. 1, 17; *F.B. Monthly*, Alameda edition, Feb., 1941, p. 12, Tulare edition, July, 1941, p. 3, Alameda edition, Aug., 1941, pp. 10, 16; C.F.B.F., The Relief Situation in California, Bulletin 38 (Berkeley, July 24, 1941), pp. 10, 16; C.F.B.F., Minutes, Nov., 1941, pp. 30, 60–61.

NOTES TO CHAPTER 11

¹ Report of Los Angeles County Farm Bureau in C.F.B.F., Minutes, Nov., 1936, pp. 64–65.
² *Pacific Rural Press*, Dec. 18, 1937, p. 652; letter of E. C. Kimball to Alex Johnson dated Jan. 19, 1938, in La Follette Committee, *Hearings*, Part 68, pp. 24945–24946.
³ La Follette Committee, *Hearings*, Part 68, p. 24957; *F.B. Monthly*, Alameda edition, May, 1938, p. 24.
⁴ "Fight Trucking Union," *Business Week*, Jan. 8, 1938, p. 36; La Follette Committee, *Reports*, Part V, p. 764, Part VIII, pp. 1584–1586; *The Associated Farmer*, June 8, 1938. See also letter of G. G. Bennett, president of the Associated Farmers of Imperial County, to Paul Shoup, president of Southern Californians, Inc., in La Follette Committee, *Hearings*, Part 58, p. 21703.

Notes to Chapters

[5] La Follette Committee, *Hearings*, Part 67, p. 24608. See also *San Francisco Chronicle*, Sept. 26–28, 1937; *Pacific Rural Press*, March 19, 1938.

[6] C.F.B.F., Minutes, Nov., 1937, p. 13; *F.B. Monthly*, Fresno edition, Nov., 1937, pp. 7, 26.

[7] *California Grange News*, Jan. 5, 1938, p. 8. The State Grange convention did not go on record on this matter.

[8] Article by Philip Bancroft in *F.B. Monthly*, Alameda edition, Nov., 1937, p. 24; *The Associated Farmer*, Oct. 10, 1937, March 21, 1938, p. 2.

[9] *F.B. Monthly*, Lake edition, March, 1937, p. 3, Alameda edition, Nov., 1937, p. 24, Merced edition, Aug., 1938, p. 3, San Joaquin edition, Aug., 1938, p. 16H, Sept., 1938, p. 3, Madera edition, Jan., 1940, p. 3.

[10] La Follette Committee, *Hearings*, Part 68, p. 24941.

[11] *California Grange News*, Aug., 1934, p. 4, Feb. 5, 1937, p. 4, Dec. 20, 1939, pp. 1, 10.

[12] The following discussion is based on La Follette Committee, *Reports*, Part IX, pp. 1660 ff; La Follette Committee, *Hearings*, Part 61, pp. 22325–22327; *The Associated Farmer* (fall and summer, 1938), *passim*; report of John B. Canning in *Transactions of the Commonwealth Club*, Oct. 4, 1938, pp. 97–99; *California Cultivator*, July 30, 1938, p. 466; *Pacific Rural Press*, Sept. 24, 1938; *F.B. Monthly*, Alameda edition, Aug., 1938, p. 13.

[13] Letter of Carl Knudsen, president of the San Joaquin County Farm Bureau, to Alex Johnson dated June 27, 1938, in La Follette Committee, *Hearings*, Part 68, pp. 24957–24958.

[14] *Ibid.*, Part 75, p. 27790.

[15] *California Grange News*, Nov. 5, 1938, p. 8.

[16] Max Radin, "Popular Legislation in California, 1936–1946," *California Law Review*, June, 1947, pp. 176–177.

[17] C.F.B.F., Minutes, Nov., 1940, p. 111.

[18] Quoted in *Sacramento Bee*, Apr. 8, 1941, pp. 1, 13.

[19] C.F.B.F., Legislative News Letter, No. 7a, May 9, 1941.

[20] The discussion of the "hot cargo" bill of 1941 was based on *Sacramento Bee*, spring, 1941, *passim*; *California Cultivator*, Aug. 23, 1941, p. 486; C.F.B.F., Legislative News Letter, No. 1, Feb., 5, 1941; report of I. H. Pfaffenberger, general counsel of C.F.B.F. in Minutes, Nov., 1941, p. 87; report of Research Department, *ibid.*, pp. 64–66; *F.B. Monthly*, San Joaquin edition, Feb., 1941, p. 16C, Alameda edition, March, 1941, p. 12, San Joaquin edition, April, 1941, pp. 16B–16C, Alameda edition, July, 1941, p. 4.

[21] Annual address of Sehlmeyer, in Grange, *Proceedings*, Oct., 1941, pp. 17–18.

NOTES TO CHAPTER 12

[1] La Follette Committee, *Reports*, Part IV, pp. 630, 694–695; La Follette Committee, *Hearings*, Part 69, pp. 25317–25331, 25679–25680; Guernsey Frazer, "Turn of the Communist Tide," *California Journal of Development*, April, 1935, pp. 11–12, 21.

[2] *The Associated Farmer*, June 19, 1937, p. 2.

³ C.F.B.F., Minutes, Nov., 1935, pp. 12–13, Nov., 1936, p. 14, Nov., 1937, p. 13, Nov., 1939, p. 16, Nov., 1940, p. 161; Edson Abel, "The Communist Menace to Agriculture," *Pacific Rural Press*, Feb. 5, 1934, pp. 88–89; *F.B. Monthly*, Kern edition, Dec., 1933, p. 3, San Joaquin edition, Aug., 1939, p. 7, Sacramento edition, Sept., 1939, pp. 6–7, San Joaquin edition, Aug., 1940, pp. 16B–16C.
⁴ La Follette Committee, *Hearings*, Part 68, pp. 24905–24906; *California Cultivator*, April 27, 1935, p. 254.
⁵ Grange, *Proceedings*, Oct., 1934, p. 118.
⁶ *Pacific Rural Press*, April 24, 1934, p. 364; *F.B. Monthly*, Ventura edition, Feb., 1934, p. 3; La Follette Committee, *Reports*, Part IX, p. 1643.
⁷ La Follette Committee, *Reports*, Part IX, pp. 1696–1698.
⁸ *Ibid.*, pp. 1656–1657, 1705–1707; La Follette Committee, *Hearings*, Part 61, p. 22346; "Licenses for Union Organizers," *Business Week*, March, 25, 1939, pp. 48–49.
⁹ Grange, *Proceedings*, Oct., 1934, pp. 134–135. This seems to be the only statement of the Grange on these ordinances.
¹⁰ La Follette Committee, *Reports*, Part I, pp. 51–53, Part IX, p. 1643.
¹¹ *F.B. Monthly*, Alameda edition, May, 1937, p. 22.
¹² *Sacramento Bee*, April–May, 1937, *passim;* Arthur Harris, "State Labor Relations Act" (Bureau of Public Administration, University of California, Feb. 10, 1939), pp. 27–28; La Follette Committee, *Reports*, Part VIII, p. 1237.
¹³ Harris, *op. cit.*, pp. 27–28; Victor Jones, "Transients and Migrants," pp. 36–37; *The Associated Farmer*, Nov. 30, 1937.
¹⁴ *San Francisco Chronicle*, Dec. 9, 1939; *The Rural Observer*, Aug., 1939; *The Associated Farmer*, July 15, 1939; *Sacramento Bee*, March 29, 1939, p. 17; La Follette Committee, *Reports*, Part VIII, p. 1233–1234.
¹⁵ *The Associated Farmer*, Dec. 14, 1937; C.F.B.F., Minutes, Nov., 1937, p. 13, Nov., 1938, p. 17.
¹⁶ The following discussion is based on C.F.B.F., Unemployment Insurance of Agricultural Labor, Bulletin 37 (Berkeley, Nov. 1, 1940), pp. 1–32; Albert Boyer, "The California Unemployment Insurance Act and Judicial Decision Interpreting the Act" (Bureau of Public Administration, University of California, May 14, 1941), pp. 1–15; *F.B. Monthly*, Alameda edition, Jan., 1941, p. 12, July, 1941, pp. 5, 25.
¹⁷ H. C. Carrasco, "The Day of Rest, Child Labor, and Labor Contractors' Law as Applied to Agriculture" (Los Angeles, Dec. 5, 1940), pp. 1–6; *Pacific Rural Press*, July 13, 1940, p. 11; C.F.B.F., Legislative News Letter, No. 1, Feb. 5, 1941, pp. 1–2; *California Cultivator*, Sept. 20, 1941, p. 542; *F.B. Monthly*, Alameda edition, July, 1941, p. 5; C.F.B.F., Minutes, Nov., 1941, p. 30.

NOTES TO CHAPTER 13

¹ John Kenneth Galbraith, "California County Expenditures; An Analysis of the Trends and Variations in Expenditures between Counties for County Services and Functions" (Doctoral dissertation, University of California, May, 1934), Table 1, p. 19.

Notes to Chapters

² *Economic Problems of California Agriculture: A Report to the Governor of California, Bulletin 504* (College of Agriculture, University of California, Berkeley, Dec., 1930), pp. 58–59, 63–64.

³ *F.B. Monthly*, Alameda edition, Oct., 1931, p. 5; *Economic Problems of California Agriculture*, pp. 59–63; Franklin Gindick and Malcolm Davisson, "Tax Delinquency in California" (Bureau of Public Administration, University of California, March 28, 1939), pp. 1–3, 8; Winston W. Crouch, *State Aid to Local Government* (Berkeley, 1939); Crouch and McHenry, *op. cit.*, pp. 252–253; California State Board of Equalization, *Summary of a Plan for Revision of California's Revenue System to Effect a Reduction in Property Taxes and a Limitation on Governmental Expenditures* (Sacramento, 1933), p. 2.

⁴ *Transactions of the Commonwealth Club*, Jan. 26, 1932, pp. 473–475.

⁵ Von T. Ellsworth, "Purposes and Program of the Research Department of the California Farm Bureau Federation" (Berkeley, March, 1934), pp. 1–2.

⁶ C.F.B.F., Enumeration of Some of the Inequities and Shortcomings of the Tax System as Seen by the Farmers of This State, Bulletin No. 1 (Berkeley, March 12, 1928), p. 6.

⁷ *Ibid.*, p. 1. Also see C.F.B.F., Presentation of the California Farm Bureau Federation to the Joint Legislative Committee on Taxation, Bulletin No. 7 (Berkeley, Nov. 1, 1929), pp. 1–16; C.F.B.F., Report of the Research Department on the Allocation of the Revenue from the Mill Tax on Intangible Personal Property, Bulletin No. 11 (Berkeley, Jan. 1, 1931), pp. 1–10; *F.B. Monthly*, Alameda edition, Dec., 1929, pp. 26–27, Dec., 1930, pp. 5–6, 12, 14, 16, Jan., 1931, pp. 10–12, March, 1932, p. 5.

⁸ Addresses of Sehlmeyer, in State Department of Agriculture, *Monthly Bulletin*, Feb., 1930, pp. 98–99, Jan., 1932, pp. 41–43; Grange, *Proceedings*, Oct., 1930, pp. 6–7; *California Grange News*, April, 1932, p. 8, Oct., 1933, p. 4; *Pacific Rural Press*, Oct. 26, 1929, p. 431, Feb. 15, 1930, p. 208.

⁹ The following discussion is based on *California Cultivator*, April 18, 1931, p. 430, April 25, 1931, pp. 453, 464–465; *Pacific Rural Press*, March 7, 1931, p. 264, April 4, 1931, p. 389; *F.B. Monthly*, Alameda edition, Feb., 1931, p. 10, Ventura edition, March, 1931, pp. 3, 30–31, Alameda edition, April, 1931, pp. 10, 23, Oct., 1931, pp. 5, 8–9, 20; C.F.B.F., Minutes, Nov., 1931, pp. 14–15; C.F.B.F., Final Report on Tax Legislation (Berkeley, May 25, 1931), pp. 1–4.

¹⁰ The following discussion is based on: Crouch, *op. cit.*, pp. 265–266; Crouch and McHenry, *op. cit.*, p. 252; V. O. Key, Jr., and Winston W. Crouch, *The Initiative and Referendum in California* (Berkeley, 1939), pp. 449–450; speech of Von T. Ellsworth, in *Transactions of the Commonwealth Club*, Jan. 26, 1932, pp. 479–483; report of Fred D. Bullock, *ibid.*, Sept. 27, 1932, pp. 200–209; *Pacific Rural Press*, June 4, 1932, p. 508, Sept. 17, 1932, p. 192; *California Cultivator*, Feb. 20, 1932, pp. 173, 179, April 30, 1932, p. 410, July 2, 1932, p. 2, July 9, 1932, pp. 21, 26, July 30, 1932, p. 66, Nov. 5, 1932, p. 291; C.F.B.F., Facts Regarding Property Tax Relief Amendment, Bulletin 16 (Berkeley, Sept. 1, 1932),

pp. 1–34; C.F.B.F., The Personal Income Tax and Education Equalization Program of California Farm Bureau Federation as Presented to the State Council of Education (Berkeley, Dec. 5, 1931), pp. 1–8; C.F.B.F., Minutes, Nov., 1932, p. 39; *F.B. Monthly*, Alameda edition, Oct., 1931, p. 3, March, 1932, p. 4, Merced edition, Nov., 1932, pp. 26–27, Alameda edition, Dec., 1932, p. 14; *California Grange News*, Jan., 1932, pp. 3–5, May, 1932, pp. 3–4, 7, July, 1932, p. 4; Grange, *Proceedings*, Oct., 1931, pp. 9–10, Oct., 1932, pp. 12–14.

[11] The following discussion of the Riley-Stewart tax plan is based on California State Board of Equalization, *Summary of a Plan* . . . , pp. 1–8; Crouch and McHenry, *op. cit.*, pp. 252–253; *Pacific Rural Press*, March 11, 1933, pp. 174–175; *Sacramento Bee*, Jan. 4, 1933, p. 10, Jan. 14, 1933, p. 1, Jan. 24, 1933, p. 2, Jan. 26, 1933, p. 2, March 13, 1933, p. 1, April 21, 1933, pp. 1, 5, April 22, 1933, p. 4, April 27, 1933, p. 6; *F.B. Monthly*, Alameda edition, Jan., 1933, p. 4, March, 1933, p. 12; *California Grange News*, Jan., 1933, p. 3, March, 1933, p. 5.

[12] The following discussion of State Constitutional Amendment Number 30 is based on Crouch, *op. cit.*, pp. 231–232, 267–268; Crouch and McHenry, *op. cit.*, p. 253; Malcolm Davisson, "Property Tax Reduction in California" (Bureau of Public Administration, University of California, Jan. 4, 1937), pp. 10–11, 21–22; *Transactions of the Commonwealth Club*, June 20, 1935, pp. 154–158; *California Journal of Development*, June, 1933, pp. 6–8; *California Cultivator*, June 10, 1933, p. 299; *Pacific Rural Press*, June 24, 1933, p. 462; *Sacramento Bee*, April 26, 1933, p. 5; *F.B. Monthly*, Alameda edition, April, 1933, p. 10, May, 1933, p. 14, Butte edition, May, 1933, p. 3, Alameda edition, June, 1933, p. 4, Butte edition, July, 1933, p. 3; C.F.B.F., Minutes, Nov., 1933, pp. 32 ff.; C.F.B.F., Facts Regarding Legislative Tax Equalization Amendment, Bulletin 17 (Berkeley, May 15, 1933), pp. 1–13; *California Grange News*, June, 1933, pp. 3, 7.

[13] Article by George Sehlmeyer in *California Grange News*, June, 1933, p. 7.

NOTES TO CHAPTER 14

[1] H. Dewey Anderson, *Our California State Taxes* (Stanford University Press, 1937), p. 129; *California Journal of Development*, Feb., 1934, p. 18.

[2] *Pacific Rural Press*, July 15, 1933, pp. 36–37, Oct., 14, 1933, p. 292; *Sacramento Bee*, July 18, 1933, pp. 1, 6.

[3] *Sacramento Bee*, July 20, 1933, pp. 1–2, July 21, 1933, pp. 1, 15.

[4] *Ibid.*, July 24, 1933, pp. 1, 5, July 26, 1933, pp. 1, 4; *F.B. Monthly*, Alameda edition, Sept., 1933, p. 12; C.F.B.F., Tax Legislation Enacted by the California Legislature, Bulletin 17b (Berkeley, July 28, 1933), pp. 1–3.

[5] Letter dated July 26, 1933, in *Senate Journal*, July 26, 1933, p. 3465.

[6] Quoted in *Pacific Rural Press*, Aug. 12, 1933, p. 108.

[7] *Sacramento Bee*, July 18, 1933, pp. 1, 6, July 21, 1933, pp. 1, 15, July 24, 1933, pp. 1, 5, July 27, 1933, pp. 1, 5.

[8] *California Grange News*, July, 1933, p. 7.

Notes to Chapters

⁹ Grange, *Proceedings*, Oct., 1933, p. 90–91; *California Grange News*, July, 1933, p. 5, Oct., 1933, p. 1.
¹⁰ Letter to the editor written by Grange member O. F. Brown, in *California Grange News*, Sept, 1934, p. 2.
¹¹ C.F.B.F., Tax Legislation Enacted by the California Legislature, Bulletin 17b, p. 3.
¹² *F.B. Monthly*, Ventura edition, Nov., 1933, p. 26. Also see *Sacramento Bee*, July 19, 1933, p. 2; C.F.B.F., Minutes, Nov., 1933, pp. 14, 32; *F.B. Monthly*, Alameda edition, Aug., 1933, p. 3, San Joaquin edition, Sept., 1933, p. 16B, Alameda edition, Oct., 1933, p. 8, San Joaquin edition, May, 1934, p. 3.
¹³ *California Grange News*, Feb., 1935, p. 1; Grange, *Proceedings*, Oct., 1934, pp. 15–16.
¹⁴ Von T. Ellsworth, quoted in *F.B. Monthly*, Alameda edition, June, 1935, p. 12.
¹⁵ Crouch and McHenry, *op. cit.*, pp. 253–254; *Sacramento Bee*, April 17, 1935, p. 10; C.F.B.F., Minutes, Nov., 1934, pp. 12, 45; *F.B. Monthly*, Alameda edition, Sept., 1934, p. 4, Feb., 1935, p. 11, July, 1935, p. 8.
¹⁶ *Pacific Rural Press*, Nov. 9, 1935, p. 468; *California Citrograph*, Nov., 1935, pp. 11, 14; *Sacramento Bee*, Jan. 10, 1935, p. 12, March 23, 1935, p. 3, April 3, 1935, pp. 1, 4; Von T. Ellsworth, "—'and all went to be taxed'—" *The Nation's Agriculture*, Dec. 1937, pp. 5–6, 11; C.F.B.F., Legislative News Letter, May 2, 1935, pp. 1–2; *F.B. Monthly*, San Joaquin edition, April, 1935, p. 24C.
¹⁷ Grange, *Proceedings*, Oct., 1936, pp. 15–16; C.F.B.F., Minutes, Nov., 1936, pp. 22, 42; *F.B. Monthly*, Alameda edition, Feb., 1936, p. 4, April, 1936, p. 4, Sept., 1936, p. 20, Oct., 1936, p. 20; C.F.B.F., Bulletin 18 (Aug. 1, 1936), pp. 3–10; *California Cultivator*, May 9, 1936, p. 368.
¹⁸ *California Grange News*, July, 1934, pp. 1, 5; *F.B. Monthly*, Alameda edition, July, 1934, pp. 4, 22–24; *California Cultivator*, March 3, 1934, p. 98.
¹⁹ *California Grange News*, June, 1936, pp. 1, 5; *F.B. Monthly*, Alameda edition, Feb., 1936, p. 4, Tehama edition, March, 1936, pp. 3, 6–7, 18A, 18D, Alameda edition, April, 1936, p. 4, Ventura edition, May, 1936, p. 3, Alameda edition, Sept., 1936, p. 10; C.F.B.F., Minutes, Nov., 1936, p. 22; C.F.B.F., Bulletin 18, pp. 11–28.
²⁰ Grange, *Proceedings*, Oct, 1938, p. 180; *F.B. Monthly*, Sacramento edition, April, 1938, p. 3, Alameda edition, June, 1938, pp. 10–11, Merced edition, June, 1938, pp. 3, 6, Alameda edition, July, 1938, p. 9; C.F.B.F., *Vote "No" on Sales Tax Repeal Proposal*, Bulletin 19 (printed leaflet, summer, 1938), pp. 1–2; C.F.B.F., Bulletin 20 (July 15, 1938), pp. 1–19.

NOTES TO CHAPTER 15

¹ E. A. Stokdyk, *Economic and Legal Aspects of Compulsory Proration in Agricultural Marketing, Bulletin 565* (College of Agriculture, University of California, Dec., 1933), pp. 32–33. Also see *California Citrograph*, Jan., 1933, pp. 69–82; address of A. J. McFadden, in *California Cultivator*,

Notes to Chapters

May 25, 1935, p. 309; H. E. Erdman, "The California Agricultural Prorate Act," *Journal of Farm Economics*, Oct., 1934, pp. 624–636; H. E. Erdman, "Market Prorates as Restrictions on Internal Trade," *Journal of Farm Economics*, Feb., 1938, pp. 170–187; Marion Clawson, The Effect of the Central Valley Project on the Agricultural and Industrial Economy and on the Social Character of California: A Report on Problem 24, Central Valley Project Studies (U.S. Department of Agriculture, Bureau of Agricultural Economics, Berkeley, March, 1945), pp. 75–76.

[2] *F.B. Monthly*, Tulare edition, Dec., 1928, p. 3, San Joaquin edition, Dec., 1932, pp. 30–31; C.F.B.F., Minutes, Nov., 1931, p. 97.

[3] *Pacific Rural Press*, Jan. 28, 1933, pp. 60–61; *California—Magazine of the Pacific*, Sept., 1938, pp. 19–20; Stokdyk, *op. cit., passim*; C.F.B.F., Minutes, Nov., 1933, pp. 14–15; *F.B. Monthly*, Alameda edition, June, 1933, p. 11, June, 1934, p. 9.

[4] Chapter 754, *Statutes of 1933*. Also see Malcolm Hamilton Watson, "An Analysis of Raisin Marketing Controls under the California Agricultural Prorate Act" (Master's thesis, University of California, 1940), pp. 11–12; *F.B. Monthly*, Alameda edition, April, 1933, p. 5, July, 1933, p. 16, July, 1934, p. 9, Sonoma edition, Feb., 1934, pp. 3, 6.

[5] Grange, *Proceedings*, Oct., 1930, pp. 9–10, Oct., 1931, pp. 13–15, Oct., 1932, pp. 14–15, 95, Oct., 1933, pp. 17–18, Oct., 1934, pp. 19–20; *California Grange News*, Feb., 1932, p. 1, Dec., 1932, p. 4, Feb., 1933, p. 4, March, 1933, p. 15, April, 1933, p. 5, Dec., 1933, p. 2, Jan., 1934, p. 3. Edson Abel, for the Farm Bureau, stated that Sehlmeyer's opposition to proration was based upon misinformation and that attempts to show the Grange Master the errors of his views were of no avail. *F.B. Monthly*, Alameda edition, June, 1933, p. 11.

[6] *California Grange News*, March, 1933, p. 15.

[7] *F.B. Monthly*, Alameda edition, Aug., 1933, p. 9, Nov., 1933, p. 23, Feb., 1934, p. 9, June, 1934, p. 9; California State Department of Agriculture, Memoranda for the Governor's Council, Aug. 29, 1933, p. 1; *Rural Observer*, Feb., 1939, p. 5; C.F.B.F., Minutes, Nov., 1935, pp. 17–18.

[8] *California Journal of Development*, Jan., 1934, p. 31, Jan., 1935, p. 5; *California—Magazine of the Pacific*, Sept., 1938, p. 20; address of A. J. McFadden, chairman of the Prorate Commission, before the U. S. Chamber of Commerce, in *California Cultivator*, May 25, 1935, p. 309; address of McFadden, in State Department of Agriculture, *Monthly Bulletin*, Jan., 1939, pp. 52–57; *Pacific Rural Press*, Sept. 1, 1934, p. 156.

[9] Speech of Hutchison before State Chamber of Commerce, in *Pacific Rural Press*, Jan. 7, 1939, p. 6.

[10] *Sacramento Bee*, Feb. 14, 1939, p. 1; *Pacific Rural Press*, June 1, 1935, p. 565, Sept. 24, 1938, p. 284, Dec. 10, 1938, p. 574.

[11] Watson, *op. cit.*, p. 23; *California Cultivator*, March 30, 1935, p. 186; *California Citrograph*, May, 1935, p. 199, April, 1936, pp. 194, 216–217; *Pacific Rural Press*, March 30, 1935, p. 332, May 4, 1935, p. 468, March 7, 1936, p. 302; *F.B. Monthly*, Alameda edition, April, 1936, p. 11.

Notes to Chapters

[12] *Sacramento Bee*, March 13, 1939, p. 2; *California Cultivator*, June 4, 1938, p. 358; remarks by Edson Abel in State Department of Agriculture, *Monthly Bulletin*, Jan., 1939, p. 64; Watson, *op. cit.*, p. 23.

[13] Erdman, *Journal of Farm Economics*, Oct., 1934, p. 634.

[14] Quoted in *Pacific Rural Press*, Jan. 7, 1939, p. 6.

[15] *Sacramento Bee*, May 6, 1935, p. 5, Jan. 12, 1935, p. 11, May 9, 1935, p. 13; Grange, *Proceedings*, Nov., 1935, pp. 18, 166.

[16] *Sacramento Bee*, June 15, 1935, p. 11; *Pacific Rural Press*, April 13, 1935, p. 390, May 25, 1935, p. 541; *California Cultivator*, April 27, 1935, p. 254.

[17] Watson, *op. cit.*, pp. 12–13; *F.B. Monthly*, Alameda edition, April, 1938, p. 12; *California Grange News*, March 20, 1938, pp. 1, 8; *Pacific Rural Press*, April 2, 1938, p. 388; *Sacramento Bee*, March 11, 1938, p. 18, March 14, 1938, p. 10.

[18] Grange, *Proceedings*, Oct., 1938, p. 9; *California Grange News*, Jan. 20, 1939, p. 1, Feb. 20, 1939, p. 5; *Sacramento Bee*, March 29, 1939, p. 17.

[19] *California Grange News*, Feb. 20, 1939, pp. 1, 8.

[20] *Ibid.*, p. 1.

[21] *Sacramento Bee*, Feb. 14, 1939, p. 1.

[22] *California Grange News*, April 5, 1939, p. 1.

[23] *Ibid.*, March 20, 1939, pp. 1, 8, June 5, 1939, p. 4; *Sacramento Bee*, March 1, 1939, p. 20, March 29, 1939, p. 17.

[24] C.F.B.F., Legislative News Letter, No. 3, April 1, 1939, pp. 2–4; C.F.B.F., Legislative News Letter, No. 3a, April 5, 1939, p. 1; *Pacific Rural Press*, April 8, 1939, p. 324; *Sacramento Bee*, April 6, 1939, p. 12; speech of Alex Johnson, in State Department of Agriculture, *Monthly Bulletin*, Jan., 1939, p. 28; *F.B. Monthly*, Tulare edition, May, 1939, p. 3, Alameda edition, July, 1939, p. 9.

[25] Grange, *Proceedings*, Oct., 1939, pp. 8, 19–20, 192, Oct., 1940, pp. 7–9, Oct., 1941, pp. 13–15; *California Grange News*, April 20, 1939, pp. 1, 3–4, Sept. 5, 1940, p. 4, March 20, 1941, pp. 1, 6; *F.B. Monthly*, Alameda edition, Aug., 1939, p. 24; *Sacramento Bee*, April 12, 1939, p. 2, April 19, 1939, p. 21, April 28, 1939, p. 15.

NOTES TO CHAPTER 16

[1] The discussion of this complex problem in the next two chapters suffers from the fact that all attempts to treat the subject comprehensively and impartially have fallen short of those goals. There is no single satisfactory treatment of the C.V.P. as a whole. The bibliographic notes may be consulted for some of the literature on this controversial subject.

[2] *F.B. Monthly*, Alameda edition, May, 1921, p. 18, Aug., 1921, pp. 7, 17, Nov., 1921, pp. 1–2, July, 1925, pp. 13, 17–18, 28, Sept., 1925, p. 11; C.F.B.F., Minutes, Nov., 1927, pp. 27, 29, 80–81.

[3] *F.B. Monthly*, San Joaquin edition, Jan., 1931, pp. 7, 16B, Alameda edition, March, 1931, pp. 13–16, Dec., 1932, p. 18, Tulare edition, Dec., 1932, pp. 6, 31; C.F.B.F., Minutes, Nov., 1933, p. 30.

⁴ *F.B. Monthly*, Alameda edition, April, 1933, p. 5, June, 1933, p. 11; C.F.B.F., Minutes, Nov., 1933, pp. 14, 31; *Sacramento Bee*, Jan. 23, 1933, p. 1.

⁵ *Sacramento Bee*, Jan. 18, 1935, p. 14, April 26, 1935, p. 1, May 9, 1935, p. 13; C.F.B.F., Legislative News Letter, June 1, 1935, pp. 1–2.

⁶ *F.B. Monthly*, San Luis Obispo edition, Aug., 1925, p. 7, Santa Barbara edition, March, 1925, pp. 7, 8b, Nevada edition, March, 1925, p. 3, Alameda edition, April, 1926, pp. 9, 24–25, San Benito edition, Aug., 1926, pp. 3, 26, Alameda edition, April, 1925, pp. 9, 22, March, 1925, p. 18, May, 1925, p. 10, Oct., 1925, p. 5, Feb., 1926, pp. 9, 16, 18, and Sept., 1926, pp. 8, 24; Grange, *Proceedings*, Oct., 1924 pp. 113–114, Oct., 1926, pp. 130–131, Oct., 1928, p. 7.

⁷ *Sacramento Bee*, March 6, 1933, p. 8.

⁸ This discussion of Clowdsley-Inman bill is based on Anderson, *op. cit.*, p. 129; McHenry, *op. cit.*, p. 120; speech of Franklin Hichborn, in *Transactions of the Commonwealth Club*, May 5, 1936, p. 234; *Sacramento Bee*, Jan. 3, 1933, p. 1, March 3, 1933, pp. 1–2, March 4, 1933, p. 1; *F.B. Monthly*, Merced edition, April, 1933, pp. 7, 26; *California Grange News*, March, 1933, pp. 3, 7, May, 1933, p. 4, June, 1934, p. 2, July, 1934, p. 6.

⁹ For a brief survey of early plans, see Robert de Roos, *The Thirsty Land, the Story of the Central Valley Project* (Stanford University Press, 1948); Osgood Hardy, *The March of Industry* (Los Angeles, 1929), pp. 205 ff.; series of articles in spring of 1939 by J. J. Deuel, in *F.B. Monthly*.

¹⁰ *F.B. Monthly*, Stanislaus edition, Nov., 1921, p. 11.

¹¹ *Ibid.*, Placer edition, June, 1921, pp. 9–10, Kings edition, Nov., 1921, pp. 10–11, Alameda edition, Jan., 1922, p. 6, Feb., 1922, p. 4, Stanislaus edition, Feb., 1922, pp. 14–15, Monterey edition, March, 1922, p. 14, Placer edition, May, 1932, p. 11, Monterey edition, June, 1922, pp. 15–16.

¹² Grange, *Proceedings*, Oct., 1921, pp. 69–70, Oct., 1922, pp. 27, 29, 45.

¹³ *F.B. Monthly*, Alameda edition, Sept., 1924, pp. 25, 28, Oct., 1924, pp. 16, 28–29, San Joaquin edition, Oct., 1924, p. 7, Santa Barbara edition, March, 1925, p. 8b, Alameda edition, Sept., 1926, pp. 4, 13, Oct., 1926, p. 9; Grange, *Proceedings*, Oct., 1924, pp. 57–58; C.F.B.F., Minutes, Nov., 1926, pp. 34–37.

¹⁴ Remarks of George Sehlmeyer, in State Department of Agriculture, *Monthly Bulletin*, Jan., 1932, pp. 141, 166; Grange, *Proceedings*, Oct., 1929, pp. 78–79, Oct., 1930, p. 8, Oct., 1931, pp. 12–13, 89, Oct., 1932, pp. 7–9, 90; *California Grange News*, Jan., 1932, pp. 4, 14, March, 1932, pp. 1, 7.

¹⁵ *F.B. Monthly*, Alameda edition, April, 1927, pp. 5, 25, Dec., 1930, p. 24; C.F.B.F., Minutes, Nov., 1931, pp. 97 ff.

¹⁶ Merrill Randall Goodall, "Administration of the Central Valley Project" (Master's thesis, University of California, 1942), pp. 99–102, 134–137; Herbert Simon, "The Central Valley Project" (Bureau of Public Administration, University of California, Feb. 24, 1941), pp. 1–19.

¹⁷ Goodall, *op. cit.*, pp. 108–112; Marion Clawson and Mary Montgomery, History of Legislation and Policy Formation of the Central Val-

ley Project (Berkeley, March, 1946), pp. 49–51; Arthur Angel, "Political and Administrative Aspects of the Central Valley Project of California" (Doctoral dissertation, University of California at Los Angeles, June, 1944), pp. 74, 183–184; *California Grange News*, Aug., 1932, p. 7, April, 1933, p. 4, Aug.–Sept., 1933, p. 3, Feb., 1934, p. 1; Grange, *Proceedings*, Oct., 1933, pp. 8–10, 16.

[18] Paid advertisement in *California Cultivator*, Dec. 9, 1933, p. 568. The advertisement was also signed by the State Federation of Labor, the State Chamber of Commerce, the California Municipal Utilities Association, and others.

[19] Grange, *Proceedings*, Oct., 1933, p. 87.

[20] *California Grange News*, Dec., 1933, pp. 1, 7, Jan., 1934, p. 7. At the height of the campaign Sehlmeyer wrote an open letter to the Railroad Commission that read, in part: "Referring to the present campaign for the adoption or disapproval of the Central Valley Project, may we call your attention to the apparent and open expenditure of a vast sum of money by the power interests to defeat this meritorious measure, and to inquire of your honorable commission whether these sums will be permitted to be charged back to the consumer in the rate which he pays. . . ." *Sacramento Bee*, Dec. 15, 1933, p. 1.

[21] For evidence of farmer opposition to the C.V.P., see *F.B. Monthly*, Napa edition, Oct., 1933, p. 5, San Joaquin edition, Oct., 1933, p. 16D, Napa edition, Dec., 1933, pp. 420–421; Angel, *op. cit.*, pp. 86–88.

[22] *F.B. Monthly*, Tulare edition, Dec., 1933, p. 3. Also see *ibid.*, San Joaquin edition, Nov., 1933, pp. 6–7.

[23] C.F.B.F., Minutes, Nov., 1933, p. 14.

[24] For discussions of the referendum campaign, see de Roos, *op. cit.*, pp. 27–33; Key and Crouch, *op. cit.*, pp. 496, 503; Goodall, *op. cit.*, p. 134; Angel, *op. cit.*, pp. 88–89; *California Grange News*, March, 1934, p. 8.

NOTES TO CHAPTER 17

[1] The introductory discussion is based on de Roos, *op. cit.*, pp. 36–44; Sheridan Downey, *They Would Rule the Valley* (San Francisco, 1947), *passim;* Goodall, *op. cit.*, p. 93; *F.B. Monthly*, Alameda edition, April, 1939, pp. 11–12, 20. For Farm Bureau support of federal financing, see C.F.B.F., Minutes, Nov., 1934, pp. 10, 14, Nov., 1936, p. 14. The acreage limitation debate is not discussed in this study because it did not begin until the 1940's.

[2] *Transactions of the Commonwealth Club*, March 26, 1940, pp. 247–258; de Roos, *op. cit.*, pp. 10–11, 104–136; Margaret Rohr and Kenneth Decker, "Water Resources Problems in California," (Bureau of Public Administration, University of California, May, 1949), pp. 10, 34–39.

[3] Grange, *Proceedings*, Oct., 1934, pp. 7–8, 16–17, Nov., 1935, pp. 6–10.

[4] The discussion of revenue bond legislation in 1935 is based on *Sacramento Bee*, Jan. 16, 1935, pp. 1, 9, May 6, 1935, p. 15, May 22, 1935, pp. 1, 22, June 8, 1935, pp. 1, 5, June 11, 1935, pp. 1, 4, June 17, 1935, pp. 1, 12; Angel, *op. cit.*, pp. 138–148. Revenue bonds, unlike general obligation

bonds, are not secured by property in any way, nor do they constitute a tax lien upon property. Funds raised by the sale of revenue bonds are used to construct public utilities, the operation of which brings in revenue with which the bonds can be retired.

⁵ Grange, *Proceedings*, Nov., 1935, pp. 140–141. For Bartlett's speech, see *Sacramento Bee*, Nov. 14, 1935, pp. 1, 5.

⁶ Grange, *Proceedings*, Oct., 1936, pp. 13, 166. There is no evidence that the Farm Bureau took an official position on this issue before 1937.

⁷ The following discussion of revenue bond legislation in 1937 is based on: *Senate Journal*, March 11, 1937, pp. 611–613; *Sacramento Bee*, Jan. 5, 1937, p. 13, Jan. 8, 1937, p. 1, Jan. 18, 1937, p. 4, March 18, 1937, pp. 1, 24, March 30, 1937, pp. 1, 4, April 2, 1937, pp. 1, 4, April 17, 1937, pp. 1, 4; *California Grange News*, Jan. 5, 1937, p. 1, March 20, 1937, pp. 1–2; Angel, *op. cit.*, pp. 148–153.

⁸ *Sacramento Bee*, Apr. 12, 1937, p. 6.

⁹ The following discussion of the referendum campaign is based on Angel, *op. cit.*, pp. 134, 141; *Transactions of the Commonwealth Club*, Oct. 4, 1938, pp. 135–149; *California Cultivator*, July 16, 1938, p. 442; *Sacramento Bee*, Oct. 24, 1938, p. P-4; Grange, *Proceedings*, Oct., 1937, pp. 5, 11–12, 33, 180, Oct., 1938, pp. 11–13, 173–175; *California Grange News*, April 20, 1938, p. 1, Sept. 5, 1938, p. 4, Oct. 5, 1938, pp. 1, 8, Nov. 5, 1938, p. 5, Dec. 5, 1938, p. 1.

¹⁰ Pamphlet in writer's possession.

¹¹ Advertisements by State Association against the Garrison Bond Act in *F.B. Monthly*, Alameda edition, Oct., 1938, p. 5; *California Grange News*, Oct. 5, 1938, p. 5.

¹² *F.B. Monthly*, Alameda edition, Sept., 1938, p. 12.

¹³ Argument for the Garrison Act in *Proposed Amendments to the Constitution, Propositions, and Proposed Laws* (California State Printing Office, Sacramento, 1938), p. 27.

¹⁴ *California Grange News*, Nov. 5, 1938, pp. 1, 8. Also of interest is a speech delivered by George Sehlmeyer on June 21, 1938, at Chico, in which he proclaimed: "Let the people decrease the burden they are carrying by the use of that which is justly theirs, and which they have the right to use. The day of the power trust has passed. It has brought benefits, it is true, but it has been outmoded and has outworn its period of service.... We have seen the impotency of regulatory bodies in bringing electrical rates to a reasonable figure. While the Railroad Commission was set up to protect the people against powerful trusts, it seems that the situation has been reversed and the trusts are being protected from the common people." *California Grange News*, July 5, 1938, p. 1.

¹⁵ *Ibid.*, Oct. 20, 1938, p. 4.

¹⁶ *Ibid.*, Nov. 5, 1938, p. 3.

¹⁷ Angel, *op. cit.*, p. 155–156.

¹⁸ *Sacramento Bee*, May 16, 1939, p. 1.

¹⁹ The following discussion of C.V.P. legislation in 1939 is based on *Sacramento Bee*, May 4, 1939, p. 25, May 9, 1939, p. 1, June 2, 1939, pp. 1,

15, June 16, 1939, p. 17, June 19, 1939, p. 6, June 22, 1939, pp. 1, 19; *California Highways and Public Works,* May, 1939, pp. 1–3; Grange, *Proceedings,* Oct., 1939, pp. 6–7, 13; *California Grange News,* March 5, 1939, p. 1, May 20, 1939, p. 1; Angel, *op. cit.,* pp. 156–159, 184–185; Goodall, *op. cit.,* p. 143.

[20] *Sacramento Bee,* May 17, 1939, p. 6.

[21] *F.B. Monthly,* San Joaquin edition, July, 1939, p. 28, June, 1939, p. 30, Madera edition, June, 1939, p. 6.

[22] The following discussion of C.V.P. legislation in 1940 is based on Goodall, *op. cit.,* pp. 140–145; Angel, *op. cit.,* pp. 159–160, 297; *Transactions of the Commonwealth Club,* March 26, 1940, pp. 260–261; *California Highways and Public Works,* Jan., 1940, pp. 1–3, Feb., 1940, pp. 1, 4; *F.B. Monthly,* Merced edition, Feb., 1940, p. 7, Kern edition, March, 1940, pp. 16B–16C, Tulare edition, March, 1940, p. 26; Grange, *Proceedings,* Oct., 1940, pp. 15–17; *California Grange News,* Dec. 5, 1939, p. 4, Jan. 5, 1940, p. 1, Feb. 5, 1940, p. 2, March 5, 1940, p. 4.

[23] *California Highways and Public Works,* Feb., 1940, p. 4.

[24] Clawson and Montgomery, *op. cit.,* pp. 102–104; Goodall, *op. cit.,* pp. 147–148; Angel, *op. cit.,* pp. 223–225; de Roos, *op. cit.,* pp. 164–165. After this proposal had been dropped, a final attempt was made in 1941 to pass revenue bond legislation; this bill failed to pass even after it was amended to provide for a two-thirds affirmative vote in bond elections.

[25] *California Grange News,* Jan. 5, 1941, p. 2.

[26] Grange, *Proceedings,* Oct., 1941, pp. 10–11, 125–126, 184–185, Oct., 1940, pp. 15–16, 195–196; *Sacramento Bee,* Jan. 17, 1941, p. 8; *California Grange News,* Nov. 20, 1941, p. 4.

[27] *F.B. Monthly,* Alameda edition, Nov., 1941, p. 25.

[28] C.F.B.F., Minutes, Nov., 1941, pp. 105–107, Nov., 1940, p. 112; *F.B. Monthly,* Alameda edition, Nov., 1941, p. 25, Lake edition, Nov., 1941, p. 3.

NOTES TO CHAPTER 18

[1] The following discussion of the enactment of the "Federal Plan" is based on Helen Marie Beck, "The Principle of Representation in the Legislature of California with Special Reference to Labor" (Master's thesis, University of California, 1948), *passim;* George W. Bemis, "Sectionalism and Representation in the California State Legislature, 1911–1931" (Doctoral dissertation, University of California, May, 1935) *passim;* Thomas S. Barclay, "Reapportionment in California," *Pacific Historical Review,* June, 1936, pp. 93–129; Legislative Apportionment (Bureau of Public Administration, University of California, Jan. 20, 1941), pp. 1–46; Elmer Patterson, Jr., "Congressional Reapportionment in California, 1849–1931" (Master's thesis, University of California, 1935), *passim; F.B. Monthly,* various editions, 1923–1931, *passim.*

[2] Some of the political consequences of the operation of the "Federal Plan" may be found in John Walton Caughey, *California* (New York, 1940), pp. 582–583; Beck, *op. cit.,* pp. 70–75, 109; Carey McWilliams,

Notes to Chapters

California: The Great Exception (New York, 1949), pp. 209–211; speech of Franklin Hichborn, in *Transactions of the Commonwealth Club,* May 5, 1936, p. 233.

³ Crouch and McHenry, *op. cit.,* pp. 23–24; *F.B. Monthly,* Alameda edition, April, 1935, p. 23, San Joaquin edition, April, 1935, p. 24C; *Sacramento Bee,* March 15, 1935, p. 18.

⁴ Grange, *Proceedings,* Nov., 1935, pp. 157–158; *California Grange News,* Oct., 1935, p. 5, Dec., 1935, p. 1.

⁵ *Ibid.,* Feb., 1936, p. 4.

⁶ *Ibid.,* Dec., 1935, pp. 7–8.

⁷ Grange *Proceedings,* Oct., 1936, pp. 77–79, Oct., 1937, p. 153, Oct., 1939, pp. 185–186; *California Grange News,* March 20, 1937, p. 3, July 5, 1937, p. 4, Nov. 5, 1937, p. 4, Dec. 20, 1937, p. 1, May 5, 1938, p. 4.

⁸ C.F.B.F., Minutes, Nov., 1935, p. 12, Nov., 1937, pp. 13, 98; *Pacific Rural Press,* Oct. 2, 1937, p. 356; speech of C. C. Teague, in State Department of Agriculture, monthly *Bulletin,* Jan., 1938, pp. 81–82.

⁹ *The Associated Farmer,* Sept. 1, 1937, p. 4.

¹⁰ *Sacramento Bee,* Jan. 19, 1935, p. S-4.

¹¹ Grange, *Proceedings,* Oct., 1936, p. 160, Oct., 1939, pp. 17, 183–185, Oct., 1940, pp. 23–24; *California Grange News,* Jan. 20, 1939, p. 1, May 20, 1939, p. 1, Dec. 20, 1940, pp. 1, 5, Jan. 20, 1941, p. 4, March 5, 1941, p, 1; *Sacramento Bee,* April 18, 1941, pp. 1, 15.

¹² See charts drawn up in *California Grange News,* May, 1936, p. 10, Aug. 5, 1939, pp. 2–3, which listed the "good" and "bad" votes of legislators in the 1935 and 1939 legislative sessions. These charts indicate that the Grange program was often supported by urban representatives, both Republican and Democratic.

¹³ *F.B. Monthly,* Alameda edition, Feb., 1931, pp. 10–11, Merced edition, Feb., 1933, p. 26; C.F.B.F., Minutes, Nov., 1933, pp. 14 ff., Nov., 1935, pp. 15–16; C.F.B.F., Legislative News Letter, May 11, 1935, p. 2.

¹⁴ *F.B. Monthly,* Alameda edition, April, 1937, p. 8, March, 1941, p. 4.

¹⁵ See, for example: *F.B. Monthly,* San Joaquin edition, Jan., 1931, pp. 6–7; Kern edition, March, 1933, pp. 3, 7, Fresno edition, March, 1933, p. 3, Merced edition, March, 1933, p. 27, San Joaquin edition, Aug., 1933, p. 7, Oct., 1935, p. 6, Ventura edition, Jan., 1937, p. 6; C.F.B.F. Minutes, Nov., 1937, p. 135.

¹⁶ C.F.B.F., Minutes, Nov., 1937, p. 56.

NOTES TO CHAPTER 19

¹ *Pacific Rural Press,* Jan. 17, 1931, p. 59, Apr. 11, 1931, p. 426, Aug. 1, 1931, p. 100.

² Front-page news stories in *Sacramento Bee,* Oct. 19–22, 1932; *Pacific Rural Press,* Oct. 29, 1932, p. 295, Dec. 31, 1932, p. 454, Jan. 14, 1933, p. 19; *California Grange News,* Nov., 1932, p. 11, Jan., 1933, p. 3. That the Farm Bureau also was dissatisfied with the Rolph administration is evidenced by a statement of J. J. Deuel in *Sacramento Bee,* Jan. 16, 1933, p. 2.

[3] *Sacramento Bee,* Jan. 25, 1933, pp. 1, 5, Jan. 20, 1933, pp. 1, 5, Jan. 27, 1933, p. 5, Jan. 28, 1933, p. 1.

[4] Front-page news stories in *Sacramento Bee,* Jan. 31–Feb. 23, 1933; *Pacific Rural Press,* March 3, 1933, p. 147, April 15, 1933, p. 275; *California Grange News,* March, 1933, p. 4.

[5] Sheridan Downey in *California Grange News,* July, 1933, pp. 14–15. See these articles by Downey: "The Desert or the Promised Land," *ibid.,* June, 1933, pp. 1, 4–6; "A Bridge from Producer to Consumer," July, 1933, pp. 4–6, 14. The editor of the *Grange News* said: "These articles are printed because it is believed they contain the elements of true information and constructive policy for future development both for agriculture and the Nation." *Ibid.,* July, 1933, p. 1.

[6] *Sacramento Bee,* Oct. 19, 1933, p. 8, Oct. 21, 1933, p. 5; *California Grange News,* Nov., 1933, p. 2, March, 1934, pp. 1–2.

[7] Upton Sinclair, *I, Candidate for Governor: And How I Got Licked* (Pasadena, California, 1934), pp. 46–48.

[8] *Sacramento Bee,* Oct. 19, 1934, p. 1.

[9] Article by Harry Hecker in *California Grange News,* June, 1934, p. 4.

[10] Paid advertisement by Merriam for Governor Farmers' Committee in *Pacific Rural Press,* Oct. 27, 1934, p. 323.

[11] *F.B. Monthly,* Alameda edition, Dec., 1937, p. 5, San Joaquin edition, Nov., 1937, p. 7; *Sacramento Bee,* Jan. 25, 1935, p. 14.

[12] *California Grange News,* May, 1936, p. 10.

[13] The account of the senatorial contest is based on: *San Francisco Chronicle,* May–Oct., 1938; "Two Who Want To Be Senator," *California—Magazine of the Pacific,* Oct., 1938, pp. 12–13, 35; "Migrants Are Becoming Voters, and What Will They Vote For? More Relief, More Pensions," *ibid.,* pp. 20–21; *Pacific Rural Press,* May 28, 1938, pp. 612–613, Aug. 20, 1938, p. 172; Richard L. Neuberger, "Who Are the Associated Farmers?" *Survey Graphic,* Sept., 1939, pp. 516–522. For "Ham-and-Eggs" aspect see Winston and Marian Moore, *Out of the Frying Pan* (Los Angeles, Oct., 1939), pp. 81–83, 92, 119–121.

[14] Editorial in the *California Commonweal,* Oct. 10, 1938, p. 8. This issue of a southern California campaign newspaper was devoted to the cause of Sheridan Downey. A copy is in the possession of the writer.

[15] H. E. Erdman noted in an appendix to "The California Agricultural Problem: A Report of a Voluntary Committee," p. 46: "The criticism of the Farm Bureau of recent years concerns its leadership. The bulk of the farmers are genuine dirt farmers, many of whom have been misled, but very, very many of whom, as a matter of fact, must be counted with those who helped elect the new governor [Olson]; in other words, they have not followed their leader's advice in this regard."

[16] *Sacramento Bee,* Nov. 12, 1938, p. 5.

[17] *Pacific Rural Press,* March 25, 1939, p. 275, July 27, 1940, p. 35, Sept. 6, 1941, p. 142; *F.B. Monthly,* Alameda edition, April, 1939, p. 16, May, 1939, p. 4, Nov., 1941, p. 19.

[18] *Pacific Rural Press,* Jan. 28, 1939, p. 75; *Sacramento Bee,* April 6, 1939,

Notes to Chapters

p. 21; address of Governor Olson, in *California Grange News*, May 20, 1939, p. 3; speech of H. Dewey Anderson, *ibid.*, Feb. 20, 1939, pp. 1, 8; speech of William B. Parker, *ibid.*, July 20, 1939, pp. 1–2.

[19] *F.B. Monthly*, Sacramento edition, March, 1940, p. 6. See also C.F.B.F., Minutes, Nov., 1939, p. 90.

[20] *F.B. Monthly*, San Joaquin edition, Jan., 1939, p. 16B, April, 1939, pp. 26–27, May, 1939, pp. 30–31, June, 1939, pp. 3, 7, July, 1939, p. 16D.

[21] La Follette Committee, *Hearings*, Part 67, pp. 24750–24751. Bancroft was, of course, exaggerating the role played by the Associated Farmers, for other groups had much greater influence in Sacramento. See also: *San Francisco Chronicle*, Dec. 9, 1939; La Follette Committee, *Reports*, Part VIII, p. 1233–1234; *The Associated Farmer*, July 15, 1939.

[22] *Sacramento Bee*, Oct. 18, 1939, p. 8. Also see *California Grange News*, March 20, 1939, p. 1, July 5, 1939, p. 4; Grange, *Proceedings*, Oct., 1939, pp. 29–30.

[23] Manuscript of Governor Olson's speech in C.F.B.F., Minutes, Nov., 1939, pp. 66–67.

[24] *California Grange News*, June 20, 1941, p. 4.

BIBLIOGRAPHIC NOTES

I. Source Material for the California Farm Bureau Federation

Reports on the proceedings of the annual conventions of the California Farm Bureau Federation, meeting in November of each year, may be found in the Minutes of the Annual Meetings of the California Farm Bureau Federation, 1919–1941. The reports contain minutes of the proceedings of the convention itself; extensive reports of the various executive officers, service departments, commodity departments, and county Farm Bureaus; detailed membership and financial statements; copies of speeches delivered at the conventions; and resolutions passed by the delegates.

The California *Farm Bureau Monthly* (various county editions, April, 1921–December, 1941) is another important source of information on the organization. The first eight pages and the last eight pages of each of the various county editions usually contain news of the state organization. The middle section of each edition, of a varying number of pages, contains news and articles of local interest. The county editions frequently printed full minutes of the monthly meetings of the boards of directors of the various county Farm Bureaus. These reports were an invaluable source of information. The editions for Alameda, San Joaquin, and Tulare counties are especially complete and valuable.

The Research Department of the C.F.B.F., directed by Von T. Ellsworth, issued special bulletins from time to time. Bulletin No. 1 was released March 12, 1928; Bulletin No. 38 was issued July 24, 1941. Bulletins No. 22, 23, and 25, prepared in the summer of 1938, dealt with certain initiative propositions that were on the ballot for that year, but, because the Board of Directors decided not to commit the state organization to support or oppose these proposals, these three bulletins were never released. With a few exceptions, most of the bulletins were mimeographed. They ran from 1 to 240 pages in length. Bulletins No. 1 through 20 (March 12, 1928–July 15, 1938) dealt with the problem of taxation and government finance. Subsequent bulletins dealt with a variety of problems: unemployment relief; old-age pensions; the construction of highways; social insurance; and miscellaneous matters of government finance and administration.

Beginning in 1935 the Research Department issued a Legislative News Letter, copies of which were sent to the various county Farm Bureaus to keep them informed of the status of certain bills in which the Farm Bureau was vitally interested. These news letters, written at irregular intervals during sessions of the state legislature, often urged local Farm Bureau units to write to their own assemblymen and senators in support of or in opposition to proposed pieces of legislation. They were mimeographed and were usually very short and concise.

Bibliographic Notes

In addition to these regular series, the Research Department occasionally issued special, mimeographed reports, such as:

"Final Report on Tax Legislation; a Summary of Final Results of the More Important Tax Bills of Interest to Agriculture." Berkeley, May 25, 1931.

"The Personal Income Tax and Education Equalization Program of the California Farm Bureau Federation as Presented to the State Council of Education." December 5, 1931.

"Purposes and Program of the Research Department of the California Farm Bureau Federation." Berkeley, March, 1934.

II. *Source Material for the California State Grange*

The material issued by the Grange is not nearly as voluminous as that released by the Farm Bureau. There are no readily available sources of information on the activities of the Subordinate and Pomona Granges, and the Grange issued no special studies or reports. For the Grange there are but two primary sources, the *Journals of Proceedings of the Annual Sessions* and the *California Grange News*.

Copies of the *Journals of Proceedings* for the years 1875–1889, 1891–1893, 1899, and 1906–1941 are available in the main library of the University of California. In addition to the official minutes of the annual conventions, each edition of the *Journal* contains addresses and reports of the state officers, the Grange Deputies, the Pomona Granges, and the standing committees; official membership and financial statements; and a list of the resolutions passed by the delegates. Until 1933 the *Journal* included membership figures for each Subordinate and Pomona Grange, but beginning in that year the Grange kept detailed statistics secret and published only one total figure for the state as a whole.

The *California Grange News* was issued monthly from January, 1932, through December, 1936; after the latter date it was issued twice a month. The editorial policy of this official journal was usually to the left of the policies outlined by the delegates to the annual conventions. For example, in 1938, when the Grange convention refused to take a definite stand on the antiunion initiative proposition, the *Grange News* felt no such compunctions; it printed extensive articles against that proposition. George Sehlmeyer undoubtedly dominated the general policies of the paper, which was edited from January, 1932, through April 20, 1938, by Ollis W. Newman and beginning on May 5, 1938 by William Ayres. One of its chief feature writers was Franklin Hichborn, prominent independent progressive journalist, who wrote articles dealing with the public ownership of utilities, taxation, banking, and state politics.

Bibliographic Notes

III. *Source Material for the Associated Farmers of California*

The Associated Farmers issued a bulletin, which appeared irregularly (but usually at least once a month), called *The Associated Farmer—From Apathy to Action.* Bulletin No. 1 was issued May 19, 1936. These bulletins were a valuable source of information on the policies, actions, and attitudes of the organization.

But of much greater importance were the *Hearings* and *Reports* of the La Follette Committee. Officially, this committee was titled:

> United States Senate, Subcommittee of the Committee on Education and Labor, 74th Congress, Pursuant to Senate Resolution 266, A Resolution to Investigate Violations of the Right of Free Speech and Assembly and Interference with the Right of Labor to Organize and Bargain Collectively. Chairman, Senator Robert M. La Follette, Jr.

Hearings were conducted by the committee in California in December, 1939, and January, 1940, and transcripts of the testimony were released soon after its work in California had been completed. Parts 46–75 of the *Hearings* deal with California material. They include testimony of witnesses and copies of official documents of the Associated Farmers, which were subpoenaed by the committee. The documents include correspondence, minutes of meetings, and financial records of the Associated Farmers. The *Hearings* reveal intimate details of the activities of the organization and thus provide an insight into the inner workings of this farm group, an insight that it is impossible to obtain for either the Grange or the Farm Bureau.

From these many, thick volumes of evidence and documents, the La Follette Committee prepared a series of *Reports*, which condensed and interpreted the data that had been collected. These were prepared and published in the five years following the hearings. They are uneven in style, interpretation, and research because of their composite authorship. There is little attempt in the *Reports* to conceal the hostility that the investigating committee felt toward the Associated Farmers.

IV. *Miscellaneous Source Material*

An extensive file of notes, newspaper clippings, pamphlets, leaflets, private correspondence, field observations, and official reports on the subject of California agricultural labor has been collected by Dr. Paul S. Taylor, Professor of Economics, University of California. This file is located in the Bancroft Library of the University of California. The collection contains extensive data on migratory labor in general, on particular racial groups that have entered into California agricultural labor, and on strikes in California agriculture during the 1930's. It contains many items not immediately available in any other single place. Leaflets distributed by county units of the Associated Farmers may be found here, as well as union and strike bulletins. Reports such as that of the Cotton Wage Hearing Board, prepared in October, 1939, are found in this collection, as is a study by Sidney Sufrin and David Ziskind, prepared for use by the State Relief Administration and not intended for general circulation, entitled "A List of the Agricultural Unions and Strikes in the United States."

Similar ephemeral material is in the library of the Bureau of Public Administration of the University of California. Here may be found several leaflets issued by agricultural unions. Here also are the following reports and transcripts, which are not generally available:

Carrasco, H. C. "The Day of Rest, Child Labor, and Labor Contractors' Laws As Applied to Agriculture." Address before the Agricultural Section, Fifteenth Annual Statewide Meeting, California State Chamber of Commerce. Los Angeles, December 5, 1940. (Mimeographed transcript of a speech delivered by the State Labor Commissioner on subjects relevant to agricultural labor legislation.)

Committee Representing Small Farmers, and Agricultural and Industrial Labor. "Brief Submitted to Secretary of Agriculture Henry A. Wallace on February 23, 1938 at Berkeley, California." San Francisco, February 25, 1938. Mimeographed. (An attack upon the Associated Farmers, the Farm Bureau, and the State Chamber of Commerce.)

"Farm Labor Policies." No place, no date (probably July, 1937). (A mimeographed statement of policy adopted by the Agricultural Department of the State Chamber of Commerce, the Agricultural Council of California, the California Farm Bureau Federation, and the Farmers' Union, California Division.)

"Important Farm Labor Developments during 1937." Speech delivered by E. F. Loescher before the Agricultural Department of the State Chamber of Commerce. No place, October 28, 1937. Mimeographed.

McWilliams, Carey. "Report on Conferences re: the Problem of Agricultural Labor in California and the Coordination of Federal and State Activities." No place, May 31, 1939. Mimeographed. (A report, presented to Governor Culbert Olson, on a conference held in Fresno, May 26–27, 1939.)

"Report of Conference on Farm Labor." Sacramento, June 27, 1939. (A typewritten copy of a report given to the library by the California Farm Bureau Federation. Includes a complete transcript of the conference of agricultural leaders on the unemployment relief problem.

"Report of the Labor Relations Committee of the California Farm Bureau Federation," Berkeley, June, 1939. Typescript. (Contains recommendations of that committee on the problem of unemployment relief.)

"Transcript of Conference on Farm Labor, Sacramento, June 12, 1939." (Typescript account of conference of government officials and farm leaders on the unemployment relief problem.)

Another valuable collection of miscellaneous source material was assembled by Dr. Robert Burke. This collection includes political pamphlets, voters' guides, and newspaper clippings concerned with the general election in California in 1938. Of special value was the material relating to the Olson-Merriam gubernatorial race, the Downey-Bancroft senatorial race, and the initiative propositions of that year.

V. *Personal Interviews*

The writer had several personal interviews with persons active in farm politics during the 1930's. On January 27, 1950, the writer interviewed S. E. Goodall, at that time executive secretary of the California Farm Bureau Federation. Goodall made many pertinent observations on the activities of the Farm Bureau and on its organizational structure and membership. He talked off the record and asked that no footnote references be made to what he said. His wishes have been followed, but parts of the interview have been incorporated in the background material in some of the chapters.

The writer had lengthy interviews with Sidney G. Rubinow on January 27 and 31, 1950. Rubinow was publicity director of the California Farm Bureau Federation from 1936 to 1939, Assistant State Director of Agriculture in the Olson administration in 1939–1940, and State Relief Administrator from July to December, 1940. Rubinow, like Goodall, was open and frank in his discussion of agricultural problems, policies, and politics during the 1930's but requested that no specific references be made to his comments.

On February 2, 1950, the writer interviewed Franklin Hichborn at his home in Santa Clara. Hichborn was a feature writer for the *California Grange News* from 1932 to 1941; he was also a personal friend of George Sehlmeyer and often lectured before Subordinate and Pomona Granges at the invitation and request of the State Master.

On February 24, 1950, the writer interviewed George Sehlmeyer, Master of the State Grange, at his offices in Sacramento. Sehlmeyer answered most of the questions put to him directly and at great length and volunteered much valuable information.

VI. *Newspapers and Periodicals*

The *San Francisco Chronicle* and the *Sacramento Bee* were the two daily papers relied upon most heavily. The clipping service of the library of the *San Francisco Chronicle* was used extensively.

References to the *Chronicle* are by date only, for pagination is omitted from the clippings made by the library staff of the paper. The *Sacramento Bee* was a valuable source of political news. Very often the *Bee* carried valuable reports of testimony of farm leaders before legislative committees, reports that were not available in any other place. The *Bee* was generally in sympathy with the policies of the Grange, especially with its program for public ownership of utilities. Because of this editorial viewpoint, the *Bee* carried many more items on Grange political action than on the activities of the other farm organization lobbies. Occasional use was also made of the *San Francisco News*, the *Western Worker*, and the *Daily People's World*.

The following farm journals were used extensively: the *Pacific Rural Press* (1929–1941), the *California Cultivator* (1929–1941), and *The Rural Observer* (September, 1937–March, 1941). The *Pacific Rural Press* was published as a weekly from January 5, 1929, to July 1, 1939, and as a biweekly beginning with the issue of July 15, 1939. Edited by John E. Pickett, it was usually in agreement with the Farm Bureau's position and occasionally with the program of the Associated Farmers. The paper rarely mentioned the State Grange. It was especially valuable on the subjects of tax reform, agricultural marketing proration, labor, unemployment relief, and state politics. It was the most conservative, the most influential, and by far the best written of all the agricultural journals.

The *California Cultivator* was published as a weekly from January 5, 1929, to February 4, 1933 and as a biweekly beginning with the issue of February 18, 1933. It contained more technical and marketing information, and less economic and political data, than did the *Pacific Rural Press*. It devoted a great deal of space to the activities of the Agricultural Council of California, some space to the Farm Bureau, and practically none to the State Grange. It usually took its policy on political matters from Ralph Taylor, executive secretary of the Agricultural Council.

The *Rural Observer* was published by the Simon J. Lubin Society of California, an independent left-wing group. It was published irregularly, but usually at least once a month. It constantly attacked the policies and activities of the Associated Farmers, but it carried very little news about the other farm organizations. Its sympathies lay with the migratory workers. The Associated Farmers was convinced that the paper was dominated by Communists.

Scattered articles in the *Monthly Labor Review*, the *Journal of Farm Economics*, and *Rural Sociology* provided background material. The *California Citrograph*, official organ of the California Fruit Growers' Exchange, provided occasional valuable bits of information on the labor problem and on the proration movement within the citrus industry. The house organ of the California State

Bibliographic Notes

Chamber of Commerce (variously titled *California Journal of Development,* 1929–1936; *California—Magazine of Pacific Business,* 1936–1937; *California—Magazine of the Pacific,* 1937–) provided frequent articles on California farm politics from a conservative point of view. Straight news items from *Business Week* often gave frank, outspoken accounts of activities of the Associated Farmers. The *Nation* and the *New Republic* carried many articles sympathetic to the migratory laborers in California.

The following magazine and periodical articles were of special value:

Adamic, Louis. "Cherries are Red in San Joaquin," *Nation,* June 27, 1936, pp. 840–841.
"Agriculture and Migratory Labor," *Monthly Labor Review,* February, 1941, pp. 338–349.
Allen, R. H. "The Influence of Spanish and Mexican Land Grants on California Agriculture," *Journal of Farm Economics,* October, 1932.
"Anti-Union Farmers Spread Out," *Business Week,* December 4, 1937, pp. 46–47.
"Associated Farmers Go National," *Business Week,* November 5, 1938, p. 32.
"A.F. Launches Anti-Red Crusade," *Business Week,* June 8, 1940, pp. 34–35.
Athearn, Leigh. "Unemployment Relief in Labor Disputes—California's Experience," *Social Service Review,* December, 1940, pp. 627–654.
Baker, Harry S. "Cotton Has Its Troubles," *California—Magazine of the Pacific,* November, 1939, pp. 18–19.
Barclay, Thomas S. "Reapportionment in California," *The Pacific Historical Review,* June, 1936, pp. 93–129.
Bartlett, Louis. "California's TVA," *Public Ownership of Public Utilities,* July–August, 1937, pp. 99–101.
Benedict, Murray R. "The British Program for Farm Labor," *Journal of Farm Economics,* November, 1940, pp. 715–728.
———. "The Problem of Stabilizing the Migrant Farm Laborer of California," *Rural Sociology,* June, 1938, pp. 188–194.
———. "Production Control in Agriculture and Industry," *Journal of Farm Economics,* August, 1936, pp. 453–468.
Benedict, Murray R., and R. L. Adams. "Methods of Wage Determination in Agriculture," *Journal of Farm Economics,* February, 1941, pp. 71–88.
"Biggest California Cotton Crop," *Business Week,* September 4, 1937, p. 28.
Bliven, Bruce. " 'Hey Rube!' The Associated Farmers and the New Deal," *New Republic,* February 8, 1939, pp. 10–12.
Blythe, Stuart O. "Agriculture is a Business in California," *California—Magazine of the Pacific,* April, 1939, pp. 9–13, 30–32.

Brindley, Ronald. "Small Farmer vs. Big Farmer?" *California—Magazine of the Pacific,* April, 1940, pp. 24, 29.
"California Organizes," *Public Ownership of Public Utilities,* April, 1939, pp. 57–58.
"California Replies to Steinbeck," *Business Week,* May 11, 1940, p. 17.
"Calpak: The Adventures of Del Monte Brand," *Fortune,* November, 1938, pp. 76–83.
Caughey, John Walton. "Current Discussion of California's Migrant Labor Problem," *The Pacific Historical Review,* September, 1939, pp. 347–354.
Clark, Frank W. "Communities Must Organize to Get Water and Power," *California Highways and Public Works,* October, 1939, pp. 5, 19.
"Coast Farmers Map War on Unions," *Business Week,* December 2, 1939, p. 29.
"Crop Control Fails," *Business Week,* April 30, 1938, p. 38.
Douglas, Katherine. "West Coast Inquiry," *Survey Graphic,* April, 1940, pp. 227–231.
"Dustbowlers Worry California!" *Business Week,* September 24, 1938, pp. 33–34.
Ellsworth, Von T. " '—and all went to be taxed—,' " *The Nation's Agriculture,* December, 1937, pp. 5–6, 11.
Erdman, H. E. "The California Agricultural Prorate Act," *Journal of Farm Economics,* October, 1934, pp. 624–636.
———. "Market Prorates as Restrictions on Internal Trade," *Journal of Farm Economics,* February, 1938, pp. 170–187.
"Farm Hands' Union," *Business Week,* March 20, 1937, p. 53.
"Farm Wage Hearings," *Business Week,* October 21, 1939, p. 42.
"Farmers Break Strike," *Business Week,* July 17, 1937, p. 26.
"Farmers Join to Smash Strikes," *Business Week,* May 22, 1937, p. 37.
"Federal-State Groups Act to Unfreeze $50,000,000 in Central Valley Project Bonds," *California Highways and Public Works,* January, 1940, pp. 1–3.
"Fight Trucking Union," *Business Week,* January 8, 1939, p. 35.
"Flee Dust Bowl for California," *Business Week,* July 3, 1937, pp. 36–37.
Frazer, Guernsey. "Turn Off the Communist Tide," *California Journal of Development,* April, 1935, pp. 11–12, 21.
Garrett, Garet. "Whose Law and Order?" *Saturday Evening Post,* March 25, 1939, pp. 8–9, 31–34.
George, Harrison. "Class Forces in California Agriculture," *The Communist,* February, 1939, pp. 156–162; March, 1939, pp. 269–273.
"Governor Olson Asks Solons to Unfreeze $50,000,000 Central Valley Bonds," *California Highways and Public Works,* February, 1940, pp. 1–4.

Green, Charles H. "Not a Hayseed Among these Farmers," *The Hat Worker*, November 15, 1939, p. 9.
"Green Gold and Tear Gas," *California—Magazine of the Pacific*, November, 1936, pp. 18–19, 54–57.
"I Wonder Where We Can Go Now," *Fortune*, April, 1939, pp. 90–100.
Institute for Propaganda Analysis. "The Associated Farmers," *Propaganda Analysis*, August 1, 1939.
Landis, Paul H. "Social Aspects of Farm Labor in the Pacific States," *Rural Sociology*, December, 1938, pp. 421–433.
"Licenses for Union Organizers," *Business Week*, March 25, 1939, pp. 48–49.
McHenry, Dean E. "Legislative Personnel in California," *Annals of the American Academy of Political and Social Science*, January, 1938, pp. 45–52.
———. "The Pattern of California Politics," *Western Political Quarterly*, March, 1948, pp. 44–53.
———. "Urban vs. Rural in California," *National Municipal Review*, July, 1946, pp. 350–354, 388.
McWilliams, Carey. "California's Migrants," *Forum*, December, 1939, p. vii.
———. "Civil Rights in California," *New Republic*, January 22, 1940, pp. 108–110.
Meigs, Peveril. "Water Planning in the Great Central Valley, California," *Geographical Review*, April, 1939, pp. 252–273.
"Migrant Households in California, 1938," *Monthly Labor Review*, September, 1939, pp. 622–623.
"Migrants are Becoming Voters, and What Will They Vote For? More Relief, More Pensions," *California—Magazine of the Pacific*, October, 1938, pp. 20–21.
"More Than Mob Terror," *New Republic*, March 21, 1934, p. 148.
Neuberger, Richard L. "Who Are the Associated Farmers?" *Survey Graphic*, September, 1939, pp. 516–521.
Ormsby, Herbert F. "The Joads—and Your Relief Problem," *California—Magazine of the Pacific*, September, 1939, pp. 13, 28–29, 31.
"P.G.& E.," *Fortune*, September, 1939, pp. 33–41, 118, 120, 122–123, 126–128, 130, 132.
Packard, Rose Marie. "The Los Angeles Border Patrol," *Nation*, March 4, 1936, p. 295.
Parker, Gilbert H. "Agriculture's Greatest Enemy," *California Journal of Development*, July, 1934, pp. 8, 25.
———. "The Farmer Accepts the Red Challenge," *California Journal of Development*, June, 1935, pp. 10, 19–20.
Pickett, John E. "Agriculture is Able to Sit Up and Take Prorate," *California Journal of Development*, January, 1934, pp. 5, 30–31.

Pickett, John E. "Rx: For That Hunger of Abundance, Take Prorate," *California Journal of Development*, January, 1934, pp. 5, 30–31.
———. "What 'Prorate' Really Means," *California—Magazine of the Pacific*, September, 1938, pp. 18–20.
Pike, Roy M. "Californians—Wake Up!" *California Journal of Development*, January, 1936, pp. 12–13, 42–44.
"Policies Split the Associated Farmers," *Business Week*, May 18, 1940, p. 32.
"Push California Land-Labor Fight," *Business Week*, August 12, 1939, pp. 32–33.
Radin, Max. "Popular Legislation in California, 1936–1946," *California Law Review*, June, 1947, pp. 171–190.
Reichard, Alice. "California's Adult Children," *Country Gentleman*, February, 1940, pp. 9, 34–35.
Rodriguez, Theodore, and W. G. Fennell. "Agrarian Revolt in California," *Nation*, September 6, 1933, p. 272.
Schuler, Loring A. "The Dust Bowl Moves to California," *California—Magazine of the Pacific*, August, 1938, pp. 5–9, 30–33.
Steinbeck, John. "Dubious Battle in California," *Nation*, September 12, 1936, pp. 302–304.
"Survey Shows Contracts for $75,000,000 Awarded to Date on Central Valley Project," *California Highways and Public Works*, December, 1939, pp. 1–4.
T.R.B. "Fink Farmers," *New Republic*, December 28, 1938, p. 228.
Taylor, Frank J. "California's 'Grapes of Wrath,'" *Forum*, November, 1939, pp. 232–238.
———. "California's Harvest Hand Crisis," *California Journal of Development*, March, 1936, pp. 6–7.
———. "Heretic in the Promised Land," *Saturday Evening Post*, December 21, 1940, pp. 27, 62–64.
———. "The Right to Harvest," *Country Gentleman*, October, 1937, pp. 7–8, 73.
———. "Trucking—A New Born Utility," *California—Magazine of the Pacific*, November, 1937, pp. 5–7, 33.
Taylor, Paul S. "Again the Covered Wagon," *Survey Graphic*, July, 1935, pp. 348–351.
———. "Central Valley Project: Water and Land," *The Western Political Quarterly*, June, 1949, pp. 228–253.
———. "From the Ground Up," *Survey Graphic*, September, 1936, pp. 526–529, 537–538.
———. "Migratory Farm Labor in the United States," *Monthly Labor Review*, March, 1937, pp. 537–549.
Taylor, Paul S., and Clark Kerr. "Uprisings on the Farms," *Survey Graphic*, January, 1935, pp. 19–22.
Taylor, Paul S., and Edward J. Rowell. "Patterns of Agricultural Labor Migration within California," *Monthly Labor Review*, November, 1938, pp. 980–990.

Taylor, Paul S., and Tom Vasey. "Contemporary Background of California Farm Labor," *Rural Sociology*, December, 1936, pp. 401–419.
———. "Historical Background of California Farm Labor," *Rural Sociology*, September, 1936, pp. 281–295.
"Terrorism in California," *New Republic*, August, 1934, pp. 305–306.
Traynor, Roger J. "Operation of the State Sales Tax," *California Journal of Development*, February, 1934, pp. 18, 32.
"Two Who Want To Be Senator: Republican Philip Bancroft, Democrat Sheridan Downey," *California—Magazine of the Pacific*, October, 1938, pp. 12–13, 35.
Vorse, Mary Heaton. "The Farm Workers Meet," *New Republic*, July 28, 1937, pp. 327–328.
"Water Authority Approves Proposed Legislation for Central Valley Project," *California Highways and Public Works*, May, 1939, pp. 1–5, 23, 26.
Weaver, F. P. "The General Property Tax as a Factor in Unsatisfactory Agricultural Situation," *Annals of the American Academy of Political and Social Science*, March, 1929, pp. 312–317.
Wiser, Ray B. "Are You Registered?" *California—Magazine of the Pacific*, September, 1939, pp. 15, 23–25.

VII. *General Studies*

The following sources and studies published by the California state government were of value:

Athearn, Leigh. *A Study of the Policies and Actions of the California State Relief Administration from 1935–1939, Regarding Aid to Persons Engaged in Labor Disputes.* Los Angeles, 1939. (A critical study, by the director of the Labor Relations Council, of unemployment relief policy under Harold Pomeroy.)
Atherton, E. N., and associates. *Legislative Investigation Report.* Submitted by H. R. Philbrick, December 28, 1938. (Sensational probe into corruption of state politics, 1935–1937; shows various methods of putting pressure upon politicians; thoroughly documented.)
California Blue Book. Editions of 1932, 1938, 1942. (Short biographical sketches of assemblymen and senators.)
California. Board of Equalization. *Summary of a Plan for Revision of California's Revenue System To Effect a Reduction in Property Taxes and a Limitation on Governmental Expenditures.* Sacramento, 1933. (The first version of the Riley-Stewart plan.)
California. Department of Agriculture. Memoranda for Governor's Council. Sacramento, 1930–1941. (Mimeographed reports of the activities of the various bureaus and offices within the State Department of Agriculture.)

California. Department of Agriculture. *Monthly Bulletin.* Sacramento, 1929–1939. (Primarily technical material, with occasional statements of department policy and surveys of agricultural legislation. January issues contain complete transcripts of the annual conventions of the California Fruit Growers and Farmers, which were attended by farm leaders from all farm groups.)

Lewis, M. H. "Transients in California." San Francisco, 1936. (Long, detailed case studies of transients illustrating conditions of migrants compiled by the State Emergency Relief Administration. Includes survey of work being done by private relief agencies.)

Richards, John R. *Reemployment: Report of the Governor's Commission on Reemployment.* Sacramento, September, 1939. (Basis of plan for "production for use" advanced by the Olson administration as an alternative to the dole.)

Wagenet, R. G. "Handbook on Farm Labor Placement in California." N.p., 1941. (Statistics on crops, seasons, acreage, income, labor, wages, and migrants.)

Woolf, Paul N. "Economic Trends in California, 1929–1934." N.p., 1935. (Analysis of how the depression affected income, price, and wage structure in California.)

The following studies published by the federal government provided valuable background material:

Bureau of Agricultural Economics. *Backgrounds of the Farm Labor Problem.* Washington, 1942. (Includes useful data on agricultural unions, strikes, and legislation.)

Bureau of Agricultural Economics. *Land Ownership and Operating Tenure in Imperial Valley, California.* Washington, D.C., 1942. (Thorough analysis of the industrial structure of agriculture in that county.)

Carpenter, G. Alvin. "Farm Size in California." Berkeley, October, 1940. (Mimeographed study of various measures of farm size and of the relation of farm size to the degree of specialization.)

Clawson, Marion. "Acreage Limitation in the Central Valley: A Report on Problem 19, Central Valley Project Studies." U. S. Department of Agriculture, Bureau of Agricultural Economics, Berkeley, September 25, 1944. (Mimeographed study written in support of the application of the 160-acre limitation to the C.V.P.)

———. "The Effect of the Central Valley Project on the Agricultural and Industrial Economy and on the Social Character of California: A Report on Problem 24, Central Valley Project Studies." U. S. Department of Agriculture, Bureau of Agricultural Economics. Berkeley, March, 1945. (Includes a description and analysis of agriculture in the Central Valley—production,

Bibliographic Notes

land tenure, land patterns, land values, income, and labor. (Overemphasizes certain spectacular features.)

Clawson, Marion, and Mary Montgomery. "History of Legislation and Policy Formation of the Central Valley Project." Berkeley, 1946. (Valuable survey, even though it weighs the scales in favor of the Reclamation Bureau and its policies. Occasional errors of fact. Greater part of the study deals with developments since 1941.)

Free, Benjamin J. *Seasonal Employment in Agriculture.* Washington, D.C., 1938. (Statistics and graphs by geographic sections and by crops; striking contrasts in Pacific Coast agriculture shown.)

Lee, J. Karl. "Economies of Scale Farming in the Southern San Joaquin Valley." Berkeley, April, 1946. (Study of the effect of size of farm upon efficiency of operation.)

Taylor, Paul S. *Migratory Farm Labor in the United States.* Washington, D.C., 1937. (Clear, concise essay on the basic problems of migratory labor.)

Vasey, Tom and Josiah C. Folsom, *Survey of Agricultural Labor Conditions in Placer County, California.* Washington, D.C., 1937. (One of a series comparing different types of farm economies in different parts of the country.)

The following studies published by the College of Agriculture of the University of California were of special value:

Adams, Richard Laban. *Seasonal Labor Requirements for California Crops, Bulletin 623.* Berkeley, July, 1938.

Crawford, L. A., and Edgar B. Hurd. *Types of Farming in California Analyzed by Enterprises, Bulletin 654.* Berkeley, September, 1941. (Analysis of geographic specialization in crops; excellent graphs, charts, and maps.)

Economic Problems of California Agriculture: A Report to the Governor of California, Bulletin 504. Berkeley, December, 1930. (Survey of production, land utilization, credit, taxation, and marketing. In addition to using the usual sources of data, the committee conducted thirty hearings throughout the state to secure first-hand accounts of the nature and extent of California's problems.)

Peterson, George M. *Composition and Characteristics of the Agricultural Population in California, Bulletin 630.* Berkeley, June, 1939. (Statistical breakdown of census data for California agriculture, 1930 and 1935.)

Stokdyk, E. A. *Economic and Legal Aspects of Compulsory Proration in Agricultural Marketing, Bulletin 565.* Berkeley, December, 1933. (In its original mimeographed form, this report was the basis for the Agricultural Prorate Act. This edition includes an analysis of the need for the act, its terms, and its expected effects.)

Stover, H. J. *Annual Index Numbers of Farm Prices, Farm Crop Production, Farm Wages, Estimated Value per Acre of Farm Real Estate and Farm Real Estate Taxes, California, 1910–1935.* Berkeley, 1936.

Tetreau, E. D. *The Objectives and Activities of the California Farm Bureau, Bulletin 563.* Berkeley, November, 1933. (Historical and analytical study; emphasis on formal structure of the organization and on the business activities of the group.)

The Bureau of Public Administration of the University of California made many studies of specific economic and political problems. Some of these were made at the request of state legislators who wanted background material on which to base legislation. These reports were usually mimeographed (occasionally typewritten), and most of them were quite short. Few of the studies received wide circulation, but many of them provide good background material. Of special value for this study were the following:

Chernin, Milton. "General Sales Taxation in the United States." Typescript, September 23, 1936.

———. "Gross Income (Gross Receipts) Taxation, 1937." 1937 Legislative Problems No. 10. March 31, 1937.

———. "Unemployment Relief Administration." 1937 Legislative Problems, No. 9. March 5, 1937.

Culver, Margaret S. "State Tax Administration." 1939 Legislative Problems, No. 8. April 14, 1939.

Davisson, Malcolm. "Property Tax Reductions in California, A Study of Tax Relief to Property Owners in California, 1931–1936." January 4, 1937.

"Farm Wage Boards." 1941 Legislative Problems, No. 8. June 2, 1941.

Gindick, Franklin, and Malcolm M. Davisson. "Tax Delinquency in California." 1939 Legislative Problems, No. 14. March 28, 1939.

Jones, Victor. "Relief and Welfare Organization in California." 1939 Legislative Problems, No. 5. April 24, 1939.

———. "Transients and Migrants." 1939 Legislative Problems, No. 4. February 27, 1939.

"Legislative Apportionment." 1941 Legislative Problems, No. 1. January 20, 1941.

McKinley, John R., and Stanley Scott. "An Index to California Special Legislative Committees and Their Reports, 1937–1947." January 23, 1948.

Rohrer, Margaret, and Kenneth Decker. "Water Resources Problems in California." 1949 Legislative Problems, No. 6. May, 1949.

Simon, Herbert. "The Central Valley Project." February 24, 1941.

These miscellaneous studies were relevant:

"The California Agricultural Problem: A Report by a Voluntary Committee." No place, October 23, 1938. Mimeographed. (The main body of the report was written before the fall elections, but an appendix, written by H. E. Erdman, was added after Governor Olson was elected. Report makes recommendations for a shift in policy by state governmental agencies toward a more liberal program.)

California. Chamber of Commerce. *Economic Survey of California and Its Counties, 1942.* N.p., 1943. (An analysis of agricultural and other economic interests, county by county.)

———. *Migrants, A National Problem and Its Impact on California.* N.p., May, 1940. (Report and recommendations of the statewide committee on the migrant problem.)

The *Transactions of the Commonwealth Club* provided another valuable source of information on opinion and policy on various political and economic issues of the 1930's. The following were of special value for this study:

"Ballot Proposals for November, 1938." October 4, 1938. (Includes discussion of the "hot cargo" initiative proposition and the Garrison Revenue Bond Act referendum.)

"Ballot Propositions for June 27, 1933." June 20, 1933. (Discussion of the Riley-Stewart tax plan. Speeches by Von T. Ellsworth for the Farm Bureau and by S. S. Knight for the Farmers' Union; the former spoke in favor of the plan, the latter in opposition.)

"California's Farm Labor Problems." April 7, 1936. (Speeches by representatives of large farmers, small farmers, and migratory workers.)

"California's Tax Problems." June 24, 1930. (Includes a speech by Von T. Ellsworth stressing the need for research on tax reform.)

"Farm, Gas, and Income Taxes." January 26, 1932. (Speeches by Von T. Ellsworth and John E. Pickett in favor of these proposals.)

"A Farm Labor Disputes Board?" December 22, 1936. (Revealing statements of attitudes toward farm labor by Philip Bancroft and Ralph H. Taylor.)

"A New Constitution and a One-House Legislature?" May 5, 1936. (Includes a speech by Franklin Hichborn, who declared that the farmers lacked real control of the senate.)

"Shasta Dam Power Distribution." March 26, 1940. (Debate on public or private distribution of power.)

"State—or County—Control of Relief Moneys and Administration." February 18, 1941.

Bibliographic Notes

VIII. Theses and Dissertations

Except where otherwise noted, the following theses and dissertations are on file in the library of the University of California, Berkeley:

Angel, Arthur Desko. "Political and Administrative Aspects of the Central Valley Project of California." Doctoral dissertation, University of California at Los Angeles, June, 1944. (This dissertation contains a great deal of material that is available in no other general work on the subject. The labor of the author was prodigious. But the interpretation and bias of the author make his conclusions unreliable; he is extremely biased against private utilities.)

Beck, Helen Marie. "The Principle of Representation in the Legislature of California with Special Reference to Labor." Master's thesis, 1948. (Traces the struggle of political forces in California about a population or a territorial basis of representation. Author concludes that the "Federal Plan" meant corporation control of rural senators, with a consequently reactionary senate.)

Bemis, George W. "Sectionalism and Representation in the California State Legislature, 1911–1931." Doctoral dissertation, May, 1933. (Traces the struggle for reapportionment in these years.)

Burke, Robert Eugene. "Cross Filing in California Elections, 1914–1946." Master's thesis, June, 1947. (Provides good background material on one of California's peculiar political mechanisms and its consequences.)

Coupe, Walter Howard. "Administration of Transient Relief California." Master's thesis, 1935. (Background material for problems of agricultural relief.)

Croutch, Albert. "Housing Migratory Agricultural Workers in California. 1913–1948." Master's thesis, 1948. (Well-written and well-balanced survey; historical and analytical.)

Ellsworth, Von Theurer. "The Property Tax in California with Emphasis on Its Relation to Agriculture." Doctoral dissertation, 1935. (Technical comparison of the tax structure of Alameda and Santa Barbara counties, by the Research Director of the C.F.B.F.)

Faustman, Stanley Paul. "Pressure Groups and the California State Relief Administration." Master's thesis, 1942. (Discusses employer and employee pressure upon administrative policy.)

Fuller, Levi Varden. "The Supply of Agricultural Labor as a Factor in the Evolution of Farm Organization in California." Doctoral dissertation, 1939. (Detailed historical study of the sources of migratory labor and the consequences of reliance upon hired labor.)

Galbraith, John Kenneth. "California County Expenditures: An Analysis of the Trends and Variations in Expenditures between

Counties for County Services and Functions." Doctoral dissertation, May, 1934. (Good background for the tax crisis in the early 1930's.)

Goldschmidt, Walter Rochs. "Social Structure of a California Rural Community." Doctoral dissertation, 1942. (Analysis of the social structure of industrialized agriculture based upon a field study in Kern County. Emphasizes, perhaps unduly, the class conflicts and dichotomies.)

Goodall, Merrill Randall. "Administration of the Central Valley Project." Master's thesis, 1942. (Very well-balanced and well-documented study; far more objective than most treatments of this controversial problem.)

Hewes, Laurence I., Jr. "Some Migratory Labor Problems in California's Specialized Agriculture." Doctoral dissertation, George Washington University, October, 1945. (Emphasis on role of the Farm Security Administration.)

Jamieson, Stuart Marshall. "Labor Unionism in Agriculture." Doctoral dissertation, 1943. (One of the best studies on this problem; much of it based on sources that have since disappeared. Detailed, exhaustive.)

Johns, Bryan Theodore. "Field Workers in California Cotton." Master's thesis, 1948. (Includes discussion of the Associated Farmers; based primarily on the La Follette investigation.)

Knight, Henry. "Social Insurance and Agricultural Labor in California." Master's thesis, 1938. (Stresses the need for social legislation to cover agricultural workers.)

Lowenstein, Norman. "Strikes and Strike Tactics in California Agriculture: A History." Master's thesis, 1940. (Traces agricultural labor disturbances from the days of the Spanish Missions through the 1930's, with less emphasis on the later period.)

McHenry, Dean E. "The Third House: A Study of Organized Groups before the California Legislature." Master's thesis, Stanford University, 1933. (Chapter vii discusses farm lobbies.)

Speth, Frank Anthony. "Agricultural Labor in Sonoma County." Master's thesis, 1938. (Final chapters contain references to the Associated Farmers.)

Watson, Malcolm Hamilton. "An Analysis of Raisin Marketing Controls under the California Agricultural Prorate Act." Master's thesis, 1940. (Includes a general discussion of the Agricultural Prorate Act and its various amendments, as well as a detailed economic analysis of the operation of the program in the raisin industry.)

Williamson, Paul Garland. "Labor in the California Citrus Industry." Master's thesis, 1947. (Covers background of the industry, type of laborers, wage structure, living conditions, and strikes.)

IX. General Books

In view of the important role played by organized interest groups in the history of California, it is curious that no serious attempt has been made to investigate and record the activities of these many organizations. General histories of California have usually neglected to discuss, and often even to mention, the actions of organized farm groups in the political and economic life of the state. The following published works provide general background, leads to more important sources, and occasionally extensive and valuable discussions:

Anderson, Hobson Dewey. *Our California State Taxes*. Stanford University Press, 1937. (Anderson was a progressive Republican state legislator from Santa Clara County and, later, State Relief Administrator in the early months of the Olson administration. Written in a semipopular style, this book is not entirely reliable in all its details.)

Bancroft, Hubert Howe. *History of California, Volume VII, 1860–1890*. San Francisco 1890. (First four chapters of this volume deal with general agricultural developments in this period. Bancroft's account of the constitution of 1879 was also used.)

Buck, Solon Justus. *The Granger Movement: A Study of Agricultural Organization and Its Political, Economic and Social Manifestations, 1870–1880*. Harvard University Press, 1913. (Frequent references to the early Grange movement in California, as well as general background for the character of the entire Granger revolt throughout the country.)

Carr, Ezra S. *The Patrons of Husbandry of the Pacific Coast*. San Francisco, 1875. (Author was a professor of agriculture at the University of California and an active leader in the formation of the California State Grange. This book, therefore, is in large part an original source. It contains many documents and many firsthand accounts of events. It would be difficult to reconstruct the early history of the California Grange without it.)

Caughey, John Walton. *California*. New York, 1940. (One of the best short, one-volume, general histories of the state, but with emphasis on the early periods.)

Cleland, Robert Glass. *California in Our Time, 1900–1940*. New York, 1947. (The best survey of economic, social, and political developments; short; pleasant reading.)

———. *A History of California: The American Period*. New York, 1939. (Includes a survey of the economic disturbances and grievances of the "discontented Seventies.")

Cleland, Robert Glass, and Osgood Hardy. *March of Industry*. Los Angeles, 1929. (Brief survey of the main trends in agricultural, industrial, and financial aspects of California history.)

Bibliographic Notes

Crawford, Harriet Ann. *The Washington State Grange, 1889–1924, A Romance of Democracy*. Portland, 1940. (One of the few nonofficial histories of a State Grange, this book was valuable in suggesting the general character of the Grange on the West Coast in the years covered.)

Crouch, Winston W. *State Aid to Local Government in California*. University of California Press, 1939. (Good background for the chapters on taxation and unemployment relief problems.)

Crouch, Winston W., and Dean E. McHenry. *California Government, Politics and Administration*. Revised edition, University of California Press, 1949. (The most valuable single guide to recent developments in California politics and in governmental organization.)

De Roos, Robert. *The Thirsty Land, the Story of the Central Valley Project*. Stanford University Press, 1948. (Popularly written account by a prominent California journalist; lacks documentation; becomes a defense of the policies of the Bureau of Reclamation; nevertheless, one of the best surveys of this controversial and complex problem.)

Fankhauser, William C. *A Financial History of California Public Revenues, Debts, and Expenditures*. University of California Press, 1913. (Chapters on tax and fiscal matters in which the Grange was interested were of value.)

Gardner, Charles M. *The Grange—Friend of the Farmer, 1867–1947*. Washington, D.C., 1949. (Official handbook and guide to history and policies of the National Grange.)

Hittell, Theodore H. *History of California, Volume IV*. San Francisco, 1898. (Political history of California, 1870–1890; passing mention of Grange's part in politics in those years.)

Hutchison, Claude B., editor. *California Agriculture*. University of California Press, 1946. (Mostly technical, but chapter by M. R. Benedict, "The Economic and Social Structure of California Agriculture," gives a brief, comprehensive, objective survey.)

Hyer, Richard V. "California: The First Hundred Years," in Robert S. Allen, editor. *Our Sovereign State*. New York, 1949. (Quick, penetrating account of the nature of California politics with some emphasis on the power of organized pressure groups and on the factor of corruption.)

Kelley, Oliver H. *Origin and Progress of the Order of the Patrons of Husbandry in the United States: A History from 1866 to 1873*. Philadelphia, 1875. (Contains some correspondence with Grange leaders in California.)

Key, V. O., Jr., and Winston W. Crouch. *The Initiative and Referendum in California*. University of California Press, 1939. (Illuminating monograph on the origins, purpose, and operation of these two measures; includes discussion of specific propositions as well as of the working of the system as a whole.)

Kile, Orville Merton. *The Farm Bureau Through Three Decades.* Baltimore, 1948. (Official history by one who was active in the events of which he writes; occasional references to the California Farm Bureau.)

McWilliams, Carey. *California: The Great Exception.* New York, 1949. (Chapters on politics are especially valuable; chapters on agriculture stress the peculiar and the sensational.)

———. *Factories in the Field: The Story of Migratory Farm Labor in California.* Boston, 1939. (Concerned primarily with the conflicts between large farmers and migratory labor; rarely mentions the role of the smaller and more numerous farmers; no mention of the Grange and only occasional references to the Farm Bureau, but much space given to the Associated Farmers.)

———. *Southern California Country. An Island on the Land.* New York, 1946. (Sociological-psychological interpretation of southern California.)

Moore, Winston and Marian. *Out of the Frying Pan.* Los Angeles, October, 1939. (Campaign book against the 1939 "Ham-and-Eggs" proposition, written by two who were on the inside of that movement.)

Packard, Walter E. *The Economic Implications of the Central Valley Project.* Los Angeles, Haynes Foundation, 1942. (Deals with technical problems involved in engineering, repayment, land use, and social aspects of the problem.)

Phillips, John. *Inside California.* Los Angeles, 1939. (Intimate glimpses of the California legislature in the 1930's by a conservative Republican from Riverside County; becomes a spirited attack upon the Olson administration.)

Schwartz, Harry. *Seasonal Farm Labor in the United States.* Columbia University Press, 1945. (A recent, brief, scholarly study of agricultural migration, wages, strikes, and unions.)

Scott, Edna A. *The Grange Movement in Oregon, 1873–1900.* University of Oregon Thesis Series, Number 1, 1939. (Short survey; indicates that movements in Oregon and California were parallel in the early years.)

Sinclair, Upton. *I, Candidate for Governor: And How I Got Licked.* Pasadena, 1934. (First-hand account by the E.P.I.C. candidate for governor of this campaign in 1934; mentions the role of Sheridan Downey as E.P.I.C. candidate for lieutenant governor.)

INDEX

Abel, Edson: and Citizens' Committee, 40; and Agricultural Prorate bill, 135; selected executive secretary of Agricultural Proration Commission, 139; testifies for Agricultural Prorate Act, 142; legal counsel for Farm Bureau, 182

Adams, R. L., and cotton strike of 1939, 74–76

Agricultural Adjustment Administration, 73

Agricultural Committee of the State Chamber of Commerce: and farm labor problem in 1933, 39; opposes repeal of Criminal Syndicalism Act, 109–110

Agricultural Council of California: founded, 54–55; opposes Yorty "Little Wagner" bill, 112; opposes "single tax," 131; supports amendments to Agricultural Prorate Act, 142; opposes Garrison Act of 1938, 166; opposes unicameralism, 178; political relationship to Governor Olson, 194; relation with Farm Bureau, 199

Agricultural Department of the State Chamber of Commerce, 53–54, 66, 199

Agricultural labor: demand for, 3; historical supply of, 3–4; conditions of labor, 4; wage rates during depression, 31; and "Dust Bowl" migrants, 32; conditions during depression, 33; unionization, 36–37; problems in 1930's, 60–61; and unemployment relief, 82–97; protective legislation proposed for, 113–114; problem of legal definition, 113–114; problems summarized, 200

Agricultural Labor Bureau of the San Joaquin Valley, 73

Agricultural labor strikes: general remarks on, 36–37; of grape pickers in Lodi in 1933, 37–38; 1934 vegetable pickers' in Imperial Valley, 38; 1933 cotton pickers', 38; 1934 Contra Costa County, 70; 1936 orange pickers' in Los Angeles County, 71; 1937 Stockton canneries', 71–72; 1933 cotton pickers', 72; 1938 cotton workers' in Madera, 72–73, in 1939, 73–81

Agricultural Labor Subcommittee of the State Chamber of Commerce, 39

Agricultural Legislative Committee, 54; supports "Federal Plan," 175–176; opposes recall of Governor Rolph, 186

Agricultural Prorate Act, 133–146, 201

Agricultural Prorate Commission, 136–137

Ahlf, A., 121

American Civil Liberties Union, 80

American Federation of Labor, 34–35

American Legion, 178

Anderson, H. Dewey: director of State Relief Administration, 89–92; speaks on Grange radio hour, 93; supports revenue bond legislation, 1935, 164

Angier, Harold, 50

Antipicketing ordinances, 41–42, 76–77, 110–111

Associated Farmers of California, Incorporated: reaction to agricultural labor unions, 33; reaction to agricultural labor strikes, 37; incorporated,

41; 1933–1934 finances, 42–46; on membership and finance, 45–46; reorganized in 1936, 46–47; 1938 shift in policy, 49; membership statistics, 50; county units, 51; coöperation with California Farm Bureau Federation, 57–58; general labor policies, 60–63; memorandum on labor relations, 63–64; "Brentwood Plan" for farm labor, 70–71; and Contra Costa farm labor strike of 1934, 70; and orange pickers' strike of 1936, 71; and Stockton cannery strike of 1937, 71–72; and cotton strike of 1938, 72–73; on relief hearings during cotton strike of 1939, 76; on violence during cotton strike of 1939, 79; attitudes toward unemployment relief policies, 85; attacks State Relief Administration, 94–95; proposes boycott of cities, 101; meets with Teamsters' Union, 101; endorses labor union 1938 initiative Proposition Number 1, 103–105; and criminal syndicalism trial, 108–109; on Communism, 109; opposes Yorty "Little Wagner" bill, 112; opposes "single tax," 131; opposes unicameralism, 178, 179; political lobby, 183; political relations with Governor Olson, 193–195; history summarized, 199–200; state leadership, 212–215

Associated Farmers of the Pacific Coast, 51–52
Atchison, Topeka and Santa Fe Railroad, 45
Athearn, Leigh, 92
Ayres, William B., 90

Backs, Edward, 50
Badger, Ray E., 49
Baker, C. L., 80
Bancroft, Philip, 48–50, 58, 183, 202; on agricultural labor unions, 61; on unionization of agricultural labor, 64; calls for defeat of Yorty "Little Wagner" bill, 112; supports Merriam for Governor, 189; candidate for United States Senator, 191–192; on defeat of Governor Olson's program, 194
Bank of America, 40
Bartlett, Louis: defends state water and power plan before 1922 Grange convention, 154; addresses 1935 Grange convention, 164
Behr, Ernst, 48
Bell, David S., 48
Biggar, George M.: introduces amendment to Agricultural Prorate Act, 143; submits 1939 compromise bill on agricultural proration, 145; 1935 stand on public utilities bill, 150; attends conference on revenue bond legislation, 165
Bishop, Holmes, 48–49; addresses Farm Bureau convention, 58; on organized labor, 62; on labor union 1938 initiative Proposition Number 1, 104
Blackburn, R. W.: elected president of California Farm Bureau Federation, 25, 190; economic interests of, 29; addresses Associated Farmers convention, 58
Booth, Newton, 10
Boycott. *See* Secondary boycott

Brittain, F. S., 149
Brock, A. A., 185, 187, 192
Building Owners and Managers' Association. *See* State Building Owners and Managers' Association
Burckhalter, F. L., 43
Burns, Michael, 142–143, 180–181
Bush, David F., 163
Busick, Charles O.: on labor union initiative Proposition Number 1, 1938, 104–105; advises Sehlmeyer, 182
Business Week, on Associated Farmers convention, 1938, 49

California agriculture: general characteristics of, 1–8; effects of depression on, 31–32, 133–134; and need for irrigation water, 147, 154–155; water problem in, 152–153; economic and social structure of, 196–197
California Committee for Peace in Employment Relations, 103
California Constitution of 1879, 11–12
California County Auditors' Association, 119
California County Tax Equalization Association: supports tax reform, 118–119; opposes "single tax," 130–131
California Employment Commission, 113–114
California Farm Bureau Exchange, 23
California Farm Bureau Federation: founded, 21–22; membership of in 1920's, 22; economic activities in 1920's, 23; organization structure in 1920's, 23; local activities in 1920's, 23; political activities in 1920's, 24; organization structure in 1930's, 25–26; commodity departments, 27; economic activities in 1930's, 27–28; membership in 1930's, 28; finances, 28; leadership, 28–29; type of membership, 29–30; and reorganization of Associated Farmers, 1936, 46; coöperation with Associated Farmers, 57–58; coöperation with State Chamber of Commerce, 59; general labor policies, 64–66; 1936 labor relations resolution, 65; unemployment relief policies of, 85–86; favors return of relief to counties, 93; and labor problem in southern California, 98–99; opposition to longshore unions, 102; endorses labor union 1938 initiative Proposition Number 1, 103–105; sponsors "hot cargo" bill, 1941, 105–106; and Communist agitation, 109; opposes Yorty "Little Wagner" bill, 112; and legal definition of "agricultural labor," 113–114; early recognition of tax problem by, 116–117; proposes income tax, 117–118; proposes tax amendment to state constitution, 118–119; opposes gross receipts tax, 122; supports Riley-Stewart plan, 123; sponsors income tax bill, 126; supports sales tax, 128; opposes repeal of income tax, 129–130; opposes "single tax," 130–132; and agricultural proration, 133; requests study of agricultural proration, 135; proposes amendments to Agricultural Prorate Act, 141–142; defends Agricultural Prorate Act, 144; submits 1939 amendments to Agricultural Prorate Act, 145; sponsors legislation on public utilities in 1933 and 1935, 150; opposes 1933 Clowdsley-Inman bill, 152; attitude toward water and power plans in 1920's, 153–154; attitude toward Central Valley Project, 155–156; atti-

tude toward 1933 Central Valley Project referendum, 158–159; favors sale of electric power through private facilities, 162–163; opposes 1938 Garrison Act, 166–168; attitude toward 1939 Pierovich bill, 169–170; attitude toward 1940 Central Valley Project appropriations, 170–171; opposes a "California T.V.A.," 172–173; supports "Federal Plan," 175–176; attitude toward unicameralism, 178; legislators friendly to, 181; political lobby of, 182–183; coöperation with Merriam, 189–190; political action in 1938, 191–192; political relations with Olson, 193–195; history summarized, 198–199; membership statistics, 207–208; state leaders, 210–211

California *Farm Bureau Monthly*, 26; on Central Valley Project referendum, 1933, 158

California Farmers, Incorporated, 55

California Fruit Growers' Exchange, 134

California Grange News, 16–17; on fraternalism, 17; on Grange membership, 18; on Extension Service, 57; on unemployment relief, 87; on waterfront strikes, 102; on income tax, 127; on Agricultural Prorate Act, 144; on Garrison Act, 168; on "Federal Plan," 177; on E.P.I.C. program, 189; on legislative session of 1941, 195

California League of Women Voters, 131

California Mutual Fire Insurance Company, 10

California Packing Corporation, 40, 44

California Property Owners' Division, 119

California Real Estate Association, 118–119, 178

California State Chamber of Commerce: and founding of Associated Farmers, 42–43; coöperation with California Farm Bureau Federation, 59; opposes "single tax," 131; opposes Garrison Act, 166; requests study of agricultural proration, 135

California State Department of Education: supports tax reform, 119; opposes repeal of income tax, 129–130; opposes "single tax," 130–131

California State Federation of Labor: opposes C.I.O., 35–36; supports Garrison Act, 166

California State Federation of Women's Clubs: opposes "single tax," 131; opposes Garrison Act, 166

California State Grange: founded, 9–10; economic coöperatives in 1870's, 10; demands political reform, 11; decline after 1870's, 12–13; revival in 1920's, 13; finances, 16; organization structure, 16; fraternal aspects, 17; membership, 17–19; expands into southern California, 17–18; supports small family farmers, 19–20; no representatives on Agricultural Committee of State Chamber of Commerce, 54; independent role of, 56; attitude toward Extension Service, 56–57; general labor policies of, 66–68; on Filipino labor, 67; labor relations resolution, 1937, 67–68; 1938 labor relations resolution, 68–69; unemployment relief policies, 86–89, 93; supports Olson's unemployment relief policy, 95; opposes anti-picketing ordinances, 111; sees need for tax revision, 117; proposes income tax, 117–118; proposes tax amendment to state constitution, 118–119; supports Riley-Stewart plan, 123; proposes amendment of sales tax, 128–129; opposes repeal of income tax, 129–130; opposes "single tax," 130–132; opposes Agricultural Prorate bill, 137–138; proposes amendment to Agricultural Prorate Act, 141–142; calls for repeal of Agricultural Prorate Act, 143; proposes amendment of Agricultural Prorate Act, 143; attitude toward state water and power plans in 1920's, 153–154; supports Central Valley Project, 155; resolution on Central Valley Project, 157–158; supports public ownership of electric utilities, 162–163; endorses revenue bond legislation, 1935, 164; sponsors 1937 conference on revenue bond legislation, 165; on 1937 Garrison Revenue Bond bill, 165; supports 1938 Garrison Act, 167–168; endorses 1939 Pierovich bill, 169–170; supports 1940 Central Valley Appropriations, 171; supports a "California T.V.A." in 1941, 172; supports "Federal Plan," 175–176; attitude toward unicameralism, 177–178; supports political reform, 179–180; legislators friendly to, 180–181; promotes recall of Rolph, 186–187; judges state legislators, 190; 1938 political action, 190–192; history summarized, 197–198; membership statistics, 205–206; state leaders, 209

California State Senate, 24, 174–175

California Taxpayers' Association: opposes Garrison Act, 166; opposes unicameralism, 178

California Teachers' Association: supports tax reform, 119; opposes repeal of income tax, 129–130; opposes "single tax," 131

California Unemployment Insurance Act, 113

California Unemployment Relief Act, 83

Camp, W. B., 49

Canners' League, 45

Cannery and Agricultural Workers' Industrial Union: and Communist party, 33; and agricultural labor strikes, 33–34, 37–38; opposed by Citizens' Committee, 42

Carrasco, H. C., 74–76, 92

Central Valley Project: plans for, submitted by Edward Hyatt, 155; introduction of bill for, 156; referendum campaign on, 157–158; struggle for control of, 160–173, 201

Chamber of Commerce. See California State Chamber of Commerce

Chambers, Pat, 34, 108

Chatters, Frank, 129

Citizens' Committee, 39–40

Clark, Frank, 171–172

Clarke, George A., 94, 181

Clowdsley, F. C.: introduces income tax bill, 126; introduces Agricultural Prorate bill, 135; sponsors Clowdsley-Inman bill, 151–152

Clowdsley-Inman bill, 151–152

Coldwell, Colbert, 42–43

Cole, Roy K., 189

Committee for California against Unicameral Legislative Initiative, 178

Communist party, 109

Congress for Industrial Organizations, 35–36

Constitutional convention of 1879, 11–12
Coöperative marketing associations: importance in economy, 3; coöperation with California Farm Bureau Federation, 27; for perishable crops, 133–134; and agricultural proration, 140; relations with Farm Bureau, 199
Cottrell, C. C., 150
County agents. *See* Farm advisers
County Auditors' Association. *See* California County Auditors' Association
County Supervisors' Association, 118–119
County Tax Equalization Association. *See* California County Tax Equalization Association
Cremin, James M., 186
Criminal Syndicalism Act, 34, 42, 108–109, 200
Crittenden, Bradford: submits compromise bill on agricultural proration, 145; defends Central Valley Project, 157
Crocheron, B. H., 22
Crown-Willamette Paper Company, 44

Decker, Carolyn, 34, 108
Deuel, J. J.: heads Law and Utilities Department of the California Farm Bureau Federation, 149, 182; testifies on utilities legislation, 1935, 150; opposes 1933 Clowdsley-Inman bill, 152
Difani, Leonard J., 164–165
Donnelly, Hugh P.: attends conference on revenue bond legislation, 165; sponsors "purity-in-elections" bill, 179; introduces bill on political lobbying, 1939, 179–180; coöperates with Grange, 181
Donnelly political reform bills: of 1939, 179; of 1941, 180
Downey, Sheridan: counsel for Inman investigation, 187; articles for *California Grange News*, 187–188; on problems of depression, 188; 1938 candidate for United States Senator, 191–192, 202
Dried Fruit Association of California, 45
Duval, Walter H.: votes on public utilities bill, 1935, 150; opposes 1935 revenue bond legislation, 164; studies utilities problem, 164–165; voting record judged by Grange, 190

Eames, Alfred W., 44
"Economy bloc": defeats 1940 appropriations for Central Valley Project, 171; blocks 1941 consideration of Donnelly bill, 180; political influence, 181; coöperation with California Farm Bureau Federation, 194
Education, State Department of. *See* California State Department of Education
Ellsworth, Von T.: director of Research Department, 26, 182; works for passage of "hot cargo" bill, 105; makes tax studies, 117; supports income tax, 118; testifies for agricultural proration, 142; analyzes agriculture bills, 182; on political influence of California Farm Bureau Federation, 183

Employment Commission. *See* California Employment Commission
"End Poverty in California," 87, 188–189, 202
Erdman, Mrs. H. E., 74–76
Extension Service of the State College of Agriculture: early activities, 21; educational program, 23; and commodity departments of California Farm Bureau Federation, 27; attitude of California State Grange toward, 56–57; evolves labor policy, 65

Farm advisers, 21
Farm Bureau. *See* California Farm Bureau Federation
Farm labor. *See* Agricultural labor
Farm Labor Code, 66
Farmers' Automobile Inter-Insurance Exchange, 15
Farmers' Clubs, 9–10
Farmers' Protective Association, 38
Farmers' Transportation Association, 100
Farmers' Union of California, 55, 199; opposes "single tax," 131; supports "Federal Plan," 175–176; opposes unicameralism, 178
Federal Emergency Relief Administration, 83
"Federal Plan," 175–176
Fisher, R. E., 42
Flood control. *See* Central Valley Project
Franklin, Robert, 49
Frazer, Guernsey, 48, 108, 110
Frick, Forrest, 189
Frisselle, S. Parker: organizes Citizens' Committee, 39–40; heads Citizens' Committee, 41; on farm labor policy, 46; Associated Farmers leader, 48; serves on Agricultural Committee of the State Chamber of Commerce, 53; on coöperation of Associated Farmers and California Farm Bureau Federation, 59; remarks to American Federation of Labor, 62
Fulcher, Clinton J., 194

Garland, Gordon: elected Speaker of the State Assembly, 94; leads anti-Olson Democrats, 181; coöperation with California Farm Bureau Federation, 194
Garrison, James Charles: attacks Agricultural Council of California, 55; opposes "hot cargo" bill, 106; votes on 1935 public utilities bill, 150; sponsors 1935 revenue bond legislation, 163; studies utilities problem, 164–165; attends conference on revenue bond legislation, 165; argues for 1938 Garrison Act, 167; sponsors 1940 Central Valley Project appropriations, 170; sponsors "purity-in-elections" bill, 179; coöperates with Grange, 180; voting record judged by California State Grange, 190
Garrison, Walter E.: action during 1933 Lodi grape strike, 37–38; on 1937 "vigilantism," 47; president of Associated Farmers, 48; on organized labor, 62–63; and 1937 Stockton Cannery strike, 71–72
Garrison-Donnelly bill, 179

Garrison Revenue Bond legislation: of 1935, 163–164; of 1937, 165–166; 1938 referendum on, 166–168
Garrod, R. V. ("Vince"): serves on Agricultural Committee of State Chamber of Commerce, 54; president of Farmers' Union of California, 55; attends unemployment relief conference, 89–92; opposes tax reform proposition, 121; opposes recall of Rolph, 186
Goodcell, Fred, 48–49
Gordon, Frank L.: sponsors "hot cargo" bill, 105; opposes 1933 Central Valley Project, 158; supports Farm Bureau legislation, 181
Grange. *See* California State Grange
Grange Canning Peach Growers' Association, 142
Grangers' Bank of California, 10
Grangers' Business Association, 10
Gross receipts tax, 122, 151
Grower-Shipper Vegetable Association, 51

"Ham-and-Egger's," 191–192
Hardison, A. C., 53, 121
Harrison, George: Master of California State Grange in 1921–1929, 13; opposes tax reform proposition, 121; works for gross receipts tax, 151; supports Merriam for Governor in 1934, 189
Hart, Fred J., 189
Hatfield, George J., 189
Hawley, C. E., 48
Hayes, Ben, 74, 77
Hays, Ray: sponsors "hot cargo" bill, 105; introduces Agricultural Prorate bill, 135; opposes revenue bond legislation, 163–164; sponsors Farm Bureau legislation, 181
Heald, Elmer W., 108
Hecke, George H., 185
Heisinger, Samuel L., 165
Henderson, Charles, 78–79
Henderson, Donald, 76
Hichborn, Franklin: favors public ownership of utilities, 151; on 1938 Garrison Act, 167–168; on California State Senate, 177–178
Hollister, John James, 170
Holly Sugar Corporation, 45
Holmes, Joseph, 187
Hoover, Herbert, 191
Horst, E. Clements, 46–47
"Hot cargo" bill, 98–107
Hulse, Ben, 150
Hunt, Thomas, 22
Hutchison, C. B.: criticizes agricultural proration, 139–140; on economic problems of small farmers, 141
Hyatt, Edward, 155
Hynes, William, 108

Index

Ickes, Harold, 172
Income tax, 117–118, 125–130, 201
Industrial Association of San Francisco, 44–45
Inman, J. M.: and public utilities legislation, 150–152; and Central Valley Project, 156–157; supports Grange legislation, 180; conducts investigation of Rolph administration, 186
International Longshoremen's Union, 34
Irrigation. *See* California agriculture; Central Valley Project
Irrigations Districts Association of California, 166

Japanese Agricultural Workers' Association, 35
Jensen, Mrs. Ida, 143–144
Jespersen, Chris N.: offers amendment in sales tax, 126; and Agricultural Prorate Act, 143; submits compromise bill on agricultural proration, 145; submits 1933 legislation on public utilities, 150; supports 1933 Clowdsley-Inman bill, 151–152; sponsors 1935 revenue bond legislation, 163–164; studies utilities problem, 164–165; sponsors 1940 Central Valley Project appropriations, 170; coöperates with Grange, 180–181; voting record judged by Grange, 190
Johnson, Alex.: serves on Agricultural Committee of State Chamber of Commerce, 53; and Associated Farmers, 58; and Works Progress Administration policy, 86; opposes Olson's unemployment relief policy, 89; endorses labor union 1938 initiative Proposition Number 1, 103; supports income tax, 118; reviews nominations to Agricultural Proration Commission, 139; testifies for Agricultural Prorate Act, 142; opposes Clowdsley-Inman bill, 152
Johnson, Hiram, 191
Jones, Herbert C.: offers amendment to sales tax, 126; favors public ownership of utilities, 151; supports 1933 Clowdsley-Inman bill, 151–152; proposes amendments to Central Valley Project, 156–157; supports Grange, 180
Jones Mortgage Moratorium bill, 182

Kearney, Dennis, 11
Kenny, Robert, 170
Kimball, E. C.: economic interests of, 29; on coöperation of Associated Farmers and California Farm Bureau Federation, 59; on labor relations problem, 102; opposes tax reform proposition, 121; supports Merriam for Governor, 189
Knight, S. S., 13, 121

Labor. *See* Agricultural labor
Labor union initiative Proposition Number 1, 103–105
La Follette Committee, 50–51, 200
Lapham, Roger, 43
Law and Utilities Department of the California Farm Bureau Federation, 26, 148–149

League of California Municipalities, 166
League of Women Voters. *See* California League of Women Voters
Livingston Chronicle, 94
Loescher, E. F., 85
Lore, Elmer E., 165

McBean, Atholl, 43
McColl, John, 157, 186–187
McCormack, Thomas, 190
McGovern, Walter, 190
McIntosh, Charles, 43
McKinney, Preston, 42
McWilliams, Carey: and 1939 cotton strike, 73–76; and "fair wage" and unemployment relief, 89; attends unemployment relief conference, 90–92
Marshall, Robert B., 153
Meeker, M. S., 135, 181
Merriam, Frank: unemployment relief policy of, 86; signs new sales tax bill, 129; signs income tax bill, 129; and agricultural proration, 142; vetoes 1935 revenue bond legislation, 164; signs 1937 Garrison Revenue Bond bill, 166; candidate for Governor, 189–190
Metzger, D. Jack: votes on public utilities bill, 1935, 150; supports 1935 revenue bond legislation, 164; attends conference on revenue bond legislation, 165
Migratory labor. *See* Agricultural labor; California agriculture
Miller, R. L., 119, 182
Millington, Seth: leader of "economy bloc," 94; sponsors "hot cargo" bill, 105; leader of anti-Olson Democrats, 181; coöperation with California Farm Bureau Federation, 194
Mixter, Frank W., 181
Morgan's Sons, 10
Moulton, Dudley, 185–187

National Committee for Agricultural Workers, 35
National Council of Cannery and Agricultural Workers, 36
Nielsen, Roy J., 163–164
Nielsen Revenue Bond bill, 165–166

O'Donnell, John H., 136, 142
Olsen, Nils A., 186
Olson, Culbert L.: and 1939 cotton strike, 73–74; on cotton strike, 80; unemployment relief policies of, 89–97; vetoes "hot cargo" bill, 106; and Yorty "Little Wagner" bill, 112; and sales tax, 129; introduces income tax bill, 129; supported by George Sehlmeyer, 143; addresses Grange meeting, 144; votes on 1935 public utilities bill, 150; supports 1935 revenue bond legislation, 164; attends conference on revenue bond legislation, 165; supports 1938 Garrison Act, 166; on 1939 Piero-

vich bill, 169; coöperation with California State Grange, 181, 190, 202; candidate for Governor in 1938, 190–191; political relations with California Farm Bureau Federation, 193–195; political relations with Associated Farmers, 193–195
Oppenheim, Arthur, 43
Osborne, Hugh, 49

Pacific Gas and Electric Company (P.G. and E.): and Citizens' Committee, 40; and financing of Associated Farmers, 45; control of electric power, 148; files 1933 referendum petitions on Central Valley Project, 157; and sale of Central Valley Project power, 162; expenditures on 1938 referendum campaign, 168
Palomares, Frank J., 39
Pardee, George, 191
Parker, Gilbert H., 48
Parker, William B.: and 1939 cotton strike, 74–76; attends unemployment relief conference, 90–92; appointed State Director of Agriculture, 1939, 192
Parkman, Harry L., 150
Patchin, Philip H., 43
Patrons of Husbandry. *See* California State Grange
Patterson, Ellis E., 142
Peek, Paul, 94
People's Independent Party, 10–11
Perry, Harry A.: opposes Agricultural Prorate bill, 136; voting record judged by Grange, 190
Pfaffenberger, I. H., 105, 182
Philbrick report, 179
Phillips, John: helps organize Associated Farmers, 46; proposes return of relief to county administration, 95; sponsors "hot cargo" bill, 105; opposes amendment of Agricultural Prorate Act, 142; submits compromise bill on agricultural proration, 1939, 145; sponsors Farm Bureau legislation, 181
Pickett, John, 30
Pierovich bill, 169–170
Pike, Roy M.: publicity for Associated Farmers, 47; serves on Agricultural Committee of State Chamber of Commerce, 54; and Agricultural Prorate bill, 135
Pinchot, Gifford, 153
Pomeroy, Harold E., 49; and 1938 cotton strike, 72; policies as Director of State Relief Administration, 84–85; supported by Associated Farmers and California Farm Bureau Federation, 85; attends unemployment relief conference, 89–92
Powers, Harold J., 170
Property Owners' Division. *See* California Property Owners' Division
Property tax, 116
Property tax relief amendment, 119–120

Proration. *See* Agricultural Prorate Act
"Purity-in-elections" legislation. *See* Donnelly bill; Garrison-Donnelly bill

Railroad Brotherhoods, 166
Railroad Commission. *See* State Railroad Commission
Real, Charles, 36, 191
Real Estate Association. *See* California Real Estate Association
Reindollar, Charles F., 150
Relief. *See* Unemployment relief
Research Department of the California Farm Bureau Federation, 26
Rich, W. P., 105
Riley, Ray L., 121
Riley-Stewart Amendment, 121–124, 150
Rivers and Harbors Act of 1935, 161
Robinson, C. Ray, 136
Robinson, Tom, 142
Robson, Fred, 182
Rogers, Will, 126–127
Rolph, James: vetoes income tax bill, 126–127; agricultural policy, 185; threat of recall against, 186–187; dismisses State Director of Agriculture, 187
Rubinow, Sidney G.: and Associated Farmers, 59; attends unemployment relief conference, 90–92; appointed director of State Relief Administration, 95–96; issues publicity on labor relations, 99–100; appointed Assistant State Director of Agriculture, 1939, 192

Sales tax, 125–130, 200–201
San Francisco Chamber of Commerce, 175
San Francisco News, 166
San Joaquin Cotton Oil Company, 45
Schottky, Andrew R.: introduces income tax bill, 129; submits legislation on public utilities, 1933, 150; sponsors Farm Bureau legislation, 181
Schulte, Ben H., 189
Scollan, Thomas P., 150
Scudder, Hubert B., 135
Seawell, Jerrold L., 164–165
Secondary boycott, 98–107
Sehlmeyer, George: early career, 13–15; on Mexican immigration, 67; and 1939 cotton strike, 74–76; opposes cash dole, 87; on unemployment relief, 96; and 1939 waterfront strike, 102–103; supports Heisinger labor bill, 107; supports income tax, 118; and tax reform, 119; attacks gross receipts tax, 122; on Riley-Stewart amendment, 123–124; and sales tax, 126; attacks Agricultural Prorate bill, 138; political friendship with Culbert Olson, 143; attacks agricultural proration, 143; favors public ownership of utilities, 151; supports Central Valley Project, 155; argues for 1938 Garrison Act, 167; as political lobbyist, 182; relation

with Olson administration, 192–193; appointed to State Board of Harbor Commissioners, 193; qualities of leadership, 198
Shelley, John F. ("Jack"), 106, 170
Sinclair, Upton, 188
"Single tax," 130–132, 201
Smith-Lever Act, 21
Snyder, Bert B., 150, 190
Southern California Edison Company, 44
Southern Californians, Incorporated, 44, 100
Southern Pacific Railroad, 40
Spreckels Investment Corporation, 45
State Association against the Garrison Bond Act, 166–167
State Building Owners and Managers' Association, 119
State Chamber of Commerce. *See* California State Chamber of Commerce
State Railroad Commission, 149, 162
State Relief Administration: policy of, during cotton strikes, 72–76; 1935 establishment of, 83–84; policies opposed by California Farm Bureau Federation, 89; administrative troubles, 92–93; criticized by farm groups, 93–95; left without funds, 97; support for, 200
State Supervisors' Association, 129–131
State Water Plan Association, 157
State water and power initiative propositions, 153–154
State-wide Council against the Single Tax, 131–132
Stevning, Don, 50
Stewart, F. A., 48
Stewart, Fred E., 121
Stokdyk, E. A., 134–135
Strathman, Stuart, 48–49, 77
Strikes. *See* Agricultural labor strikes
Strobel, Henry L. ("Hank"), 48–50; on collective bargaining in agriculture, 63; calls for defeat of Yorty "Little Wagner" bill, 112
Supervisors' Association. *See* California Supervisors' Association
Swank, Amon, 189
Swett, Frank T., 116

Tax Research Department of the California Farm Bureau Federation, 116–117
Taxation, 115–116, 200–201. *Also see* Gross receipts tax; Income tax; Property tax; Sales tax; "Single tax"
Taxpayers' Association. *See* California Taxpayers' Association
Taylor, Ralph: serves on Agricultural Committee of State Chamber of Commerce, 54; serves as executive secretary of Agricultural Council of California, 54; attends unemployment relief conference, 90–92
Teachers' Association. *See* California Teachers' Association
Teague, C. C.: leads opposition to "single tax," 131–132; reviews nominations to Agricultural Prorate Commission, 139; heads special committee against unicameralism, 178

Teamsters' Union, 34, 98–99
Thorp, C., 135
Tickle, Edward H., 150
Tyler, U. Butte, 29, 189

Unemployment relief: general nature of the problem of, 82–83; policies of Harold Pomeroy, 84–85; attitudes of Associated Farmers toward, 85; attitudes of Farm Bureau Federation toward, 85–86; Merriam's policies, 86; attitudes of Grange toward, 86–89; Olson's policies, 89–97; "fair" wage concept in, 89; 1939 conferences on state government policy of, 89–92; 1939–1941 state appropriations for, 93–97; disappearance of problem of, 97; problems summarized, 200
Unemployment Insurance Act. See California Unemployment Insurance Act
Unicameralism, 177–178
United Cannery, Agricultural, Packing and Allied Workers of America: early activities, 36; leads cotton strikes, 72–81; on Associated Farmers' role in cotton strike, 78; on Associated Farmers, 79–80
Utilities Act of 1911, 149

Vandeleur, Edward: on agricultural labor, 35; testifies against "hot cargo" bill, 105–106
Vehlow, Ernest, 182

Wagner, Walter D., 167
Wagy, James I., 181
Ware, Allison B., 154
Warren, Earl, 81
Water Plan Association. See State Water Plan Association
Water and power initiative propositions. See State water and power initiative propositions
Water Project Authority, 156
Watson, John, 49–50, 182
West, Percy G., 117, 180
Western Growers' Protective Association, 51
Westover, Harry C., 165
Wilson, George, 182
Wilson, R. N., 40–42, 48, 90–92
Wirin, A. L., 80
Wiser, Ray B.: economic interests of, 29; serves on Agricultural Committee of State Chamber of Commerce, 53; and cotton strike, 74–76; attends unemployment relief conference, 89–92; on "hot cargo" bill, 106; testifies for Agricultural Prorate Act, 142; testifies on agricultural proration, 145; on Olson, 193
Wood, Leonard E., 42–43
Worden, Charles A., 48
Workers' Alliance, 73, 91
Workingmen's Party, 11

York, George K., 186
Yorty, Samuel W., 165
Yorty "Little Wagner" bill, 111–112
Young, Sanborn, 103, 190

Zion, E. H., 136

www.ingramcontent.com/pod-product-compliance
Lightning Source LLC
Chambersburg PA
CBHW021654230426
43668CB00008B/621